Wharton Edward Ross

Etyma Latina

An Etymological Lexicon of Classical Latin

Wharton Edward Ross

Etyma Latina
An Etymological Lexicon of Classical Latin

ISBN/EAN: 9783337217341

Printed in Europe, USA, Canada, Australia, Japan

Cover: Foto ©Thomas Meinert / pixelio.de

More available books at **www.hansebooks.com**

ETYMA LATINA

AN ETYMOLOGICAL LEXICON OF CLASSICAL LATIN

BY

EDWARD ROSS WHARTON, M.A.

FELLOW AND LECTURER OF JESUS COLLEGE, OXFORD

RIVINGTONS
WATERLOO PLACE, LONDON

MDCCCXC

PREFACE

In Lewis and Short's 'Latin Dictionary' (1880) the etymological element is both fragmentary and uncritical: a
lexicographer cannot fairly be expected to be also an
etymologist. Bréal and Bailly's 'Dictionnaire Etymolo-
gique Latin' (1885) embraces but two-thirds of the words
used by ordinary classical Latin writers, and the etymological element in it is avowedly secondary. Pre-scientific
work like that of Hintner and Zehetmayr, both of whom
published in 1873, is hardly worth mentioning: it was
not till the publication in 1876 of Brugmann's discoveries
that anything was known about vocalic laws.—For other
languages also etymological dictionaries are rare. For
Umbrian we have Bücheler, for Oscan Zvetaieff, for
Greek my 'Etyma Graeca,' for Gothic Feist, for German
Kluge, for Old Slavonic Miklosich, for Armenian Hübschmann: for Irish and Welsh, Old Norse and Anglosaxon,
Lithuanian, Zend and Sanskrit, we have no complete
etymological dictionary at all.—It may thus appear,
both that an etymological Latin dictionary was wanted,
and that it was not easy to compile one. Kluge had
Weigand to work on: I have had to find my material
where I could.

The dictionaries which I have chiefly used are the foll

Latin—Lewis and Short.	English—Skeat.
Greek—Liddell and Scott.	Old German—Schade.
Gaulish—Stokes (' Celtic Declen-	Modern German—Klug
sion ').	Lithuanian—Kurschat.
Old Irish—Zeuss.	Lettish—Ulmann.
Middle Irish—Windisch.	Prussian—Nesselmann.
Modern Irish—O'Reilly.	Old Slavonic—Miklosicl
Welsh—Pughe.	Armenian—Hübschmann.
Gothic—Balg.	Zend—Justi.
Old Norse—Vigfusson.	Old Persian—Spiegel.
Anglosaxon—Leo, Grein.	Sanskrit—Böhtlingk.

Excluding (as all writers of etymological diction
have agreed to do) Proper Names,[1] I find that the wr
of the classical period of Latin literature, down to
death of Trajan in A.D. 117, use 26,326 words: all of w
except 4320 sufficiently explain their own formation,
are derivatives or compounds of these 4320 words. In
present work I have treated 3055 of these 4320 wo
being those found in the sixteen Latin authors of the l
rank (fragments in each case excluded): viz., in chro
logical order, Plautus, Terence, Cicero Caesar Catul
Lucretius Sallust, Vergil Horace Livy Tibullus Prop
tius Ovid, Persius, Tacitus, Juvenal.[2] Setting aside so:

[1] Among these I reckon some words sometimes spelt with a sm
initial, Ciris Cocles Februa Liburna Pege Surena Triones Venetus:
which I have nothing new to offer. On the other hand I have includ
in my work the words *ligustrum polluceo puniceus quirito veneror*,
being derivatives of Proper Names but successfully concealing the
real character.

[2] I need hardly apologise for omitting the conjectural *hir thyius*, tl
misreading *matta*, and the ' ghost-words ' *liroe nico*: the proper readinj
are—Cic. Fin. 2. 23 (from Lucilius) *hirsizon* (whatever that may cor
ceal), Propert. 4. 7. 49 *Chio*, Ov. Fast. 6. 674 *lata*, Plaut. Poen. 13
collyrae, Plaut. Truc. 624-625 *viceris* . . . *vicerim*.—I have omitted als
Adverbs and Conjunctions of which the sole peculiarity lies in th
termination (such being sufficiently explained by Stolz ,or Victo:
Henry); and loanwords from the Greek of which the originals are
sufficiently treated in ' Etyma Graeca ' or (in the case of derivatives)
in Liddell and Scott.

380 words of obscure origin, which cannot as yet be classified, these 3055 words fall into the following three classes :

I. 'inherited' words, having cognates in other Indoceltic languages : about 1130.

II. 'manufactured' words, derivatives or compounds of the words in class I. : about 930.

III. 'imported' words, borrowed from Greek or other languages : about 615.

So much for the scope of the work : next for details of its arrangement. The sign † preceding a 'head-word' (i.e. the first word of an article) denotes that the word is borrowed from some foreign language. (It is often however difficult to draw the line : Latin *derivatives* from loanwords, e.g. *topiarius*, are left unmarked.) Loanwords which are not 'head-words' are marked either by † preceding, or by being put in brackets : thus after the translation of each head-word I give in brackets the more interesting of the English words borrowed (often through many stages) from the Latin word. For details on these English loanwords I would refer to Skeat's 'Concise Etymological Dictionary of the English Language' : where he puts several words under one head I have given the leading word and added the sign '&c.'. It is of course often difficult to decide whether a word is borrowed or not : I suppose Gothic *haban* to be borrowed from Latin *habeo*, the Teutons originally having no word for 'have' (the Welsh still have none, and in Latin itself we may say 'est mihi pater' for 'habeo patrem'). When two loanwords in any language are nearly identical in form the sign † is put before the first only, e.g. †*balneum balineum*, †τάπης δάπις.

A numeral after a word denotes that the word concurs in form with another word, or even several other words, of

distinct origin : I have thus been obliged to divide *praest*
into two words, *stringō* into three, *ruō* into four.

Cognates in Umbrian and Osco-Sabellian are given only
when they are in themselves instructive. The cognates
from other languages are given in the following order
Greek, Celtic, Teutonic, Balto-Slavic, Armenian, Arian.
I have not thought it necessary to give a cognate from
Welsh when I had given one from Irish, nor from Old
Norse or Anglosaxon or German when I had given one
from Gothic, nor from Lettish or Prussian when I had
given one from Lithuanian.—When possible, Nouns are
given in the Nominative Singular (a rule embracing words
from Hesychius which he gives in some other case) : Verbs
are given in Zend and Sanskrit in their roots, in Teutonic
and Old Slavonic (unless the translation shows otherwise)
in the Infinitive, in other languages in the First Singular
Present Indicative. Roots, stems, and words found only
as the first element of a compound are marked by a dash
following; which is itself accented (∠) when we know from
Verner's Law (that after a barytone vowel a Tenuis becomes
in Teutonic not an Aspirate but a Media) that such was
the original pitch-accent. (The accent, when marked,
always denotes pitch-accent or 'tone,' not stress-accent.)
Greek disyllabic Prepositions are marked as paroxytone.
Enclitics in Greek have a grave accent, in other languages
a dash preceding. Sanskrit words unaccented in the MSS.
are left unaccented.—Hypothetical forms are denoted either
by prefixing an asterisk or by putting a letter in brackets :
e.g. ἔλαι(Ϝ)ον denotes that ἔλαιον was originally ἔλαιϜον.—
The position of a single letter (or combination of letters) is
denoted by a dash; e.g. "*a-*" denotes initial *a*, "*-a-*"
medial *a*, "*-a*" final *a*.—When a word is given partly in
Roman partly in Italic type, the part in italics is alone to
be compared with the other words mentioned.—The sign

'fr.' may roughly be read as 'from,' more exactly as 'connected with'; it denotes that the two words have the same root, or are 'Ablauts' of each other.

The translation of a word, where no translation is given, is the same as that of the next-preceding translated word; translated, i.e., into English (for convenience' sake the translation is sometimes into Latin or Greek). Parentheses are not considered as interrupting the sequence of construction. The abbreviation 'E.' followed by a comma denotes that the English cognate has just been given as a translation of some other cognate word: the abbreviation 'E. E.' denotes not 'Early English' but that the English cognate has just been given and that one or more English cognates follow. A Latin or Greek word quoted simply for the sake of its form is left untranslated.—When a word is the same (as to both form and meaning) in two related languages, I write it only once: e.g. "Zd. Sk. *mā-* measure" shows that *mā-* means 'to measure' alike in Zend and Sanskrit. Similarly "Ags. E. *fin*" denotes that Anglosaxon *fin* and English *fin* are cognate words and of the same meaning.

As a rule a vowel not marked long is to be reckoned short. But to this rule there are some limitations:

(1) When a vowel in Latin stands before two consonants I have endeavoured to mark it according to its etymological quantity, not according to the quantity it may have acquired from the nature of the consonants; and where the etymology is obscure or ambiguous the quantity, if marked, is not to be taken as a guide to the possible etymology, *fōrma* may go with *ferio* 'strike' (as τύπος 'form' with τύπτω) though in deference to authority I have marked the *o* long (see note at end of preface):

(2) As to marks of length in other languages than Latin: I have, following my authorities, left unmarked the quantities of Umbrian, Oscan, and Welsh vowels. I have

marked Gothic and Sanskrit ē ō, though always long, bu
left unmarked Lithuanian y ú ė o and Old Slavonic i y u a
which likewise are always long. In Irish and Old Norse]
mark vowels as long, not with an accent : in Anglosaxon]
write eā eō (not, as Sweet does, ēa ēo), and use ae oe foɪ
the long diphthongs, ä ö for the short. In Lettish I write
ē not eh, in Old Slavonic ē not ě.

A note of interrogation at the end of an article is meant
to apply to the words preceding after the last colon or
semicolon. In the explanation of a Compound, e.g. *mani-
festus*, the note of interrogation implies that the second half
of the Compound is of obscure origin.—Where no etymology
at all is given, it is to be understood that none yet proposed
is satisfactory : in many of such cases the ordinary (un-
scientific) etymology may be found in Lewis and Short.
The following 360 derivations are, so far as I know (it is
difficult in such matters to speak with certainty), my own :

abdo	arma	caelebs	cicuta
abdomen	arvina	caepe	clandestinus
abundo	as	caerimonia	coepi
accerso	asper	caliga	colocasium
acervus	assula	callis	coluber
adeo	ast	cantharus	comis
adulor	ater	capistrum	comissor
aequus	atrox	carbo	como
agnitus	auster	carduus	concipilo
aha	autem	careo	condalium
alacer	bajulus	caries	condo
alapa	balneum	cataractria	conquinisco
allex	balo	catasta	corbis
almus	boletus	census	corbita
alucinor	boreas	cepolendrum	cortina
aluta	bubulcus	cervix	cottidie
ambulo	bufo	ceu	crambe
amo	bulla	cicada	crocio
apium	cachinnus	cicatrix	cucumis
apricus	cacumen	ciconia	culex

culus	fore	jejunus	minus
cumulus	formīca	jento	mirus
cunctus	formido	juxta	miser
cuniculus	fortassis	lacertus	mitis
de	fritillus	lacuna	monedula
delibero	fuligo	lambero	moretum
demo	furca	lamina	morus
densus	furfur	lanista	mucro
dirus	fusus	lanius	mutus
discipulus	gemini	laterna	nempe
doceo	genesta	lens	nihilum
dodrans	germanus	lēvis	nimbus
doleo	glans	libo	nimis
domicilium	gravastellus	libum	niteo
drapeta	grex	lignum	non
dubius	gutta	lima	norma
dudum	guttur	lis	nota
duplex	hapalopsis	littera	numella
ecce	hira	liveo	nutrio
edepol	hospes	locuples	obliviscor
ehem	humanus	luridus	obturo .
elegans	icio	luscus	officium
ellum	identidem	lŭstrum	omentum
emineo	ideo	mancus	opimus
emusitatus	igitur	mando	oportet
enim	ilex	mane	optimus
erga	ilia	manipulus	opto
eruca	imitor	manubiae	paedico
euax	immanis	marceo	paelex
exploro	impraesentiarum	marsupium	palear
fames	inanis .	materia	palpo
farfarus	incilo	medeor	panicum
ferula	incolumis	memor	papilio
ficus	inferus	mensa	parra
finis	infestus	mensus	parricida
firmus	inquam	mentula	patior
fistuca	invidus	meo	patro
fistula	invitus	mereo	pectus
flaccus	ipse	merops	perinde
flamma	ita	merus	perperam
focus	item	mico	piget
foedus Adj.	itidem	minae	pignus
fons	jam	minor	pingo

pituita	quantus	scrinium	sudiculum
placeo	quidem	seria	sumo
placusia	quoque	serperastra	suspicio
plaustrum	radius	sileo	tabula
ploro	ramus	siler	taeter
ploxenum	renideo	sin	tamen
pluteus	repudium	sincerus	tantus
polio	reus	sirempse	tardus
pollex	rima	sirpe	territorium
polluceo	rivus	sisymbrium	testa
populor	robur	sobrius	titillo
porrigo	rorarii	sodalis	turgeo
portorium	rudis Adj.	soleo	uligo
praefica	rudus	sollemnis	ulva
praestigiae	ruo[1]	solvo	urtica
prior	ruscum	specus	ûter
privus	ruta	spiro	vaco
proinde	rutilus	sponda	varius
promo	sacer	stilus	vehemens
proprius	saeculum	stimulus	venor
protelum .	salaputium	stipula	venter
prox	saltem	strages	verrunco
pudeo .	saltus	strigilis	vidulus
pulcher	sapa	stringo[1]	vilis
pulmentum	sartago	stuprum	villa
puppis	savium	suavium	vito
quadra	scapulae	subtemen	vitricus.

I have as far as possible avoided the use of strange symbols. In words given (in small capitals) as from the 'Ursprache,' the 'sonant' liquids are denoted by a dot below, and the long sonants are further marked as long: for the consonants corresponding to i and u I use j and v, to be pronounced like English y in *yet* and w in *wet* respectively: the 'velar' gutturals I write with a v following (the sign k-v, see *equus*, denotes that the k and the v are distinct elements), the distinction of 'fixt' and 'labialisable' velars being left to be gathered from a comparison of the cognate forms or from the notes in Part II.—In Old Umbrian I write ḍ, not ḍ or ṛ; in Lithuanian iė, not ė; in Old Sla-

vonic **h**, not **ch**. In Armenian, for the aspirates I write
ph, th, kh; for Hübschmann's 25th letter I use **thš**, for
his 33rd **ths**. In Zend I write **aē** not **aẹ**, **ç** not **s**, **q** not
hv. For the Hebrew Aleph I give no sign, for Ayin ', for
Shevā '; for He I write **h**, for Cheth **ḥ**.

A few points of pronunciation may be noticed :

(a) Umbrian **ç** or (New Umbrian) **ŝ** = Eng. *s* in *see*; **ḋ** = Eng. *th* in
the :

(β) Welsh **au** = German *ai* (Eng. 'Aye'), **aw** = Eng. *ow* in *cow*;
dd = Eng. *th* in *the*, **ll** = an aspirated *l* (i.e. *h* + *l*, or, when
final, *l* + *h*) :

(γ) Gothic **gg** = Eng. *ng*, **q** = Eng. *qu* :

(δ) Lithuanian **y** = Eng. *i* in *machine*; **ŭ** = *û* + *o*; **ė** and **o** are pronounced 'close' (see p. xv); **ą** and **ą̄** are now pronounced as
a and *ā* respectively. The 'falling' tone is marked ' on a short
vowel, ' on a long; the 'rising' tone (as in Eng. 'Why?') is
marked ˜ or ˆ. A consonant followed by i + another vowel is
pronounced soft, like German **k** in *kind* as opposed to **k** in *kahn* :
sz = Eng. *sh*, **z** = Eng. *z*, **ž** (Lettish **š**) = French *j* (Eng. *s* in
leisure), **c** = Eng. *ts*, **cz** = Eng. *ch*.

(ε) Old Slavonic **y** = a (long) 'modified' or French *u*; **ę** = French
in in *vin*, **ą** = French *on* in *bon*. Of the consonants, **š** = Eng.
sh, **č** = Eng. *ch*, while z ž c are pronounced as in Lithuanian.

(ζ) Armenian λ is a 'guttural' *r*, **ṙ** a 'hard' *r*; **j** = Eng. *dz* in *adze*,
ǰ = Eng. *j* in *jet*; **š** = Eng. *sh*, **z** = Eng. *z*, **ž** = French *j* (see
above), **c** = Eng. *ts*, **č** = Eng. *ch*.

(η) Zend **aē** = German *ai*, **ao** = German *au* : **c** = Eng. *ch*, **ç** = Eng.
sh, **j** and **z** are pronounced as in English : **q** = Eng. *h* + *w* (as
in the dialectic Eng. pronunciation of *when*). The pronunciation of **ḋ** and **ḣh** is unknown.

(θ) Sanskrit **y** as Eng. *y* in *yet*; **c, ç, j**, as in Zend (Sanskrit **sh** has a
stronger aspiration than **ç**). The 'linguals' (or 'cerebrals') **ṭ ḍ**
ṭh ḍh ṇ are pronounced 'with the tip of the tongue turned up
and drawn back' (Whitney), but are not by us distinguishable
from ordinary dentals.

The notes in Part II. on the various cognate languages
embrace only the words quoted in Part I., and of course are
not meant to be exhaustive.

I have to acknowledge many obligations to Professor Macdonell, Margoliouth, Nettleship, Rhys, and Sayce; to Dr. Neubauer, Dr. Whitley Stokes, F. Y. Powell, and my colleague W. M. Lindsay; and, on points of natural history to my brother, H. T. Wharton, editor of 'Sappho'.

I hope in some future year to complete the subject by an analysis of the 1265 'sub-classical' words found in fragments of our sixteen authors or in less important authors of the classical period. But in England even the worst etymologist meets little encouragement.

E. R. WHARTON.

Oxford, *St. David's Day*, 1890.

NOTE ON HIDDEN QUANTITIES

It seems that certain combinations of consonants in Latin lengthened the preceding vowel, others shortened it, others (which is most perplexing of all) sometimes lengthened sometimes shortened it, probably in different dialects; and, to complicate matters still more, each of our rules has numerous exceptions. For the determination of these 'hidden' quantities I have used Seelmann's 'Aussprache' pp. 69-108, Marx's 'Hülfsbüchlein,' and (for the Romance languages) Gröber's 'Vulgarlateinische Substrate Romanischer Wörter' in Wölfflin's 'Archiv'. The authorities on which these writers rely are:

(α) the testimony of Latin Grammarians ('Gramm.'), and the old spellings of ī ū as ei ou:

(β) the usage of Plautus and Terence, who before Mute + Liquid allow a vowel to be long only when it was long by nature:

(γ) the marks given in Inscriptions ('Inscrr.'), the ī carved taller than usual, the other long vowels accented:

(δ) the Greek transcription of Latin words ('Gk.'), ī ū = ει ου, ē ō = η ω:

(ε) the evidence of the Romance languages ('Rom.'), which represent ī ū by *i u* but ĭ ŭ by *e o*, and ē ō by close *e o* (pronounced i.e. with the tongue convex) but ĕ ŏ by open *e o* (pronounced with the tongue flat).

A. Combinations which lengthen the preceding vowel:

(a) **ns nf** (according to Cicero and the Latin Grammarians), Cic. *cōnsuevit insanus cōnfecit infelix*, Inscrr.[1] and Gk. *cōnsul*, Gramm.

---

[1] The signs 'Gramm.' 'Inscrr.' 'Gk.' 'Rom.' in these pages may be read 'according to the Latin Grammarians, inscriptions, the Greek transcription, the Romance languages': i.e. the abbreviation denotes the source from which we learn the quantity of the vowel.

and Rom. *īnsula*, Inscrr. *īnferus*. Yet one dialect must hav
allowed the natural quantity, Gk. *Cōnstantinus* (1st century A.D
cōnsul (6th century, beside *Cōnstantīnus !*), Priscian *mānsi*, Rom
cōnsilium cōnficio īnfans.

(β) **nqv** in *quīnque* (Inscrr. Gk. and Rom.), **ngv** apparently in *pīngui*
(Rom., Gröber 'Grundriss der Romanischen Philologie,' p. 50
note). Yet not in one dialect, Rom. *propīnquus līngua ūnguis*.

(γ) **gn** (according to Priscian), Inscrr. *dīgnus sīgnum*. Yet not ii
one dialect, Gk. *cōgnitus*, Gramm. and Rom. *dīgnus*, Rom. *līgnun*
pīgnus pūgnus sīgnum.—Apparently also **gm** (Marx p. 2), Inscrr
and Rom. *pīgmentum*, Gk. *sēgmen*.

(δ) **ct** from **g** + **t** (Seelmann pp. 78, 90), Inscrr. *lēctus* ('bed') *līctor*
Rom. *lūctor*. Yet not in one dialect, Gk. and Rom. *lĕctus.*—S(
x from **g** + **s** (Seelmann pp. 78-79, 91) seems to have had ɛ
lengthening effect, Inscrr. *māximus*, Inscrr. and Gk. *vēxillum*.

B. Combinations which shorten the preceding vowel:

(a) **nt** (Marx p. 1-2), Gramm. *cŏntio* from *coventio*, Gk. *frŏntem mŏntem*
pŏntem vĕntus. Yet one dialect allowed the natural quantity,
Gramm. *nūntius*, (Inscrr. Gk. and Rom. *quīntus*), Inscrr. *frōntem*,
Rom. *fōntem mōntem pōntem* (so Gröber in his articles in Wölfflin's 'Archiv'; in his 'Grundriss' p. 522 he makes the **o**
short).—So **nd**, Rom. *harŭndo hirŭndo ŭndecim* (from *ūnus*), cf.
splĕndeo (Lithuanian *splĕndžiu*) from σπλήν, *vindex* (βίνδιξ) from
vēnum. Yet not in one dialect, Gramm. *harūndo hirūndo*, Inscrr.
nōndum nūndinum, Rom. *frōndem* (Gröber is ambiguous, as above)
prēndo vēndo.

(β) **l** + any consonant, Gramm. *remŭlcum* (ῥῠμουλκοῦν), Rom. *corŏlla*
(from *corŏna*) *ŭltra *ŭlcem* (from *ilicem*: so even with a vowel
between, *pŭlegium*), and *văllum* whence Anglosaxon *veal*. Yet
not in one dialect, Inscrr. *ūltra vāllum*, Inscrr. and Rom. *mīlle*
ōlla vīlla, Rom. *anguīlla favīlla mūllus stīlla trūlla*: which cannot be *lengthenings*, as the Romance languages substantiate
capīllus cucūllus ('cuckoo') *īlle mŏllis pŭllus* ('dark') *sĕlla vīllus*,
pŭlmo pŭlpa sīlva.

(γ) Before Mute + Liquid a vowel is generally short, and hence *ēbrius*
nūtrix (Plautus) show in the Romance languages a short root-
vowel.

C. Combinations which in one dialect lengthen, in another
shorten, the vowel:

(*a*) nc lengthens the vowel in Inscrr. *cūnctus fūnctus jūnctus sānctus* and so *conjūnx*, Gramm. and Rom. *ūnctus*, Rom. *cīnctus tīnctus pūnctus*. Yet one dialect allowed the natural quantity, Rom. *pŭnctus ŭnctus* (Seelmann p. 90).—But it shortens the vowel in Rom. *jŭncus* (Ἰούγκος) *ŭncia* (οὐγκία).

(*β*) r + another consonant lengthens the vowel in Inscrr. *ārca ārvum hōrtus quārtus* (*ārma pērnix* are marked as barbarisms), Rom. *cōrtina pērtica*. Yet not in one dialect, Plaut. *ĕrgo*, Gramm. *ărs ărx părs*, Gk. *cŏrtina pĕrtica*, Gk. and Rom. *cĭrcus fŏrtis vĭrga*, Rom. *fŭrnus stĕrcus*.—But it shortens the vowel in Rom. *lărdum* (lāridum) **lŭrdum* (= lūridum) *fŭrca* (which I would derive from *fūr*). Which represents the natural quantity, *fĭrmus* (Inscrr., Seelmann p. 92, cf. *fŭlus*) or *fīrmus* (Rom., cf. *fīdes*), we cannot tell; nor of course where the etymology is unknown, Inscrr. *sĕrvus* Rom. *ŏrca* do not prove that the vowel was by nature long, nor Gk. *fŏrmica ŏrbis ŭrna* Rom. *stĭrps ŭrceus* that it was by nature short. More perplexing still, our authorities sometimes differ, Gramm. Gk. and Rom. have *fōrma* but Gk. also *fŏrma*, Inscrr. and Rom. *ōrdo* but Gk. (and Irish) *ŏrdo*, Inscrr. and Rom. *ōrnŏ* but Gk. *ŏrnŏ*, Inscrr. *vīrgo* but Rom. *vĭrgo*.

(*γ*) s + any consonant lengthens the vowel in Gramm. *hēsternus*, Gk. *fōssa*, Rom. *hibīscum ūsque*, and cf. Priscian's *austrum* from *ōstrum*. Yet not in one dialect, Gk. Rom. *fŏssa*, Rom. *lŭscus misceo nŏster vĕster tĕsta*.—But it shortens the vowel in Gk. *ŏstium* (Inscrr. and Gk. *ōstium*), Rom. *fĕstus* (Inscrr. and Gk. *fēstus*) *fŭscus* (Inscrr. *fūscus*) and perhaps *gŭstus* (cf. γεύω), and I think in Gramm. *ăsper lanīsta* and Gk. *crăssus*. Where the etymology is unknown, or consonant with either supposition, we cannot tell whether the vowel was by nature short or long, Inscrr. *manifēstus viscus* Inscrr. and Rom. *tristis* Gk. *sōspes* Gk. and Rom. *cūstos* Rom. *ēsca fūstis hispidus* do not prove that the vowel was by nature long, nor Gk. *rĕstis* Gk. and Rom. *crĭsta* Rom. *fĭstula fŭscina mŭsca mŭstela* that it was by nature short. Sometimes too our authorities differ, Gk. has *bēstia* but Rom. (and later Gk.) *bĕstia*, Gk. *crĭspus* but Rom. *crĭspus*, Inscrr. *crūstum* but Rom. *crŭstum*, Inscrr. and Gk. *prīscus* but Gk. also *prĭscus*, Rom. has both *pĭscis* and *pĭscis*.

ABBREVIATIONS

Aen.	Aeneid.	*NHG.*	New High German.
Aeol.	Aeolic.	*NUmbr.*	New Umbrian.
Aesch.	Aeschylus.	*OE.*	Old English.
Ags.	Anglosaxon.	*OHG.*	Old High German.
anal.	analogy.	*OIr.*	Old Irish.
Ar.	Aristophanes.	*onomatop.*	onomatopoeic.
Arab.	Arabic.	*ONor.*	Old Norse.
Arm.	Armenian.	*OPers.*	Old Persian.
BB.	Bezzenberger's Beiträge.	*opp.*	as opposed to.
cf.	compare.	*orig.*	originally.
Dimin.	Diminutive.	*Osc.*	Oscan.
Diosc.	Dioscorides.	*OSlav.*	Old Slavonic.
Dor.	Doric.	*OUmbr.*	Old Umbrian.
E.	English.	*OW.*	Old Welsh.
EM.	Etymologicum Magnum.	*Part.*	Participle.
Etrusc.	Etruscan.	*Pers.*	Persian.
etym.	etymology.	*Plut.*	Plutarch.
fr.	connected with.	*Polyb.*	Polybius.
Fr.	French.	*pop.*	popular.
Geo.	Georgics.	*praeced.*	preceding word.
Got.	Gothic.	*Pruss.*	Prussian.
Heb.	Hebrew.	*Redupl.*	Reduplication.
Hes.	Hesiod.	*Rom.*	Roman.
Hesych.	Hesychius.	*Sab.*	Sabine.
Hom.	Homer.	*sc.*	scilicet.
Instrum.	Instrumental.	*Schol.*	Scholiast.
Interj.	Interjection.	*sec.*	according to.
Ion.	Ionic.	*Sicil.*	Sicilian.
Ir.	Irish.	*Sk.*	Sanskrit.
Ital.	Italian.	*sq.*	following word.
Lett.	Lettish.	*Subst.*	Substantive.
Lit.	Lithuanian.	*syll.*	syllable.
Loc.	Locative.	*term.*	termination.
Metath.	Metathesis.	*Umbr.*	Umbrian.
MHG.	Middle High German.	*Vb.*	Verb.
MIr.	Middle Irish.	*W.*	Welsh.
Neut.	Neuter.	*Zd.*	Zend.

Other abbreviations may be seen in Lewis & Short.

* denotes a hypothetical form.

† preceding a word denotes that it is a loan-word; † following a Sanskrit word, or meaning of a Sanskrit word, denotes that the word or meaning is unauthenticated (being found only in Sanskrit grammarians, not in literature).

SELECT LIST OF AUTHORITIES

(The numeral above the line indicates the number of the edition. — sq. here denotes 'and following years'.)

Balg, Comparative Glossary of the Gothic Language. 1887.

Bartholomae, Handbuch der Alt-Iranischen Dialekte. 1883.

Bedrossian, New Dictionary Armenian-English. 1875-1879.

Bezzenberger's Beiträge zur Kunde der Indogermanischen Sprachen. 1877 sq.

Bielenstein, Die Lettische Sprache. 1863.

Böhtlingk, Sanskrit-Wörterbuch in kürzerer fassung. 1879-1889.

Braune, Alt-Hoch-Deutsche Grammatik. 1886.

Bréal et Bailly, Dictionnaire étymologique Latin. 1885.

Brugmann, Griechische Grammatik.[2] 1889.

„   Grundriss der vergleichenden Grammatik der Indogermanischen Sprachen. 1886-1889.

Bruppacher, Versuch einer Lautlehre der Oskischen Sprache. 1869.

Corssen, Aussprache Vocalismus und Betonung der Lateinischen Sprache.[2] 1868-1870.

Curtius, Grundzüge der Griechischen Etymologie.[5] 1879.

Delitzsch, Assyrische Studien I. 1874.

Dioscorides, in Kühn's Medicorum Graecorum Opera vol. 25, 26. 1821.

Douse, Introduction to the Gothic of Ulfilas. 1886.

Ducange, Glossarium Mediae et Infimae Latinitatis. 1840-1850.

Feist, Grundriss der Gotischen Etymologie. 1888.

Festus, edited by C. O. Müller. 1880.

Fick, Vergleichendes Wörterbuch der Indogermanischen Sprachen.[3] 1874-1876.

Fritzner, Ordbog over det Gamle Norske Sprog. 1867.

Georges, Ausführliches Lateinisch-Deutsche Handwörterbuch. 1879-1880.

Graff, Alt-Hoch-Deutsche Sprachschatz. 1834-1846.

Grein, Bibliothek der Angelsächsischen Poesie. 1857-1864.

Hehn, Kulturpflanzen und Hausthiere.[3] 1877.

Helfenstein, Comparative Grammar of the Teutonic Languages. 1870.

Hesychius, edited by Moriz Schmidt. 1858-1862.

Hübschmann, Armenische Studien I. 1883.

Hübschmann, Indogermanisches Vocal-system. 1885.
  „   Umschreibung der Iranischen Sprachen. 1882.
Isidore of Seville, in Lindemann's Corpus Grammaticorum Latinorum vol. III. 1832.
Jablonski, Opuscula. 1804-1813.
Justi, Handbuch der Zend-sprache. 1864.
Keil, Grammatici Latini. 1857-1880.
Key, Latin-English Dictionary. 1888.
Kluge, Etymologisches Wörterbuch des Deutschen Sprache.⁴ 1888.
Kuhn's Zeitschrift für vergleichende Sprachforschung. 1852 sq.
Kurschat, Grammatik der Littauischen Sprache. 1876.
  „   Wörterbuch der Littauischen Sprache. 1883.
Lagarde, Arica. 1851.
Leo, Angelsächsisches Glossar. 1877.
Leskien, Handbuch der Alt-Bulgarischen Sprache. 1871.
Lewis and Short, Latin Dictionary. 1880.
Liddell and Scott, Greek-English Lexicon.⁷ 1883.
Mahlow, Die Langen Vocale A E O in den Europäischen Sprachen. 1879.
Marx, Hülfsbüchlein für die Aussprache der Lateinischen Vocale in positionslangen Silben.² 1889.
Mémoires de la Société de Linguistique de Paris. 1869 sq.
Meyer G., Griechische Grammatik.² 1886.
Miklosich, Etymologisches Wörterbuch der Slavischen Sprachen. 1886.
  „   Lexicon Palaeo-Slovenico-Graeco-Latinum. 1865.
Murray J. A. H., New English Dictionary. 1888 sq.
Nesselmann, Thesaurus Linguae Prussicae. 1873.
Nettleship, Contributions to Latin Lexicography. 1889.
Noreen, Alt-Nordische Grammatik. 1884.
O'Reilly and O'Donovan, Irish-English Dictionary. 1864.
Osthoff, Zur Geschichte des Perfects in Indogermanischen. 1884.
  „   *und Brugman*, Morphologische Untersuchungen. 1878-1880.
Paul, Principien der Sprachgeschichte.² 1886.
Pauli, Preussische Studien, in Kuhn's Beiträge VII. 1870.
Peyron, Lexicon Linguae Copticae. 1835.
Phrynichus, edited by Lobeck. 1820.
Pierret, Vocabulaire Hiéroglyphique. 1875.
Plautus, edited by Ritschl, Loewe, Goetz, and Schoell. 1871 sq.
Pliny, Natural History, edited by Jan. 1857-1880.
Pughe, Welsh Dictionary.³ 1866-1873.
Rhys, Hibbert Lectures. 1888.
  „   Lectures on Welsh Philology.² 1879.
Roby, Grammar of the Latin Language.⁴ 1881-1882.

Saalfeld, Tensaurus Italo-graecus. 1884.

Saussure F. de, Mémoire sur le système primitif des Voyelles. 1879.

Sayce, Introduction to the Science of Language. 1880.

Schade, Alt-Deutsches Wörterbuch. 1872-1882.

Schmidt Johannes, Zur Geschichte des Indogermanischen Vocalismus. 1871-1875.

Schneider Engelbert, Dialecti Latinae priscae et Faliscae exempla selecta I. 1886.

Seelmann, Aussprache des Latein. 1885.

Sievers, Angelsächsische Grammatik. 1882.

Sittl, Lokalen Verschiedenheiten der Lateinischen Sprache. 1882.

Skeat, Concise Etymological Dictionary of the English Language. 1882.

  ,,   Etymological Dictionary of the English Language.[2] 1884.

Sophocles, Greek Lexicon of the Roman and Byzantine periods. 1870.

Spiegel, Alt-Persischen Keil-inschriften. 1881.

  ,,   Vergleichende Grammatik der Alt-êranischen Sprachen. 1882.

Stokes, Celtic Declension. 1886.

  ,,   Neo-celtic Verb Substantive. 1885.

  ,,   Remarks on the Celtic additions to Curtius' Greek Etymology. 1875.

  ,,   Three Irish Glossaries. 1862.

Stolz, Lateinische Grammatik.[2] 1889.

Sweet, Anglosaxon Reader. 1879.

Ulfilas, Heyne's edition of Stamm.[8] 1885.

Ulmann, Lettisches Wörterbuch. 1872-1880.

Van Eys, Dictionnaire Basque-Français. 1873.

Vaniček, Fremdwörter in Griechischen und Lateinischen. 1878.

  ,,   Griechisch-Lateinisches Etymologisches Wörterbuch. 1877.

Varro de Lingua Latina, edited by A. Spengel. 1885.

Vigfusson, Icelandic-English Dictionary. 1874.

Weise, Griechischen Wörter im Latein. 1882.

Wharton E. R., Etyma Graeca. 1882.

  ,,   Latin Vocalism (Philological Society). 1888.

  ,,   Loanwords in Latin (do.). 1889.

  ,,'   On Latin Consonant-Laws (do.). 1889.

Whitney, Sanskrit Grammar.[2] 1889.

Windisch, Irische Texte I. 1880.

  ,,   Kurzgefasste Irische Grammatik. 1879.

Wölfflin, Archiv für Lateinischen Lexicographie. 1884 sq.

Zenker, Türkisch-Arabisch-Persisches Handwörterbuch. 1866-1876.

Zeuss, Grammatica Celtica.[2] 1871-1881.

Zvetaieff, Inscriptiones Italiae mediae dialecticae. 1884.

  ,,   Sylloge Inscriptionum Oscarum. 1878.

CONTENTS

INTRODUCTION

THE languages spoken by the nations of Europe, with isolated exceptions (the ancient Etruscans, the modern Basques of north Spain, the Magyars, Turks, Esthonians, Livonians, Ugrians, Finns, and Lapps), and of Asia from the Caucasus to Ceylon, resemble each other sufficiently to justify the supposition that they all descend from one common original or 'Ursprache'; the speakers of which, issuing from Scandinavia in search of a warmer climate, separated in various directions. The Teutonic stock remained in Scandinavia or occupied central Europe; the Celtic race proceeded to the British Isles, Gaul, and Spain; the Italic to Italy; the Albanian to the east side of the Adriatic; the Hellenic to Greece; the Balto-Slavic to eastern Europe; the Armenian, probably through Thrace and Asia Minor, to the district south of the Caucasus; the Arian to Persia and India.

The family of languages here described has been denoted by several names, none quite satisfactory. The quasi-biblical term 'Japhetic' has died out, though the corresponding term 'Semitic' has survived: all the other terms hitherto suggested labour under the defect of insinuating that the race came originally from India, a view wholly untenable. Max Müller's 'Aryan,' from Sanskrit *aryas* 'a high-caste man,' has the merit of being short, and of lending itself to the convenient compound 'un-Aryan,' but is in pronunciation indistinguishable from 'Arian,' the term applied by the Germans to Zend and Sanskrit: of the three compound designations, 'Indo-Germanic,' by far the worst, as excluding the Celtic branch, has been adopted by the Germans, Bopp's 'Indo-European' is cumbrous and not quite accurate, while the French 'Indo-Celtic' is logical enough, as giving the two extreme branches of the family, and might perhaps be adopted in the modified form 'Celtindic'.

Albanian, with a literature dating only from the 17th century, is of too little importance to be here noticed : sufficient information on it will be found in Gustav Meyer's 'Albanesische Studien' (1883-1884). The remaining seven branches of the family may be thus distributed : ·

(1) Teutonic:
> *Gothic*, preserved in Ulfilas' translation of the New Testament, 4th century of our era.
> *Old Norse* or Icelandic, with literature from the 12th century.
> *Anglosaxon* or Old English, from the 7th to the 13th century.
> *Old High German*, with glosses from the 8th century; *Middle* do., the language of the Nibelungenlied, 12th century; *New* do., from the 16th century.

(2) Celtic:
> *Gaulish*, a few remains derived from Latin authors or inscriptions.
> *Old Irish*, glosses of the 8th and 9th centuries: *Middle Irish*, the earliest MS. A.D. 1100.
> *Welsh*, glosses of the 8th and 9th centuries: the earliest MS. of the 12th century.

(3) Italic:
> *Latin*, the first inscription perhaps 300 B.C.; earliest author (Plautus) 224 B.C.
> *Umbrian*, preserved in the Eugubine Tables, the first part ('Old Umbrian,' perhaps 200 B.C.) written in Etruscan characters, the last ('New Umbrian,' perhaps 100 B.C.: from V. b. 7 to the end) in Latin.
> *Osco-Sabellian*, inscriptions from about 200 B.C.

(4) *Greek*, from Homer (B.C. 800?).

(5) Balto-Slavic or Lithu-Slavic:
> *Lithuanian*, with literature from the 16th century.
> *Lettish*, from the 16th century.

Prussian or Old Prussian, of the 15th and 16th centuries, now extinct.

Old Slavonic, Church-Slavonic or Old Bulgarian, from a translation of the Bible by Methodius and Cyrillus, 9th century.

(6) *Armenian* or Old Armenian, 5th to 11th century.

(7) Arian:

Zend or Old Bactrian, the language of the Avesta, the oldest parts of which are said to date from 1000 B.C.

Old Persian, the language of the Behistun inscriptions, about 500 B.C.

Sanskrit, said to date from 1000 B.C., and divided into two periods, Vedic and Classical Sanskrit, the latter from about 400 B.C. The earliest Indian inscriptions date from about 250 B.C.

The Ursprache, if the speakers of it had known how to write, would perhaps have had the following alphabet:

Vowels: I, U, Ü, E, O, A: Ī, Ū, Ǖ, Ē, Ō, Ā.

Diphthongs: EI, OI, AI: EU, OU, AU: ĒI, ŌI, ĀI: ĒU, ŌU, ĀU.

Sonants: Ṃ, Ṇ, Ḷ, Ṛ: Ṃ̄, Ṇ̄, Ḹ, Ṝ.

Liquids: M, N, L, R.—Semivowels: J, V.

Explosives:

Labial P, B, PH, BH.

Dental T, D, TH, DH.

Palatal K, G, KH, GH.—Velar KV, GV, KHV, GHV.

Sibilants: S, Z.

The Ursprache must have possessed a 'modified' or French u (which I write ü), short and long, written sometimes **u**, sometimes (apparently later) **i**: it appears frequently in Latin, see p. 119, less often in Greek (e.g. ὕψος-ἶψος) and Old Slavonic (see *stipula*), and in Sanskrit in **ul il** as representing sonant L.—The Arian languages sometimes have **i** where other languages have **a**, see *pater;* but the **i** may be due to foreign influence, and hardly necessitates the theory of an 'indefinite' vowel (which Brugmann writes as an inverted **e**), in sound between **a** and **e**.—Diphthongs beginning in a long vowel are rare.— For sonant or vocalic **r** Sanskrit uses a single letter, ṛ:

the other sonants in Sanskrit, and all the sonants in other languages, are represented by a liquid + a vowel (usually *before* the liquid) differing in different languages, and of course different in the short form and in the long. A sonant may stand either in the accented syllable, e.g. **re** in Eng. *pretty*, or (more often) in the unaccented, e.g. **en** in Eng. *seven*, **le** or **il** in Eng. *able, evil*.

Whether we ought to recognise 'spirants' **j** and **v**, as distinct from the semivowels **j** and **v**, is extremely doubtful: the 'spirant' **v** is nowhere distinguishable from the semivowel **v**, and the 'spirant' **j**, distinguished only in Greek (where it appears as initial ζ, see *jam jugum jūs*[1] *zōna*), may be only a strongly-pronounced semivowel **j**.—The Tenues Aspiratae, PH, TH, KH, KHV, are rare except in Greek, in which φ θ χ represent both kinds of Aspirates.— Palatals and Velars alike are usually called Gutturals: the palatals seem to have been pronounced nearer the front of the mouth (as **k** in Eng. *kill*), the velars further back (as **c** in Eng. *cool*). The palatals are preserved in the Western languages (Teutonic Celtic Italic and Greek), but in the Eastern (Balto-Slavic Armenian and Arian) become spirants: the velars in the Eastern languages are written as **k g gh** (or their equivalents) with no **v** following, while in the Western languages they vary in different words, i.e. are sometimes written as **k g gh** (or their equivalents) with no **v** following, and sometimes with a **v** following or (dialectically) as Labials or (in certain positions) Dentals. It is thus possible that we ought to recognise two different sets of velars, which have been kept apart in the Western languages and confused in the Eastern: the 'fixt' velar in the roots given below under *secó garrió congius gradus* shows no sign of a **v** in any language, the 'labialisable' velar given under *sequor venió ninguit* regularly shows a **v** (or is labialised) in the Western languages. But how the two sets were distinguished in pronunciation, or how to represent them, does not appear.

The perhaps insoluble question of the origin of language does not fall within our province. It may suffice to observe that onomatopoeic words, imitations of sounds, are rare in the daughter-languages, and must have been correspondingly rare in the Ursprache. Of this kind in Latin are the following :

(1) from human sounds : Nouns *amita mamma pappus* (all infantile), *balbus stloppus* : Verbs *lallō pappō* (both infantile), *screō*, and see *bibō* : Interjections *ā ō, hahae hau hei hēja heu hui, ēheu ehō ōhē, ēm ēn, bat, fū fī, *vā* (spelt *vah* or *vaha*), *ātāt tat tatae, prō prox, st, heus.*

(2) from sounds of animals : dog see *baubor*, sheep *bālō* ; chicken *pīpō*, cuckoo *cucūlus*, hoopoe *upupa*, owl *būbō strix tū*, raven *crōciō*.

(3) from inanimate sounds : *strepō strīdō tīniō tintinō, tax tuxtax* (these two expressing the sound of blows).

A kind of Onomatopoeia appears in the initial Reduplication of some words : either the whole root is given twice over, *cincinnus* (of obscure formation) *tintinō ululō*, or to it is prefixt the initial consonant + i in Verbs, *gignō sīdō sistō titubō* (see also *jējentō jējūnus*), u in Nouns, *cucurbita susurrus.*

The Ursprache was doubtless, like each of the daughter-languages, a congeries of different dialects. In one of these initial s before a Tenuis was dropt, whence we have by-forms in **sp-** and **p-**, **st-** and **t-**, **sc-** and **c-**, see p. 127. So also the variation in the ending of certain numerals, see *decem novem septem*, may have been dialectic.—Other pairs of forms are more difficult to understand, see under *juvenis, rāpum rēte, quattuor quinque sex, alcēs grūs turdus.*—Apparently one dialect preferred (as Old Slavonic does) open syllables, i.e. those ending in a vowel : hence the occasional instances of Metathesis in the case of liquids, **on-no** see *umbilīcus umbra unguis*, **ir-ri** *circus*, **ur-ru** *socer*, **er-re** *crēdō terreō*, and in one dialect the vowel in such cases was lengthened, see *frētus plēnus.* So the two ways of representing ̦L and ̦R in Latin point to different dialects in the Ursprache: one had LĀ, RĀ, the other *ăl, *ăr, and thence (if a consonant followed) AL, AR.

In the Ursprache, as in the daughter-languages, the majority of words were disyllabic; and we may call the first part of the word the 'root' and the rest the termination, without supposing that either root or termination was ever used independently. The root, and to some extent the termination, were subject as to their vocalism to definite changes of form ('vowel-gradation' or 'Ablaut'), probably originally depending on grammatical construction: i.e. the word acquired a stronger meaning by copying the vocalism of some forcible word, an ordinary meaning by copying the vocalism of most ordinary words, a weaker meaning by copying the vocalism of less emphatic words. Such Ablaut may be of three kinds: any vowel may be either long or short, certain vowels (especially **e** and **o**) may interchange, **e** (and in some few cases **o**.[1]) may disappear entirely. Latin examples of Ablaut are the following:

(1) vowel long or short:

     I *liquor-liquŏ strĭx vĭbēx-vibrŏ.*

     U *nūbō-prōnuba pūsus-pusillus pūteŏ-puter rŭdō scūtum-scutica*, and see *suppus.*

     E *lēx-legō rēx-regō sēdēs-sedeō tēgula-tegō*, and see *sŏpiō.*

     O *glŏmus mōles-molestus* (?) *nōs-noster prō-pro- scrōfa-scrobis vōx-vocŏ,* and see *cŏmis cŭpēs offa persŏna.*

     A *ācer-alacer flāgitŏ-flagrum indāgŏ-agō lābor-labŏ mācerŏ-macō mānemanus sāgiŏ-sagāx stŏ-destinŏ vādō-vadum,* and see *mamma.*

     Sonants: ṇ *gnārus-ingens,* ̦L *flāvus-fulvus lātus-tulī largus-indulgeŏ,* ̦R *grātus-hortor prāvus-por- marceŏ-morior pars-portiŏ.*

(2) different vowels:

     E-O: *meditor-modus necŏ-noceō nectō-noxa* (?) *pendō-pondus precor-procus regō-rogŏ sedeō-solium sequor-socius tegō-toga.* So *gemō-gumia jaciō-jocus niteō-nota,* and see *foveō-faveō meminī-moneō.*

---

[1] So sometimes **a**, see *ambi- ante arduus horreum latus, sŏrex sŭdus.*

E-ō only in the terminations -tĕr -tōr (both later shortened).
Ē-A imbēcillus-baculum, and see langueō reor: in satus beside sēmen the **a** may be pretonic for **e**.
Ō-A only in dōnum-dare nōscō-agnitus: in catus beside cōs the **a** may be pretonic for **o**.

(3) vowel omitted:

   E : (α) in a diphthong: EI dīcō-dicāx fĭdō-fĭdēs, EU dūcō-dux trūdō-trudis, EÜ jūgis-jugum līber-libet.

      (β) initial before an explosive in dens sum.

      (γ) between two explosives, one disappearing in Latin, see hospes sīdō quartus.

      (δ) between explosive and liquid, the latter becoming a sonant, N see tenuis, L pulmentum, R extorris fors mordeō sors storea urgeō.

      (ε) between liquid and explosive, the former becoming a sonant, M infit (?), N infula (?), R fortis gurges pōscō (= *poroscō) turpis, and with long sonant flaccus.

   O : (α) in a diphthong, see faveō-fuī :

      (β) between two explosives, -pte :

      (γ) between explosive and liquid, the latter becoming a (long) sonant, lāna :

      (δ) between liquid and explosive, the former becoming a sonant, pulcer.

So in terminations :

(1) vowel long or short: Nom. abiēs ariēs pariēs, Gen. abiĕtis &c.
(2) different vowel: E-O lītera-litus temperō-tempus, and see annus.
(3) vowel omitted: E between consonants, aes ansa fār, and see amnis annus, corylus sōl, ascia mēnsis. So Ē of the (original) Nom. drops in the oblique cases, ācer pater and on this analogy ager &c. ; and so ō of stem nepōs-neptis soror-sobrīnus, or of Nom. carō-carnis cf. homō-hominis, and see collis cornīx.

A phenomenon akin to Ablaut is the insertion of a nasal before explosive or sibilant at the end of the root: pampinus nimbus, prehendō (?), sanciō, fringilla jungō langueō ninguit pungō, fimbriae pinsō.

When a new idea arose, or a modification of an old idea, it was apparently expressed in the Ursprache not by a wholly new word, which would have been unintelligible, but by giving some existent word a fresh termination. Sometimes the initial consonant of the new termination necessitated a change in the final consonant of the 'root' or first syllable : hence we may explain occasional fluctuations in the root-ending, between **b** and **bh** *cubó*, **k** and **g** *pāx pāgina*, **kv** and **gv** *mūgilis sūcus*.

A sufficient account of the various terminations of words in the Ursprache is given in Brugmann's 'Grundriss,' vol. ii. The following list of Noun-endings contains only those found in words with which in this work we are concerned, with one or two examples of each ending :

(A) Vowel-stems ending in

  (1) o (Fem. **ā**): mo *fūmus fāma*, no *pugnus lūna*, lo *oculus pīla*, ro *ynārus fibra* : *jo i.e. io *lanius ascia* or eo (the 'plebeian' form) *cuneus līnea*, vo *flāvus* : bho *acerbus probus superbus morbus*, to *lectus crūsta*, do *crūdus*, ko *juvencus vacca* kvo *fūscus fūrca*. With two consonants, or consonant + sonant : mno *auctumnus* **mno** *fēmina*, nto *ventus* ndo *merenda* : bdo = *blo plo *duplus* or plo *dīscipulus* : tmo *optimus*, tno *prīstinus*, tlo = clo *saeclum* or clo *surculus pericutum*, tro *monstrum dextra*, dhlo = *blo blo *vēstibulum fībula* or by Dissimilation bro *crībrum crēbra* : skvo or sko *vēscus ēsca pōsca*.—Compound endings :

  (*a*) double :

    ū + vo *mīluus cernuus*, + no *opportūnus supīnus*, + ro *mātūrus*, + to *hirsūtus cerrītus*, + kvo *festūca aprīcus*, + sko *corūscus labrūsca* : ē + ro *sevērus*, + to *facētus morētum* : ā + ro *amārus*, + to *arquātus* + do *cicāda*, + kvo *opācus*.

    no + *jo i.e. io *scrīnium lacinia* or eo *idōneus* : lo + lo *capillus axilla* : ro + io *māceria*, ri + no see *hibernus taberna* + kvo *lūbricus noverca* : bho + io *dubius* : to + eo *pluteus*.

    mno + io *calumnia*, mōn + io *caerimōnia* : nt + io *nūntius* : mn + to *armentum*.

    is + tro *sinister* : es + ro *cerebrum tenebrae* : s + lo *aesculus* + no *lūna* + to *jūxtā*.

  (*β*) treble :

    ū + no + io *vaccīnium*, + ro + io *pēnūria*, + kvo + lo *vēnūcula*, + gvo + io *fāstīgium* : ē + lo + io *contumēlia fidēlia* : ā + lo + io *spondālium*, + ro + io *rōrāriī*, + kvo + eo *mustāceum*.

to + lo + lo *pastillus*: tā + ro + io *stlātārius mortārium*: tu + ŏ + to *pītuīta*: kvo + lo + io *domicilium*: s + lo + io *auxilium*, + lo + lo *paxillus vexillum*.
ntā + ro + io *ferentārius*.
In *mediastīnus prōvincia* even more terminations are combined.

(2) i *cinis*: ri *ācer*, ti *tussis vestis rēte* and see *dōs nox*, si see *anser*, tri *puter*. Double: ŏ + li *bubīle monīle*, ā + ri *laquear palear*, nt + ri *venter*: treble ļ + tā + ti *simultās*, es + tā + ti *tempestās*.

Most -i- stems in Latin are formed from -o- stems, *lēvis piscis*, and see *similis*: in mo *sublīmis vermis*, no *acclīnis amnis collis mūnis omnis-segnis*, lo *tālis*, ro *imber*, to *fortis mitis tristis*, dhro *celeber*. So with double ending: ǎ + lo *canālis fērālis rīvālis*, jā + lo *mājālis*, nā + ro .*sescēnāris*, to + lo *fūtilis*. See also *conchis hilaris, palumbēs tābēs.*—Also from -u- stems, *brevis dulcis gravis levis pinguis tenuis*; and from consonant-stems, *canis juvenis mēnsis*.

(3) u *gradus metus nurus socrus, cornū*: tu *aestus artus* (Subst.) *fāstus gressus passus portus rītus saltus*.

(4) ē after ī, *cariēs faciēs pernitiēs rabiēs saniēs*.

(5) Sonant: ņ *femen inguen sanguen*, ŗ *augur femur furfur jecur memor murmur*: mņ *carmen crīmen germen nōmen*. Double: to + ŗ *guttur*, s + mņ *lūmen ōmen*.

(B) Consonant-stems ending in

(1) n: ōn *umbō* and ōn (ņ) *homō margō ordō virgō*: mōn *pulmō sermō tēmō* and mōn (mņ) *flāmen.* Double: ī + ōn *condiciō regiō relligiō scīpiō*: n + ōn *fullō*, ro + ōn *crābrō mūcrō*. Treble: ŏ + d + ōn (ņ) *hirūdō formīdō*, + nd + ōn (ņ) *harūndō hirūndō*, + gv + ōn (ņ) *porrīgō*: ā + gv + ōn (ņ) *imāgo*: tā + gv + ōn (ņ) *sartāgō*. In *fūlīgo ūlīgo* even more terminations are combined.

(2) l *pugil vigil*.

(3) r: ōr *soror*, tēr (tr) *frāter māter pater*, tōr *nōmenclātor*. Double: m + ōr *rūmor*.

(4) bh *caelebs*.

(5) t *caput, comes dīves līmes seges stīpes*, and see *ingens locuplēs* : ōt *nepōs* : nt *cliens dens frequens repens rudens, fōns sons.* Double : m + it *fōmes trāmes*, j + it *abiēs ariēs pariēs.*

(6) d *lapis pecus*, and after long vowel *palūs hērēs mercēs custōs.*

(7) kv *culex senex, fīlix silix varix.* Double : ī + kv *cervix pernix rādix vībīx*, ē + kv *vervēx*, ā + kv *procāx sagāx* : mo + kv *pūmex*, no + kv *fornix pollex*, lo + kv *allex* : bdo (= *blo, plo) + kv *duplex simplex.* Treble : no + ī + kv *cornīx*, + ā + kv *fornāx* : lo + ō + kv *vēlōx*, ro + ō + kv *atrōx.*

(8) s *fār* : is *anser*, ōs *ador honōs* and see *tellūs*, os (es) *genus opus rōbur vetus.* Double : n + os (es) *pignus vellus volnus* : ī + es *mulier* : t + os *pectus.* Treble : ā + vo + es *cadāver papāver.*

Verb-stems are mostly similar to Noun-stems : only the termination **dho**, *claudō tendō*, does not appear in Nouns. Simple Verbs have stems in **n** *cernō linō spernō temnō fallō tollō vellō*, **t** *flectō nectō plectō stertō nītor*, **sk** *crēscō nōscō pāscō pōscō* (and double, **i** + **sk** *apiscor nanciscor paciscor ulciscor*, see *conquiniscō*), **u** *acuō arguō minuō sternuō.* Verbs in **do**, *abdō* &c., are (except *crēdō*) formed from Adjectives : other derived Verbs have stems in

ī *grundiō* : double, mo + ī *dormiō*, ro + ī *nūtriō*, do + ī *audiō condiō* : treble ū + to + ī *frigūtiō.*

ē *moneō* : double, mo + ē *ūmeō*, no + ē *polleō*, do + ē *gaudeō splendeō*, kvo + ē *marceō.*

ā *amō* : mā *clāmō*, nā *dēstinō lancinō mūginor*, lā *fēlō vāpulō violō stipulor*, rā *blaterō flagrō ignōrō lamberō mācerō migrō penetrō tolerō vibrō* : tā *confūtō mactō nūtō putō temptō hortor luctor meditor*, dā *mandō* : kvā *fricō peccō* : sā *vexō.* With two consonants trā *intrō lātrō lūstrō* : with consonant + sonant tṛnā *autumō aestimō.* Double : ū + nā *opīnor* : treble sko + to + lā *pōs(ci)tulō.*

ETYMA LATINA

almus must go with **ad** (cf. προσῆκον 'fitting,' from πρός 'to ').

an -cilla fr. *ambi-* + *colō*, cf. ἀμφί-πολος.

arvīna ' accretion,' Adj. **ar-vus* from *ar, ad.*

assula from **ad-tula, ad-*, ' rising up '.

at, Got. *ath-* than ' but '.

concipilō : ' offatim conficiam ' in Plaut. Truc. 613 is a mere conjecture, and the reading in 621 is ' quem ego jam jam jam concipulabo '.

crepida κρεπ- ONor. *hriflingr* shoes, cf. κρῆπ- κρηπίs.—The meaning must be ' something to stand on,' cf. *crep-ĭdō.*

cūdō : ποίη can hardly be connected.

doceō = ' cause to receive,' cf. δέκομαι receive.

ē- castor cf. ἤ Interj., ed-ĕ-pol cf. ἔ. So *eccerē* = **ĕ-cerē*, ' O Ceres '.

e-hem disyllabic in Plaut. Mil. 1382 must be a compound like *e-heu.*

fār.

formīca = ' architect,' fr. *forma.*

juvenis, add OSlav. *junŭ.*

musca, OSlav. *muha* fly.

novus, Ags. *neōve.*

proceres fr. **pro-cus* Adj. of *pro-*, cf. Fest. *procum* (ieu.

reor, add E. hund*red.*

sarrācum : cf. MIr. *sessrech* wagon ?

ungula, Ags. *nägel* with inserted *e*.

ETYMOLOGICAL LEXICON

ā ante-consonantal form of sq.

ab from: for **ap* (from **apo*, see *aperiō*): orig. used in compounds before a Media, e.g. *abdicō*, then became the prevalent form.

†abacus board: **ἄβακος*, by-form of †ἄβαξ.

abdō hide: fr. **abdus* Adj. from *ab*, see *-dō*.

abdōmen abdūmen paunch: 'containing,' fr. **habdus *habidus* Adj. of *habeō* (cf. *albūmen* fr. *albus*).

abiegnus of fir-wood: for **abiet-nus *abiennus* fr. sq., with *g* on anal. of *īlignus salignus* (in which the *g* is from *c*).

abiēs white fir: Hesych. ἄβıs:

ab-oleō destroy: 'check the growth of,' see *ad-olescō²*.

abolla cloak: Dimin. of †**abola*, from ἀβολῆ Acc. of Sicilian ἀβολεύς (Hesych.), see *amphora*:

†abrotonum southernwood: †ἀβρότονον, Sk. *mrātanam*† a marsh-plant.

†abs aps from: *ab* + *s* (a case-ending?), cf. *ex obs-*.

absinthium wormwood (Fr. *absinthe*): ἀψίνθιον, Hesych. ἀσπίθιον (*i.e.* from Aspendus in Pamphylia?): spelt quasi from *ab*.

ab-sur-dus out of tune: from SUR-, see *susurrus*.

abundē in profusion, **abundô habundô** (see Key) abound: fr. **habundus* 'possessing,' Gerundive of *habeō*. (Popularly connected with *unda*.)

†acalanthis goldfinch: ἀκαλανθίς, fr. **ἀκάλη* thorn (see *acuō*), from its habitat.

accērsō summon: = **ad-cēr-tō* from **cērō = cēdō*, with *-sō* on anal. of *arcessō*.

accipiter hawk: = **ācupéter*, cf. ὠκυπέτης swift-flying (epithet of hawk in Hes. Op. 210), Sk. *āçupátvan-*: fr. *ōcior + petō* 'go'.

ac-clīnis leaning: cf. κλίνω turn κλίνη couch, and (with *l*) Ags. *hlinian* lean E.: KLI-, see *clivus*, cf. KLI- Zd. *çri*- go Sk. *çri*- resort, KLEI- Lit. *szliéti* lean.

acer maple: AKES-, cf. Hesych. ἄκασ-τος, OHG. *ahor-n*.

ācer sharp (E. *eager vinegar*): fr. *ōc-ior*, with 'pretonic' *ā*; see *alacer*.

acerbus sharp: = **acri-bus* from **acru-*, Lit. *asztrùs* OSlav. *ostrŭ*: fr. *aciēs*. Term. BHO-, cf. *dubius probus superbus*.

acerra incense-box: foreign?

acervus heap : = **acri-vus* fr. *acer-bus,* 'pointed '.
acētum vinegar (NHG. *cssiŋ* from **atēcum,* Metathesis) ; Part. Neut. of *aceō* am sour, fr. sq.
aciēs edge : ΑΚ- ἀκίς point, Ags. *ecy* edge E., E. *egg* Verb, cf. ᾹΚ- W. *awch* edge : fr. *acuō.*
†acīnacēs soimitar : †ἀκῑνάκης, Persian.
acinus berry :
†acipēnser aquipēnsis sturgeon : cf. †ἀκκιπήσιος for **ἀκϝιπήνσιος* : Gaulish, the first element fr. *aqua !*
†aclys javelin :
†aconītum monkshood : ἀκόνῑτον :
acr-ēdula thrush (for the term. cf. *ficēdula monēdula querquēdula, nītēdula, alcēdō*) :
†acta shore : ἀκτή headland :
acuō sharpen (E. *aguʋ eglantine*) : cf. sq. Not fr. *ōcior.*
acus needle : fr. praeced.,.cf. Arm. *aseλn.*
ad at to : OIr. *ad,* Got. E. *at.*
ad- up (in *adimō adsurgō āscendō attollō*) : = **ed-* (with pretonic *a*), Sk. *ádhi,* see *af ergā iterum.*
adeō so far : 'up from that,' praeced. + *eō* Abl. of *is* ; see *af.*
adeps fat : *adip-* (quasi fr. *adipiscor* acquire) for †*alīp-* from ἄλειφα.
ad-miniculum vine-stake : 'handle,' fr. *manus.*
ad-oleō offer ('bring out the fragrance '), **ad-olescō**[1] smell (Georgics 4. 379) : *oleō,* cf. OUmbr. *uḍetu* let him kindle.
ad-olescō[2] grow up : fr. *alō,* cf. *aboleō indolēs subolēs prōlēs,* 'survivals' for **abuleō* &c.—Festus' *olescō* is a figment.
ador spelt : cf. Got. *atisk* cornfield : ?
ad-ōrea glory : **aurea,* cf. ἐπ-αυρέω partake of.
ad-ūlor fawn on : **ad-ūdiō* (cf. *assentor* beside *assentiō*) pay attention to, from *audiō.*
ad-ulterô pollute : 'mix with something else,' fr. *alter.*
aedis dwelling : 'where the fire is kept up,' fr. αἴθω burn, MIr. *āed* fire, Ags. *ād* pyre E. *oast*-house (cf. ONor. *eld-hūs* 'fire-house,' *i.e.* hall or parlour).
aeger sick (E. *malinger*) : 'shaking,' ΑΙG- Sk. *ḗj-* stir ? Hardly for **aesger* fr. αἰσχρός ill-favored.
†aegis shield : αἰγίς (either 'of goatskin,' fr. αἴξ goat, or 'of oak,' see *aesculus*).
†aelinos dirge : †αἴλινος, Heb. *ai* woe *lanu* to us.
aemulus emulous : Fest. *aemidus* swelling :
aequus level : = **aeviquus* continuous, fr. *aevum.*
†āēr air (E.) : ἀήρ, fr. ἄημι blow (see *ventus*).

aerumna trouble: 'burden' cf. Fest. *aerumnula* forked stick to carry a bundle:

aes copper: AIS- short form of AJES-, see *ahēneus*.

aesculus winter-oak: dialectic (see *ascia*) for **aexulus*, **aexus*, AIGV-*αἴγειρος* poplar (see on *frāxinus*) *αἰγανέη* spear, Ags. *āc* oak E., + -s-.

aestumô value (E. *aim*) : **aestumus* calculating, fr. *aes*.

aestus heaving motion, heat : ONor. *eisa* to dash, foam?

†**aethēr** sky : *αἰθήρ*: 'burning,' see *aedis*.

aevum time (E. *age*): cf. (1) AIVOS Got. *aivs* E. *ever* (see Kluge on *immer*) *aye* *either* *or* *no*; (2) AIVÓN *αἰών* age; (3) AIVES- OIr. *āis* (= **aives-tu-*), Loc. *αἰεί* (= **αἰϝεσί*) always. Orig. 'continuance,' see *aequus*.

af from (used before consonants): dialectic for **ab* EDH'- see *ad-*, 'up from '.

af-fatim enough : 'to weariness,' *ad* + **fatis*, see *fatigô*.

ager field : *ἀγρός*, Got. *akrs* E. *acre* *acorn*, Sk. *djras* plain : 'place to move in,' fr. *agô*.

āgnitus known : *ad* + **gnatus* by-form of *gnōtus*, see *nōscō*.

āgnus lamb: ĀGVNOS, OSlav. *agnę*; by-form AGVNÓS, *ἀμνός* (for **ἀβνός*)? MIr. *ūan* can hardly be connected.

agō move (E. *squash* *squat*): AG- *ἄγω* I drive, MIr. *agaim*, ONor. *aka* to drive Ags. *acan* to ache E., Arm. *acem* I bring, Zd. *az-* drive Sk. *aj-*.

ah ā (cf. *oh ō, proh prō*) Interj.: *ā*, MHG. *ā-* E. *ah*, Lit. *à*, Sk. *ā*.

aha Interj. (in Plaut. a monosyllable): dialectic spelling of *ā* (praeced.), see *trans*.

ahēneus aēneus of copper: = **aës-neus* from ĀJES-, Got. *aiz* copper Ags. *ār* brass E. *ore*, Zd. *ayañh* iron Sk. *áyas*, see *aes*.

†**ai** Interj. : *αἴ*, cf. Ir. *ē*, MHG. *ei*, Lit. *aî*, and ĀI Zd. *āi* Sk. *āi*†.

ājō say : = **ag-jō*, cf. *adagiō* proverb, AGH- OIr. *āi* a saying (Stokes, Celtic Declension, p. 22), Sk. *ah-* say.

āla wing : = **axla*, cf. *axilla*.

alacer lively : 'sharp,' *ad* + **acer* OK- cf. ŌK- *ācer*.

alapa blow : *ad* + *apiscor* reach.

albus white (E. *auburn* *daub*): ALBH- *ἀλφός* white leprosy, OHG. *elbiz* swan (whence OSlav. *lebedĭ*).

alcēdō (for term. see *acrēdula*) a bird: cf. *ἀλκυών*: hardly from Teutonic, OHG. *alacra* little auk (Graff) ONor. *alka* auk E.

alcēs elk: *ἄλκη* (Pausanias), cf. ELK- Ags. *eolh* ONor. *elgr* E., ḶK- Sk. *ṛças* antelope, LAK- OSlav. *losĭ* elk.

ālea gaming :

†**ālēc allēc hallēc** pickle :

alga seaweed:

algeō am cold: ἄλγος pain (as ῥίγιον 'more horrible' is fr. ῥῖγος 'chill').

alius other: ALJ- ἄλλος, OIr. *aile*, Got. *aljis* E. *else*, Arm. *ail*.

allex hallex thumb: *allus* Fest., i.e. **ad-lus* from *ad*, 'additional' finger.

allium ālium garlick: cf. *alum* wild garlic Plin. 19. 116, if its *a* is long:

almus propitious (a religious term): = **admus*, cf. NUmbr. *arsmor* ceremonies (and Hesych. ἀδμαίνω am well?).   ⸞⸝⸍ ⸰⸰ ⸝   ⟍ ⸝ ⸍ ⸝

alnus alder: = **elsnós*, Lit. *clksnis* (for **elsnis*), ELS- cf. ELIS- OHG. *clira* E. (E. with 'excrescent' *d*), OSlav. *elìha*.

alō nourish: AL- ἄν-αλτος insatiate, OIr. not-*ail* alit te, Got. *alan* grow.

†**aloē** aloe: †ἀλόη, Assyrian *uduu*.

†**alpha** A: †ἄλφα, Heb. *eleph* (see *elephās*).

altus high (E. *haughty hawser*): Part of *alō*, 'grown up'. Hardly add Got. *althcis* old E.

ālūcinor allūcinor (also **hāl- hall-**) prate: 'breathe out' (cf. *fatuus* 'foolish' fr. *fatisco* 'gape'), **hālūcus* Adj. fr. *hālô*.

alūta soft leather: = **adūta* put on, Part. of **ad-uō*, cf. *ind-uō ex-uō*.

alvus belly: 'hollow,' αὐλός pipe, αὐλών a hollow.

†**tamāracus** marjoram (E.): †ἀμάρακος:

amārus bitter: OM-, MIr. *om* raw (so Ags. sūr 'sour' goes with OSlav. syrŭ 'raw'), Sk. *am-las* sour; cf. ŌM-, ὠμός raw, Arm. *hum*, Sk. *āmás*.

†**tambactus** vassal (Got. *andbahts* servant, spelt quasi from *and* towards, see *ante*: Eng. *ambassador*): Gaulish (Fest.), cf. W. *amaeth* husbandman: 'sent around,' fr. sq. + *agō*.

ambi- around: AMBHÍ ἀμφί, cf. (1) MBHÍ OIr. *imme*, Ags. *ymb* E. *ember*-days MHG. *um*; (2) ABHÍ OSlav. *obi-*, Zd. *aibi* over Sk. *abhí* around; (3) BHÍ (?) Got. *bi* by E.

ambō both: AMBHŌ ἄμφω, cf. (1) ABHṒ Lit. *abù* OSlav. *oba*; (2) BHṒ (?) Got. *bai baj-ōths* E., and U-BHṒ Zd. *uba* Sk. *ubhá*: fr. praeced.

†**tambrosia** ambrosia: †ἀμβροσία, cf. Arab. 'amber ambergris (E. E. amber) Zenker 639 b.

†**tambūbāja** flute-player: Adj. fr. **ambūba* pipe, Arab. *embūbe* Zenker 99 c.

ambulō walk: 'move both feet,' fr. **amb-lus* Adj. from **amb-* by-form (properly before vowel) of *ambi-*.

amb-ūrō scorch: *ambi-* + *ūrō*: wrongly divided *am-būrō*, whence *cumbūrō* and *būstum*.

amellus starwort: Gaulish for **ampellos* 'loved by bees,' fr. **ampis* bee (ᴍ spelt *am*, and *p* disappearing in Celtic: see Stokes B B. 9. 194), cf. OHG. *impi* and ἐμπίς gnat?

āmentum amm- adm- arm- thong: *ad*, 'attachment'.

ames pole of bird-net:

amita aunt (E.): ᴀᴍᴀ onomatopoeic, cf. ᴀᴍᴍᴀ Hesych. *ὰμμὰs* mother, ONor. *amma* grandmother, Assyrian *ummi* mother; with participial ending quasi fr. *amô*.

amnis river: = *abnis* ᴀʙʜ-ɴ-, cf. ᴀʙʜ-ᴇɴ- MIr. *abann* (E. *Avon*), and ᴀᴍʙʜ- Gaulish *ambe* rivo, Sk. *âmbhas* water.

amô love: 'choose,' fr. *emô* take.

†amômum balsam: †*ἄμωμον* : Semitic, cf. *cinn-amômum*.

amplus large: = *am-blus* from am- *ambi-* + term. *-blus*, see *duplex*, 'comprehensive'.

ampulla bottle: = *ampor-la* fr. †*ampora* amphora (NHG. *eimer* pail) from *ἀμφορᾶ* Acc. of *ἀμφορεύς* (see *abolla*).

†amurca oil-lees: = *amurga* (see *spēlunca*), *ἀμόργη* :

†amussim carpenter's rule: 'line scratched,' *ἄμυξιν* (Aco.) tearing, fr. *ἀμύσσω* I tear.

†amȳgdalum almond (E.): *ἀμύγδαλον*, †*ἀμυγδάλη*, Semitic.

an or: cf. *ἄν* in that case, Got. *an* then (Interrogative).

anās duck: ᴀɴᴀᴛ́-, Ags. *äned* OHG. *anet*-recho drake ('duck king') E. drake *decoy*; cf. ɴᴛꜰ- *νῆσσα νᾶσσα* (= *νᾱ́rja) duck, Lit. *ántis* OSlav. *ųty*, Sk. *âtis* a water-fowl.

ancīle oval shield: = *am-cīde* 'cut around,' am- (see *amplus*) + *caedô* !

ancilla handmand: Dimin. of *ancula*, cf. Fest. *anculô* serve:

†ancora anchor (E.): *ἄγκῦρα*, cf. *ἀγκών* arm ('bent'): ending on anal. of *remora* 'hindrance'?

†andabata blindfolded gladiator: Gaulish (cf. *Gallus* for *mirmillo*, Fest.)?

†anēthum dill: †*ἄνηθον*, *ἄνῑσον*, oriental.

anfr-āctus winding: Osc. *amfr-* around (formed from amb-, see *ambulô*, as *super* from *sup, sub*: cf. Fest. *ambr-icēs* bars, fr. *jaciô*) + *agô*: *-fr*-retained (for *-br-*) quasi fr. amb- + *frangô*.

angō choke (E. *anguish*), **angustus** narrow: ᴀɴɢʜ- *ἄγχω* choke, OIr. cum-*any* narrow, Got. *agg*-vus E. *ag*-nail ONor. *angr* grief E. *anger*, Lit. *anksztas* narrow OSlav. *ązŭkŭ*, Arm. *anjuk*, Zd. *âzanh* distress Sk. *anhas* need.

anguilla eel: = *engvīla*, ᴇɴɢʜᴠ- cf. *ἔγχ-ελυς* ; and ᴏɴɢʜᴠ- Lit. *ung-urȳs* (initial vowel obscure) OSlav. *ęg-oriŭlŭ* ; fr. sq. ?

anguis snake: ɴɢᴠꜰ́-, Lit. *angis*, cf. ɴɢᴠ- OHG. *unc* snake. Hardly add OIr. esc-*ung* eel (Stokes, Celtic Declension, p. 29) quasi 'fen-snake'.

angulus corner: OSlav. *ąglŭ*, cf. (without the nasal) Sk. *ágram* point.

anhēlus panting: = *anēlus* (*h* from *hālô*) Adj. (cf. *crūd-ēlis*) from ᴀɴ-, sq.

anima air, **animus** soul: ἄνεμος wind, OIr. *anim* air, from AN- Got.
us-*anan* expire, OSlav. vonja odor, Zd. *ainika* face Sk. *an*- breathe.
annus ānus year: = *asnos, ASN- cf. ASON- Got. *asans* harvest E. *earn*,
Pruss. *assanis* autumn, ASEN- OSlav. *jesenĭ*.
Rather than *atnos, Got. *athn* year. Not *amnos, see *sollemnis*:
mn would remain.
ansa handle: Lit. q̄sà: = *omsā, fr. *umerus*.
anser goose: = *hansis, MIr. *gēis* swan, Lit. ž̄qsis goose OSlav. *gąsĭ*
(with *g*- from Teutonic), cf. (1) GHANS- Ags. *gōs*, Sk. *hansas*, GHĀNS-
χήν; (2) GHAN-, Ags. *gandra* gander E., *ganot* gannet E.
Not add Arm. *sag* goose quasi = *gas: as soon make *dog* the Classical form whence Teutonic *cat* quasi = *tac.
ante before (E. *advance enhance vamp vanguard*): = *anti 'in the row,'
Locative fr. *antēs*: ἀντί opposite, cf. Got. *and* towards E. *and* answer
+*elope*, Lit. *ant* on, and ꞚTI Sk. *ánti* opposite, ꞚTÍ Got. *und* to E.
unto, ꞚT- OIr. *étan* forehead.
ante-cellō excel: 'rise before,' *cel-nō, see *celsus*.
ante-mna (for the ending cf. *lā-mna*) **antenna** (quasi fr. *ten-dō*) sail-
yard: *ante*, 'against' the mast, cf. *Antemnae* 'opposite' the junction
of Anio and Tiber.
antēs rows: ANTÍ- Got. *andeis* end E., cf. ÁNTO- Sk. *ántas*, see *ante*.
antēstor call to witness: = *ante-tēstor.
†**antrum** cave: ἄντρον: from AN- *anima*, cf. Plin. 2. 208 quae spiracula
vocant . . . scrobes mortiferum spiritum exhalantes?
ānulus ring **ānus** δακτύλιος (in two senses): OIr. *ānne* ring.
anus old woman: OHG. *ana* grandmother, Pruss. *ane*, cf. Hesych.
ἀννίς.
aper boar: EPRÓ- Ags. *efor* (and *Efor-vic* York).
Hardly add OSlav. *veprĭ*.
ap-eriō uncover (E. *malapert*): Sk. *apa-ar*-: *ap (see *ab*) Got. *af* from
E. *of off after awkward ebb evening*, from APO ἄπο, Zd. *apa* Sk. *ápa*
away, + ER- raise, see *orior*.
apex top: 'point of junction,' fr. *apiscor*.
apis bee: 'builder,' *apō* fasten, sq.
apiscor get **aptus** fitted: Fest. *apō* fasten, Ags. *äfnian* to complete,
Zd. *ap*- reach Sk. *āp*- (i.e. ā to + *ap-) obtain.
apium parsley (E. small*age*): 'used for garlands,' fr. *apō*, praeced.
†**aplustrum** stern: = *aplust-trum from *aplustum = *ἄφλοστον by-form
of ἄφλαστον (as μολόχη of μαλάχη):
aprīcus lying in the sun: 'basking' like a boar, fr. *aper*.
apud apur apor with: 'reaching,' fr. *apiscor*.
aqua acua water (E. *ewer sewer*): Got. *ahva* Ags. *ī-ge* (= *eā-jā, *eā-
from *au-, av-, ahv-*) island E. *i-s-land ey*-ot Angles-*ey*.

aquila eagle (E. : the 'dark' bird) **aquilō** north wind ('dark' with storm) **aquilus** dark: = *aquudus* *ak-vo-dos, cf. Osc. *Akudunniad* Aquilōniā: *ak-vos, cf. Hesych. ἄκ-αρος blind.

ar to (before consonant, *arbiter arcessō arfuērunt arvehō,* Plaut. *ar mē*): cf. NUmbr. *arfertur* adfertor, from *ars-* NUmbr. form of OUmbr. *ad-* = Lat. *ad.*

āra āsa altar, sunken rock (Key's Dictionary): hardly fr. *āreō.*

†**arānea** spider: fr. *arāna *aracna* from ἀράχνη. So *arāneus* from ἄραχνος.

arbiter witness: *ar* + GVOT-, OUmbr. *ad-putrati* arbitratu, cf. GVĒT-ONor. *at-kvaeda* decision ; see *vetō.*

arbos tree : ARDH-, Lit. *ardai* frame made of bars OSlav. *ras-tą* (= *rad-tą) I grow, Zd. *ared-* grow Sk. *ardh-* thrive. ·

arbutus strawberry-tree : 'fast-growing,' fr. praeced.

arca chest (E. *ark*), **arceō** confine : ARKV- ἀρκέω keep off, OIr. *tess-urc* I keep, Lit. *rakìnti* (Metathesis, from Slavonic) to lock, Arm. *argelum* I restrain.

arcēssō summon: fr. *arcēssus* Part., *ar* + *cēdō.*

†**arctus** bear : ἄρκτος, see *ursus.*

arcus bow (E. *arch*): cf. Got. *arhv-az-na* arrow Ags. *earhv* E.: 'defence,' fr. *arceō.*

ardea heron : 'plebeian' for *ardia* i.e. ₴DIΑ̅, ἐ-ρωδιός ῥωδιός, cf. ONor. *arta* teal.

ārdeō burn : fr. *ārdus* (Plaut.) = *āridus* dry, fr. *āreō.*

arduus steep: ₴DHVÓS MIr. *ard* high, Sk. *ūrdhvás* rising, cf. ₴DHVÓS Zd. *eredhwa* just ('upright') ; and ARDH-, *arbos.*

But ὀρθός erect = ƒορθός, cf. Βορθ-αγόρας.

ārea āria ground (E. *aery* ?) :

āreō am dry :

argentum silver (OIr. *arget*): ₴GENTO- cf. ₴GETO- Osc. *aragetud* Abl., and ₴GETO- Arm. *arcath*, Zd. *erezata* : 'white,' from ₴G- ἀργός white ἄργυρος silver, cf. ERG- W. *eira* snow, Got. *un-airkns* unholy, Sk. *drjunas* white *drjunam* silver *arj-* shine.

†**argilla** (quasi Adj., sc. *terra*) white clay: ἄργιλλος ἄργιλος, fr. praeced.

arguō prove ('make clear') **argūtus** clear: fr. *argentum.*

ariēs ram : *eriēt-, cf. Lit. *éras* lamb OSlav. *jarina* wool.

arista awn : hardly = *osistä, ὀιστός arrow, from the shape.

arma tools : *ar*, 'appendages'.

armentum beast: *ar*, 'appendage'.

armus shoulder: ₴MÓS, Got. *arms* arm E., OSlav. *ramę* shoulder, Zd. *arema* arm Sk. *ir̥nds* ; cf. ₴MÓS, Pruss. *irmo*, Arm. *arm-ukn* elbow.

arô plough : cf. ἀρόω, W. *ar* tilth, Got. *arjan* to plough OE. *ear* Verb,
Lit. *árti* OSlav. *orati*, Arm. *arōr* a plough.

arquātus jaundiced : 'yellow as the rainbow,' *arquus* = *arcus*.

†**arrabō** pledge (E. *earnest* Subst.) : †ἀρραβών, Heb. *ěrabhōn*.

ars skill : §τῐ-, Sk. *r̥tis* attack, cf. OHG. *art* nature ; 'going,' see *orior*.

artus Adj. close (also spelt *arctus* quasi fr. *arceō*), Subst. joint : AR-
ἀρ-αρ-ίσκω fit.

arvīna fat : cf. *arbilla* Fest. :   ∟ ∤ ✕ ✕ ✕ ∕ιι.

arvum field : = *ervóm*, W. *erw* acre, OHG. *ero* earth.

arx citadel : 'defence,' fr. *arceō*.

ās assis pound (E. *ace*) : = *ed-tis* fr. *elementum*, 'unit'.

ascia axe : dialectic for *acsia* AGVSI-, ἀξίνη, AGVESI- Got. *aqizi*, AGVS-
Ags. *eux* E.

asīlus gadfly : foreign ?

†**asinus** ass (W. *asyn* ; Got. *asilus* E. *eascl* ; Lit. *ásilas* and OSlav.
oslŭ from Teutonic : Ags. *assa* E. is obscure) : *ἄσινος Ionic for *ἄτινος
from Heb. *athōn* she-ass, with ι quasi an Adj.-ending -ινος.

†**asparagus** asparagus : ἀσπάραγος (whence Pers. *espereg* a dyer's plant,
Zenker 36 b) :

āsper (**ăsper** late, Diomedes Keil 1. 431) rough : = *abs-per* unattrac-
tive, *abs* + *parô* (see *pauper*).

†**aspis** asp : ἀσπίς : foreign ?

asser pole : *ad* + *scrō*.[2]
    Not cf. Got. *ans* beam.

assula astula acsula (Catullus 17. 3, see *pessulus*) splinter : ᒡ ✕ ✕ ✕ ✓∕ᒧ

assus roasted : = *ad-tus*, cf. ἅζα dryness (= *ἄδ-ja).

ast but : = *ads-te*, i.e. *ad-s* from *ad* (see *abs*) + TI Loc. fr. TO, see *tam*,
'thereto'.

†**astrum** star : ἄστρον, see *stella*.

†**astu** city : †ἄστυ :

astus craft :   *a*

at ad but : ἀτ-άρ, Got. *ath* thén, OIr. *aith-* back (= *ati-*), Lit. *at-* OSlav.
otŭ from, Sk. *āt* further (= *ă* to + *at*).

ātāt attāt Interj. : cf. (with short vowels) ἀτταταί, ONor. *atatata*, Lit. *at.*

at-avus ancestor in the 5th degree : *at* 'further' + *avus.*

āter black : NUmbr. *adro* μέλανα : ŌDH-RÓ-, cf. Lit. *júdas*, and ONDH-RĪ,
see *umbra.*

†**ātrium** hall : Etruscan (Varro).

atrōx fierce : fr. *atrus* (cf. *ferōx* fr. *ferus*), OD-RÓS fr. *odium.*

†**attagēn** hazel-hen : †ἀτταγῆν : Lydian ('Ionicus' Hor.) ?

†**attegia** hut : Moorish (Juv. 14. 196) ?

auctumnus autumnus autumn : 'season of increase, harvest-time,' fr.
augeō.

ETYMOLOGICAL LEXICON   9

audeō dare : fr. *audus = avidus greedy, fr. aveō.
audiō hear: by-form (see condiō) of *audō from *au-dus *aus-dus Adj.,
   fr. aur-is + term. -DO-.
au-ferō take away : Pruss. au- away (see clepō) OSlav. u-, Sk. áva.
augeō increase : AUGV- OIr. ōg entire, Got. aukan multiply E. ekc
   Verb n-ick-name y-ean, Lit. dugu I grow, Arm. oiž strength, Zd.
   aojańh Sk. ójas: see ōmen.
augur auger soothsayer: 'authority,' fr. praeced.
†aula court: αὐλή:
†aura breeze, gleam Aen. 6. 204 (E. soar): αὔρα breeze:
†aurichalcum (as though fr. aurum) ōrichalcum copper ore: *ὀρίχαλκος
   by-form of ὀρεί-χαλκος fr. ὄρος mountain + χαλκός copper.
aurīga ōrīga driver : = *aure-iga fr. OLat. aurea bridle (from ōs) + agō.
auris ear: = *ousis, Lit. ausis, cf. oὖs (= *oὖσ-as), OIr. ō, Got. ausō
   Ags. ēāre E., OSlav. uho: 'orifice,' cf. ōs.
aur-ōra (an Adj.-ending) dawn: ous-, cf. Ags. ēās-t east E., Lit. ausz-rà
   dawn OSlav. u-tro (i.e. *us-t-ro), and us- Zd. ushańh Sk. úsh: fr. ūrō,
   'when the sun begins to burn'.
   Not add (1) αὔριον to-morrow : (2) αὔως ἠώς dawn, i.e. *ἀ-Fώ-s (cf.
   Hesych. ἀβώ early), fr. ἀ-(F)η-μι blow, from the morning
   breeze.
aurum ōrum gold (E. oriel ori-flamme oriole): Pruss. ausis Lit. duksas:
auscultō listen (E. scout): fr. *auscula Dimin. of aur-is (as caecultô
   'am dim-sighted' fr. *caeculus).
†auster south wind: *αὔστρος, fr. αὖos dry, see sūdus.
aut or: OUmbr. ute: fr. αὖ again, Got. au-k also E. eke Adverb, + -te,
   see ast.
autem but: praeced. + a quasi-numeral ending (on anal. of septem
   novem decem), see item saltem enim quidem : cf. Osc. avti.
autumô say: fr. *autumnus Adj. (see aestumô) = *avi-tumus from ou-,
   ὄίω (= ὀF-ίω) suppose.
   Hardly add avis in the sense of 'omen'.
auxilium help: AUX- αὔξω increase, Lit. duksz-tas high, fr. aug-eō + s.
avēna oats: 'rustic' for *avīna = *ovis-na, cf. Lit. awiž-à OSlav. ovis-ŭ:
   'eaten by sheep,' fr. ovis?
aveō haveō desire: 'watch for,' ἀίω (= ἀF-ίω) perceive, OIr. conn-ôi
   qui servat, OSlav. u-mŭ mind, Sk. av- favor.
avis bird (E. ostrich): = *ovi-s, cf. οἰωνός (= ὀFι-ωνός).
av-unculus (cf. fūr-unculus lēn-unculus rān-unculus) mother's brother
   (E. uncle): Dimin. fr. sq., cf. Ags. eā-m NHG. o-heim, Pruss. awis
   Lit. awýnas OSlav. uj.
avus grandfather: cf. Got. avō grandmother, Arm. hav grandfather.
axicia shears: 'turning on a pivot,' fr. *axicus Adj. of axis.

axilla armpit (MIr. *ochsal*): sq., cf. W. *echel* axle, OHG. *ahsala* shoulder E. *axle.*

axis assis axle (E. *ashlar*): Lit. *aszis* OSlav. *osǐ*: AKS-, ἄξων, OHG. *ahsa*, Sk. *ákshas.*

†babae Interj.: βαβαί, Lit. *babà*, cf. Lat. *babulus* fool, Sk. *bababā* crackling.

bāca bacca berry (E. *bay*-tree):=*bat-ca*, Cyprian βάτια mulberries BB. 15. 93?

†baccar Celtic valerian: †βάκκαρις, Lydian (Schol. Aesch. Pers. 41 Λυδῶν μύρον).

baculum staff: cf. βάκ-τρον, Hesych. βάκτης strong: 'supporter,' see *imbēcillus.*

bājulus porter (E. *bail*): *bagiolus* =*baciolus* fr. praeced. (see *pūlējum*).

‒†bālaena ballēna bellāna whale: Northern, cf. †φάλαινα φάλλαινα:

†balanus acorn: βάλανος, GVL- cf. Lit. *gilè*, Arm. *kałin*, and GVEL- OSlav. *želǫdǐ*: 'dropt,' GVL- βάλλω throw, GVEL- OHG. *quellan* gush, GVOL- Sk. *gal*- drop.

†balatrō buffoon: 'devourer,' = *baratrō* fr. *baratrum* = *barathrum.*

balbus stammering (Ir. *balbh* dumb): Sk. *balbalā* a stammering, ‾onomatopoeic.

▸ baliolus brown (of an African, Plaut. Poen. 1301): Dimin. of *badius*, see *varius.*

  Not fr. βαλιός dappled.

†balneum balineum bath: βαλανεῖον: 'dropping, vapor-bath,' see *balanus.*

bālō bleat: fr. *bāla* Adj. Fem. from *bā* cry of sheep E. *baa.*
So Varro's *bēlō* bleat fr. *bēla* Adj. Fem. from *bee* (i.e. *bē*, βῆ) cry of sheep.

†balsamum balm (E.): †βάλσαμον (for the λ see *palma*[2]), Heb. *besem.*

†balteus belt (Ags. E. *belt*): Etruscan (Varro).

†barathrum pit: βάραθρον, fr. *vorō.*

barba beard (W. *barf*): dialectic for *farba*, BHARDH-, Ags. *beard* E., OSlav. *brada*, cf. Lit. *barz-dà.*

†barbarus foreign (E. *brave*): βάρβαρος, BRB- Lit. *birbiù* I buzz, cf. BERB- βερβερίζω stammer.

†barbitos lyre: †βάρβιτος Aeol. βάρμιτον βάρμος Sappho 154:

▸†barditus German warcry:

bardus stupid: GVERDH' Spanish *gurdus* dolt (Quint.), Sk. *jaḷhús* dull, cf. GVRDHÚs *βραθύs* slow (whence βράσσων slower) by-form of βραδύς.

†bārō vārō blockhead: Gaulish for 'soldier's servant' (Schol. Pers. 5. 138 Jahn).

— †**barrus** elephant: = *bārus, Babylonian biru (Sayce).

†**bascauda** tub: British (Mart. 14. 97. 1).

Not E. basket (whence W. basged), etym. unknown.

†**bāsium** kiss: Gaulish (first in Catullus)?

bat Interj.: cf. βαττολογέω stammer, Sk. bata Interj.

— **batillum vatillum** firepan:

hardly fr. βατάνη Sicilian for πατάνη dish, borrowed from patina.

battuō bātuō beat (E. abate battle combat, but not beat): dialectic for *fatuō, cf. BHATÚ- Ags. beadu combat.

— **baubor** bay: βαυβάω sleep ('snore'), cf. Lit. bubauti roar, onomatop.

†**baxea** shoe: fr. *bax = *βάξ, Hesych. †πάξ, MIr. hais.

— †**bdellium** a gum: †βδέλλιον: Arabian (Diosc. 1. 80), Heb. b'dolaḥ.

bellum (E. revel) = duellum.

bēlua bellua beast:

bene well: = *beni (cf. beni-gnus) Loc. of *benus good (cf. bellus fine), DVŅ-, cf. DVON- bonus.

beô gladden:

†**bēryllus** beryl (E. brilliant): †βήρυλλος (Arab. billūr crystal Zenker 208 b), Sk. vāiḍūryas catseye.

bēs bessis two-thirds: = *du-essis, duo + assis, see ās ('unit').

bēstia beast (E.):

bēta Fem. beet (E.):

†**bēta** Neut. B: †βῆτα, Heb. bēth.

bibō drink (E. beverage imbrue): onomatopœic for *pibō, OIr. ibid drink ye, Sk. píbāmi I drink.

bi-fāriam in two parts:

bīlis gall:

bīmus two years old: = *bi-hīmus two winters old (cf. Got. tvalibvintrus 'twelve years old,' E. twinter 'beast two years old'), fr. bis + χεῖμα winter (see hiems), with which go also χίμαρος goat ('yearling'), MIr. gamuin yearling calf, ONor. gymbr yearling lamb Scotch gimmer.

bi-pennis bi-pinnis two-edged (E. pimpernel): OLat. pennus sharp Isid. Orig. 11. 1. 46:

bis duis (Fest.) twice: = *dvís, δίς, MHG. zwis, Sk. dvís, Zd. bi- two-, fr. duo.

†**bītō bētō baetō** go: Osc. baíteís thou comest, GVAIT- cf. OIr. fo-bíth because of, Lett. gaita going, Zd. yaēth- come.

bitūmen asphalt: GVETÚ-, Ags. cvidu resin (Kluge s. v. kitt), Sk. jatu gum (E. guttapercha).

†**blaesus** lisping: βλαισός bandylegged, GVLAIS-VOS, cf. ONor. kleiss inarticulate.

blandus agreeable : GHVLANDH- Pruss. *glands* comfort, cf. GHVLĀDH-, see *glaber*.

blaterô blatiō babble : dialectic for *flat-* BHLAT- ONor. *bladr* nonsense Scotch *blether*.

blatta cockroach : dialectic for **flacta* BHLAKV-, Lett. *blakts* bug, cf. Lit. *blāke̜*.

†blennus dolt : βλεννός driveling, cf. βλέννα mucus.

†blitum orach : βλίτον : = **μλίτον* fr. μέλι honey (see *mel*), cf. NHG. *melde* orach (OHG. *mouhlta* in Graff is a mis-writing for *molta*).

bōjae collar of iron, wood, or leather (E. *buoy*) :

†bōlētus mushroom (NHG. *pilz*) : **βωλητός* globular, fr. βῶλος clod, cf. Galen's βωλίτης mushroom.

†bombax Interj. : βομβάξ, fr. sq.

†bombus booming (E. *bomb bound* Vb. *bumper*) : βόμβος : onomatop., cf. βαμβαίνω chatter.

†bombȳx silk (E. *bombast*) : †βόμβῦξ, cf. Pers. *pembe* cotton Zenker 210 c.

bonus duonus good (E. *bonny boon*-companion) : = **dvonus* :

†boô bovô roar : βοάω (**βοϝάω*), GVOV- GVOU- Lit. *gauju* I howl, cf. GVU-Sk. *gu-* be heard.

†boreās north wind : βορέᾱς, Thracian for **φορέᾱς* 'ventus ferens' fr. φέρω (see *ferō*), cf. ONor. *byrr* fair wind (E. *pirouette*).

bōs ox (E. *beef bugle*) : Oscan (the Rom. form would be **vous*, **vōs*) : GVŌU-, βοῦς, OIr. *bō*, Ags. *cū* cow E., Lett. *gōws* OSlav. *govędo* ox, Arm. *kov* cow, Zd. *gāus* ox Sk. *gāus*.

brācae braccae breeches : Gaulish (Diodorus Siculus), from Teutonic, Ags. *brōc* E.

†bracchium brāchium arm (W. *braich*, E. *brace* &c. *branch*) : = **bracchium* from **βρακχῖον* for **βράχῖον* (as βρόκχος for βρόχος), by-form of βραχίων : fr. βραχύς (see *brevis*), 'shorter' than the leg.

† bractea brattea gold-leaf :

†brassica cabbage (Hesych. βράσκη, W. *bresych*) :

brevis short : MREGHV-, cf. MEGHV- βραχύς, Got. *ga-maurgjan* shorten.

brūma winter solstice : = 'dull' time, fr. sq.

brūtus heavy : Lett. *grūts*, fr. con-*gruō*.

–bubīle ox-stall : dialectic for **buvīle bovīle* from *hov-*, *bōs*.

būbō owl : onomatop., Redupl. fr. βύας eagle-owl, Arm. *bu* owl.

bubulcus ploughman : fr. **bubulus* for **bovulus*, see *bubile*.

būbulus of oxen : = **bovi-blus* fr. *bōs*.

bucca puffed cheek (W. *boch*, E. *buckle debouch* &c. *rebuke*) :

būcina buccina horn (Polyb. βυκάνη) : BŪKV- OHG. *pfūchen* snort, cf. BOUKV- OSlav. *bučati* bellow, BUKV- βύκτης howling, Sk. *buk-kāras* lion's roar.

bŭfō toad: cf. Low Lat. *buffāre* (E. *buffer buffet* &c. *pop puff*) to inflate (as φῦσαλος toad fr. φῦσάω blow) :
†**bulbus** onion : βολβός :
bulla bubble, knob (E. *bill boil* Vb. *bull²* &c.) : dialectic for **folla* fr. *follis*.
būris ploughbeam : = **gvō-ris* cf. GVO- γύης ?
būstum tomb : see *ambūrō*.
†**buxus** box (E. E. blunder-*buss booze bushel bust*) : **βύξος* for †πύξος : Paphlagonian, cf. Catull. 4. 13 Cytore buxifer (in Paphlagonia) ?

†**caballus** nag (E. *caper*-cailzie *cavalry chivalry*) : Plut. †καβάλλης, cf. W. †*ceffyl* (= **kappilos*), OSlav. †*kobyla* mare (= **kvabūlā*) :
†**cachinnus** laugh : **καχῖνος*, fr. καχ-άζω I laugh (as γελασῖνος dimple fr. γελάω).
caco : KAKV- cf. κάκκη stercus, MIr. *cacc*, Sk. *çákam*.
cacula servant : KAKV- cf. Ags. on-*hagian* to suit, Sk. *çak-* be able.
cacūmen top : fr. **cacuō* fit, praeced. (cf. *apex* top fr. *apō* fasten).
cadā-ver (cf. *papā-ver*, term. -VES) corpse : fr. **cadō* by-form of sq. (cf. πτῶμα fr. πίπτω fall).
cadō fall (E. *cadence* &c. *chance cheat decay*) : KAD- MIr. *casir* (= **cad-tric-*) hail, Sk. *çad-* fall.
†**cādūceum** herald's staff (formed quasi fr. *cādūcus*, stick of 'fallen' wood ?) : **κάρὑκιον* Dor. for κηρύκιον, fr. κῆρυξ herald.
†**cadus** jar (E. *albatross*) : †κάδος, Heb. *kad*.
caecus cēcus blind : KOIKŎS κοικύλλω gape about, OIr. *caech* one-eyed, cf. KOÍKOS Got. *haihs*.
caedō cut (E. *chisel excise scissors*) : KVAIDH-, cf. SKVAIDH- Got. *skaidan* divide E. water-*shed sheath shoddy skid*, Lit. *skiēdziu* I separate.
caelebs cēlebs single : ' separate,' = **caedi-b-* fr. praeced. + -BH- cf. -BHO- *acerbus*.
caelum¹ chisel :
caelum² sky : 'dark' (cf. *caerulus*) :
caenum dirt :
†**caepe cēpe** onion (E. *chive*, NHG. *zwiebel*) : quasi Adj. Neut. (like *turpe*) for **caepium*, **κήπιον*, cf. Hesych. κἆπια (Plur.) garlic, fr. κῆπος garden, see *campus*.
caerimōnia cērimōnia reverence : 'seclusion,' fr. *caedō* 'separate'.
caerulus dark-blue : = **caelulus*, fr. *caelum*.
caesariēs hair : = **caesār-jēs*, cf. Sk. *kēsaram* ?
caesius light-blue : = **caed-tius*, KVAIDH- Ags. *hādor* clear, cf. SKVAIDH Lit. *skaid-rùs*.
caespes cēspes sod :
Osc. *kaispatar* caedatur (?) is too obscure to compare.

caestus gauntlet:

†**caetra cētra** shield: Spanish, Hesych. καιτρέα.

calamitās cadamitās (Isid.) injury (orig. 'hail,' Donatus, or 'mould,' Servius):

†**calamus** reed (E. *calumet shawm*, W. *calaf* stalk): κάλαμος, see *culmus*.

†**calathus** basket: κάλαθος:

caleō glow (E. *caldron caudle chafe nonchalant scald*): KEL'-, cf. KĻ- Lit. *szilti* grow warm.

†**caliendrum** headdress: slang form of **callintrum*, κάλλυντρον ornament, fr. καλλύνω beautify.

†**caliga** soldier's sandal: 'covering,' **κάλιγα* = κάλυκα (as ὔρτυγα = ὔρτυκα) Acc. of κάλυξ husk.

cālīgō darkness: Sk. *kālas* blue-black?

†**calix** cup (E. *chalice*): **κάλιξ* by-form (cf. μαλάχη-μολόχη) of **κόλιξ* i.e. κύλιξ (see *mola*), cf. Sk. *kaldças* pot.

callis hill-path (Fr. *chalet Chaux*): KVĻNIS, cf. KVOLNIS *collis*.

callum hard skin (E. *gall* Vb.): KVĻNOM, cf. KVĻNOS Sk. *kinas*.

calô summon: KĻ-, cf. KĻ- καλέω call, KEL- κέλομαι, KOL- OHG. *halōn* summon.—Not = **cadô*, OUmbr. *kaḍctu* vocato.

†**cālō** soldier's servant:

†**caltha** pot-marigold: = **calcantha*, χαλκ-άνθη (sulphate of copper) in the etymological sense of 'with copper-coloured flowers'?

calumnia (fr. **calumnus* Adj.) intrigue (E. *challenge*), **calvor** deceive: KALU-:

calvus bald: KVĻVOS, cf. KVĻVOS Sk. *kulvas*.

calx[1] heel (E. *caltrop caulk*):

calx[2] small stone, lime (E. *causeway chalk*):

†**camēlus** camel: †κάμηλος, Heb. *gāmāl*.

†**camera** vault (E. *chamber comrade*): †καμάρα, cf. Zd. *kameredha* skull ('arched').

†**camīnus** furnace (E. *chimney*): κάμῑνος: 'stone hearth,' cf. Ags. *hamor* hammer E. (orig. of flint), and (with ā) OSlav. *kameni* stone.

†**cammarus** lobster: †κάμμαρος, †κομαρίς, ONor. †*humarr*: praeced., 'like a stone'?

campus field (E. *camp* &c. *scamp shamble*): cf. KĀP- κῆπος garden, Ags. *hōf* house E. *hovel hover* OHG. *hōba* piece of land.

camur bent:

canālis pipe (E. *canal channel kennel*[2]): from †**cana*, **κάνη* by-form of †κάννη, see *canna*.

cancellī lattice (E. *chancel chancery*): *cancrī* Fest.: 'like a crab's claws,' sq., see *carcer*.

cancer crab (E. *canker*): Dissim. for **carcer*, cf. καρκ-ίνος (Sk. *karkin*).

candeō shine: = **cendeō*, cf. *ac-cendō* fire, KVEND- Sk. *cand* shine.

canis dog (E. *canary kennel'*) : κ-voνίς, cf. κ-voν- Sk. çván-, κ-vōν κύων (for *κϝών, *κών: ν from oblique cases), Arm. *šun*, Zd. çpān-: short form κυνίς Lit. *szunis*, cf. κυν- κύνα Acc., OIr. *con* Gen. (Nom. *cŭ*: E. *cub*), Sk. çún- (and κυν-τός Got. *hunds* E. *hound*?).

†**canistrum** basket : †κάνιστρον, fr. sq., 'made of reeds'.

†**canna** reed : †κάννα, Heb. *qāneh*.

†**cannabis** hemp (Ags. *hänep* E.; and E. *canvas canvass*) : †κάνναβις, Arab. *kunneb* Zenker 709 c.

canō sing (E. *cant* &c.) : OIr. *canaid* canit, Got. *hana* cock E. *hen*.

†**cantharis** beetle : κανθαρίς, κάνθαρος : Egyptian (the beetle worshipped in Egypt)?

†**cantharus** tankard (E.) : κάνθαρος, praeced., 'like a beetle inverted'.

†**cantherius** gelding: Gaulish (Plaut. Aul. 491 Gallicis cantheriis), cf. †κανθήλιος pack-ass.

†**canthus** tire (EM. κανθός) : Spanish (Quint.).

cānus white : = *cas-nus*, cf. Ags. *hasu* grey E. *haze*?

caper goat (E. *cab caper*[1] *capricc*) : κάπρος boar, Ags. *häfer* goat: 'strong-scented'?

Hesych. κάπρα. αἴξ, Τυρρηνοί is obscure.

⌐**capērō caperrō** am wrinkled:

capillus hair (Got. *kapillōn* shave the head, E. *dishevel*) : fr. *caput*.

capiō take (OIr. *cacht* capta, E. *cable casket catch cater chase regatta window-sash scaffold*) : = *cepiō*, κvEP-, cf. κvOP- Got. *hafts* joined, κvĒP- *cēpi* Perf., κvOP- κώπη handle, and κvOMP- Lett. *kampt* seize.

Hardly add Got. *hafjan* raise E. *heave behove*, on account of the meaning.

capis bowl: 'capacious,' praeced.

capistrum halter (E. *capstan* ?) : 'headstall,' = *capit-trum* fr. *caput*.

†**capparis** caper (E.) : †κάππαρις, Sk. *çapharī* a plant (or borrowed from Gk. ?).

†**capsa** box (E. *case*[2] *cash chase*[2]) : cf. †κάμψα κάμπτρα.

caput head (E. *achieve cabbage cad cadastre cape*[2] *cattle chattel chief corporal* &c.) : κvAP- Ags. *hafela*, Sk. *kapálam* pot, skull.

†**carbasus** flax: *κάρβασος by-form of †κάρπασος, Sk. *karpāsas* cotton (or borrowed from Gk. ?).

⌐†**carbatina carpatina** (Catull. 98. 4 Ellis) shoe : †καρβατίνη καρπατίνη, Carian (Pollux).

carbō charcoal : κᾱβ-όν-, cf. *corbis*, 'carried in a basket' (Ar. Ach. 333 λάρκος charcoal-burner's basket).

carcer enclosure (Sicil. κάρκαρον) : 'grating,' see *cancelli*.

†**carchēsium** beaker : †καρχήσιον : from a place-name ?

cardō pivot : κᾱᵈD-όν-, cf. κᾱᵈD- *cor*, 'heart, centre,' κERD- OSlav. *srěda* middle.

carduus thistle (E. *card* Vb.) : ᴋᴠ̄ᴅ-, 'shaking,' cf. κόρδαξ a dance, Sk. *kū̆rd-* leap, and ᴋᴠ̣ᴅ- κραδάω shake, W. *cryd* ague.

careō want : = *cadeō* am deprived of, cf. κεκαδών depriving.

cārex rush :

cariēs decay : = *cadiēs* fr. *cadō*.

carīna hull (E. *careen*) :

carmen song (E. *charm*) : = *canmen *canimen*, fr. *canō*.

carō flesh (MIr. *carna*, E. *carnage carrion charnel crone*) : Nom. ᴋᴀʀόɴ Gen. ᴋᴀʀɴόs : 'portion' at a feast, Osc. *carneis* part Gen. :

—**cārō** card : ᴋᴠ̄ᴀs, cf. ᴋᴠᴀs- Lit. *kasýti* scratch, Sk. *kash-*.

†**carpentum** chariot (OIr. *carpat*, E. *carpenter*) : Gaulish (Florus).

carpō pluck (E. *carpet scarce*) : ᴋᴠᴇ̣ᴘ-, cf. ᴋᴠᴇ̣ᴘ- καρπός fruit, Sk. *kṛpāṇas* sword, ᴋᴠᴇʀᴘ- Lit. *kerpù* I cut, ᴋᴠᴏʀᴘ- Ags. *härfest* harvest E.

†**carrus** wagon (E. *career carry chariot, cargo caricature carking charge*) : Gaulish? cf. MIr. *carr* (E. *car*).

cārus dear (E. *caress charity cherish*) : ᴋᴀ̄ʀ- Got. *hōrs* μοιχός E. *whore* cf. ᴋᴀʀ· OIr. *cara* friend.

casa hut (E. *casemate casino cassock chasuble*) :

_†**cascus** old : Sabine (Varr. L. L. 7. 28) :

cāseus cheese (E., W. *caws*) : hardly cf. OSlav. *kvasŭ* leaven.

cassēs hunting-net :

†**cassis** helmet : Etrusc. (Isid.).

cassus empty (E. *cashier* Vb.) : = *cad-tus*, fr. *careō*.

†**castanea** chestnut (E. E. *castanets*) : †κασтανέα : Arm. (Hehn)?

_†**castēria** cuddy : = *catastatēria*, *κατασтαтηρία fr. *κατασтαтέω settle, καθ-ίστημι.

†**castōr** beaver : †κάσтωρ :

cástrô : fr. *castrum* knife, Sk. *çástram* from *ças-* cut?

castrum fort, **castra** camp (W. *caer* city) :

castus pure (E. *caste chaste*) : ᴋᴀs- Arm. *sast* rebuke, cf. ᴋᴀ̄s- Sk. *çās-* to order.

†**catamītus** : Etrusc. †*catmite* Ganymede (Deecke BB. 2. 186), from *κατάμισθος venal.

†**catapulta** catapult : καταπέλτης, fr. πέλτη shaft.

_†**cataracta** portcullis : καταράκτης down-rushing, fr. ἀράσσω strike (cf. Plut. καταρράκτης portcullis, fr. ῥάσσω push).

†**cataractria** a spice : *καταράκτρια Fem. fr. praeced., 'rushing down' as it is sprinkled.

†**catasta** stage : *καταστή, κατά + ἵστημι.

_†**catēja** spear : Gaulish (Serv. Aen. 7. 741).

catēna chain (E. E. *chignon*) : 'capturing,' ᴋᴇᴛ-, cf. ᴋᴇɴᴛ- Got. *frahinthan* seize.

†**caterva** troop: Gaulish (Isid. Orig. 9. 3. 46), = *cates-va*, cf. OIr. *cath* fight.

catīnus dish (Sicilian κάτινον Varro; E. *kettle*): foreign?

catulus whelp:

†**catus** sharp (MIr. *cath* wise): Sabine (Varr. L. L. 7. 46): cf. Zd. çā-cut Sk. *çā-* sharpen, see *cōs*. (Ablant A: ō; or *catus* may = *cotós*.)

cauda tail (E. *coward cue*): cf. SKAUD- Got. *skauts* hem of a garment E. *shoot* &c. *scout* Vb. *scut* tail, 'projection'.

caudex trunk of a tree: 'projection,' praeced.

caulae passages, **caulis** stalk (E. *cole kail*): καυλός, Lit. *káulas* bone ('hollow').

caupō cōpō huckster: foreign?

Got. *kaupōn* to traffic (Lit. *kupczius* merchant OSlav. *kuplcĭ*) E. *chaffer chapman cheap cope* Vb. *keep* go rather with Got. *kaupatjan* strike (sc. a bargain).

‿ **caurus** N. W. wind: Lit. *sziduré* N. wind.

causa caussa cause (E. *kickshaw ruse*):

hardly = *coud-tā*, fr. *cūdō* (as *dēcīdō* fr. *caedō*): change of meaning too violent.

†**causia** hat: καυσία, Macedonian.

cautēs rock:

caveō take care: KVOV-, κο(F)έω perceive ἀ-κούω hear, Lit. *kawóti* attend to, Sk. *kavís* wise; cf. SKVOV- θυο-σκό(F)ος priest, Got. us-*skavs* prudent Ags. *sceāvian* look E. *show sheen* †*scavenger*.

cavilla raillery: 'bit of knowledge,' fr. praeced.

cavus hollow (E. *cage cajole gabion gaol*): = *covos*, κοῖλος (= *κόϜιλος*) Hesych. κόοι cavities.

-ce Demonstrative: MIr. *ce* this, Got. -*h* (in thau*h* yet E. *though*), Arm. *s* this.

cedo give thou: *ce-dō*, praeced. (cf. Osc. *ce-bn-ust* vēnerit) + root of *dō-num*.

cēdō go:

†**cedrus** cedar (E.): †κέδρος, cf. Sk. *kadaras* mimosa (late: borrowed from Gk.?).

celeber frequented: *qucle-bri-*, see *colō*.

celer quick: KVEL- cf. κέλης racehorse κελεύω urge, Zd. *car-* go Sk. *car-* move.

cella storeroom: 'covered place,' see sq.

cēlō hide: KEL-, cf. KEL- MIr. *celim* I hide, KḶ- Got. *huljan* to cover E. *hell helmet holster hull husk housings*.

‿ †**celōx** (term. from *vēlōx*) cutter: κέλης, see *celer*.

celsus high: Part. of *cellō* raise (-*sus* for -*tus* from Perf. *celsī*), τέλλω rise, Lit. *kélti* raise, fr. *celer*.

cēna caena caesna (Fest.) coena dinner (E.): NUmbr. *ƀesna* Acc.; =
caers-na, see *silicernium*, KAIBS-NĀ :

census registering (OIr. *cís*): KENS- cf. KONS- κοννέω understand.

centō patchwork: KVENT-, cf. KVONT- Sk. *kanthā*, KVOT- OHG. *hadarā*
rag.

centum 100: KMTÓM, *ἑ-κατόν*, OIr. *cēt*, Got. *hund* E. *hund*red, Lit.
szimtas OSlav. *sŭto*, Zd. *çatem* Sk. *çatdm*.

†cēpolendrum a spice: κῆπος garden (see *campus*) + ?

cēra wax (Ir. *cēir*): κηρός :

†cerasus cherry-tree (E. *cherry*, OHG. *kirsā* whence Lit. *czeresna* OSlav.
črĕšinja): †κερασός :

†cercūrus a ship: Cyprian κέρκουρος: Phoen. ?

cerebrum brain (E. *saveloy*): KERĒS- cf. KRES- κάρā (= *κάρεσα), Sk.
çíras; also KERS- ONor. *hjarsi* crown of the head, KRS- Arm. *sar*
(= *sars) top, and KĒS- κόρση temple, Sk. *çírshâm* head.

cernō separate: KVER-, MIr. *cert* right ('decided'), cf. SKVER- Ags.
sceran cut E. *shear* &c., SKVR- Lit. *skirti* to separate.
    Not = *crīnō, κρίνω decide (see *cribrum*), or Perf. would be *crīvi.

cernuus headlong: KVERN- skull, Got. *hvairnei*; 'concave' (cf. E.
skull beside ONor. *skál* bowl), κέρνος dish, ONor. *hverna* pan.

cerrītus crazed: KVERS-, cf. KVRS- ἐγκάρσιος slantwise, SKVERS- Lit.
skersas crooked OSlav. *črĕsŭ* beyond.

†cērūssa white lead: 'wax-like,' *κηροῦσσα Fem. of *κηρόεις Adj. of
κηρός wax.

cervīx neck: = *crīvīx fr. KREIVOS bent, Lit. *kreĩwas* OSlav. *krivŭ*
(cf. OSlav. *vratŭ* neck fr. *vratiti* to turn).

cervus stag: KVERVOS W. *carw*, cf. KVORVĀ Lit. *kárvė* cow OSlav.
krava: 'horned,' fr. κέρ-ας horn.

†cestrosphendonē an engine: *κεστροσφενδόνη, fr. κέστρα bolt + σφεν-
δόνη sling.

cēterī caeterī the rest:

†cētus sea-monster: κῆτος :

ceu whether: *queu = quī-ve (as seu = sī-ve), quī (Abl. of quī) + -ve.

cēveō move the haunches:

†chalybs steel: †χάλυψ, from the Chalybes (iron-workers in Pontus).

†chara horse-radish:

†charta paper (E. *card cartridge*): †χάρτης, Egyptian (see *papȳrus*).

†chēlē chaelē claw: χηλή :

†chelys tortoise: χέλυς, GHELU- OSlav. *želŭvĭ*.

†chlamys mantle: †χλαμύς, cf. Thracian ζαλμός skin.

†chorda string: χορδή :

†chorus dance: χορός, cf. Lit. *žáras* way of going.

†chrȳsos gold: †χρῦσός, Heb. *hârûts*.

†cibōrium cup: †κιβώριον seed vessels of colocasia : Egyptian (from its habitat).

cibus food :

cicāda tree-cricket : fr. *cicur.*

cicātrix scar: fr. *cicur,* 'taming,' subduing (being the end of) the hurt, cf. Varr. L. L. 7. 91 nulla res neque cicurare neque mederi potis est (Pacuvius).

†ciccus doit: *κίκκος, cf. κίκκαβος : Phoen.?
  In Varr. L. L. 7. 91, ciccum dicebant membranam tenuem, the best MS. reads *ciccur.*

cicer chick-pea: = *cecir, Pruss. *keckirs* pea.

†cichorēum endive (E. *succory*): *κιχόρειον †κιχόρεια, Egyptian (Plin. 20. 73).

†cīcilendrum a spice: †*κικίλενδρον, cf. cēpo*lendrum* :

†cīcimandrum a spice: †*κικί-μανδρον, cf. praeced.:

cicōnia (for the term. cf. *Favōnius*) stork: sq., from its reputed affection for its parents.

cicur tame: *cecur, KVEKV-, cf. Hom. τέπων gentle.

cicūta hemlock (W. *cegid cecys,* whence OE. *kex*): praeced., 'domesticated, grown in gardens,' from a Vb. *cicuō.*

cieō ciō move (E. *cite*): cf. κίω go, Corn. *ce* go thou Zeuss 586 a.

cīmex bug:

†cinaedus wanton: †κίναιδος:

cincinnus curl: κίκιννος, Redupl. (cf. *tintinō* beside τιτανισμός):

cingō gird (E. *shingles*): = *cungvo from *congvō, cf. κόμβος band.

cinis ashes (not E. *cinder*): = *cunis from *conis, κόνις dust.

†cinnamōmum cinnamum cinnamon: †κιννάμωμον *κίνναμον, Heb. *qinnāmōn.*

cippus cīpus stake:

circus circle (E. *carcanet scarch*): Metath. κρίκος ring, cf. KRINKÓS Ags. *hring* E. E. *rink rank range rung* †harangue.

cirrus curl: = *cirsus, OHG. *hirsi* millet ('tufted ')?

cis within: cf. -κι (in οὐκί not πολλάκι often), Got. *hi-na* this Ags. E. *he,* Lit. *szès* OSlav. *sĭ.*

†cisium gig: Gaulish ?

†cista box (E. *chest*): †κίστη :

†cithara lute (E. *guitar*): †κιθάρα: Semitic ?

citrā within : Got. *hidra* hither E., fr. *ci-s.*

†citrus Rom. form of *cedrus.*

cīvis ceivis citizen :
  hardly cf. Got. *heiva-* house.

clādēs loss: 'breaking,' KĻD- cf. KĻD- κλαδαρός brittle.

clam secretly: = *clā-m, KĻ-, see cēlō and *tam.*

clāmô shout (E. *claim*) : fr. Subst. **clāma* (cf. *fā-ma*), Κ̣-, see *calô*.

clandestīnus secret : = **clandestrīnus* (see *mcdiastīnus*) fr. **clandcster* formed (on anal. of *equester pedester*) from **clande=clam* (as *quamde=quam* : so *clāde* Müller on Fest. p. 47 = **clā* i.e. *cla-m*).

clangō clang (E.) : ΚVLANGV- *κλαγγή* Subst., cf. ΚVLAGV- Lit. *klagéti* cackle.

clārus bright (E. *clear claret*) :

classis division : = **clād-tîs* cutting, fr. *clādês* ?

claudō clōdō clūdō shut (OHG. *sliozan* from *exclūdcre*) : **claudus* Adj., fr. *clāvis* + term. -DO-.

claudus lame : ΚLAU-, cf. Sk. *çrō-náš*, + term. -DO-.

clāva club :

clāvis key : *κλη(ϝ)îs* :

clāvus nail, helm, stripe (OIr. *clôi* nails, E. *clove cloy*) :

clēmens mild :

clepō steal : Got. *hlifan* E. shop-*lifter*, Pruss. au-*klipts* hidden, cf. *κλέπτω* steal.

cliens client : Part. of *cluēō*, 'obedient'.

clipeus clupeus shield : =**clopeus* cf. *clepō*, 'cover,' OSlav. po-*klopŭ* lid.

clītellae pack-saddle : 'sloping,' Dimin. of **cleitrae*, OUmbr. *kletra* litter, Got. *hlcithra* tent, from ΚLEI-, see *acclīnis*.

clīvus slope : = **cloivos*, Got. *hlaiv* tomb ('mound') E. Lud-*low*, from ΚLOI- Ablaut of ΚLEI-, see *acclīnis*.

cloāca cluāca clouāca sewer : from **clou-ācus* Adj. (see *opācus*), ΚLOU- cf. ΚLU- *cluô* cleanse and ΚLU-D- *κλύζω* wash, Got. *hlutrs* clean.

clueō am reputed : ΚLU- *κλύω* hear, Zd. Sk. *çru-*, see *inclutus*; cf. ΚLEU- *κλέ(ϝ)os* glory, OIr. *clū* rumour, Got. *hliu-ma* hearing E. *lumbering*, OSlav. *sluti* be famous, Sk. *çrávas* sound, and ΚLOU-S- OW. *clustcu* ears Zeuss 285 b, Ags. *hlÿstan* listen E., Lit. *klausÿti* (with *k-* from Teutonic) OSlav. *sluhŭ* hearing, ΚLU-S- Sk. *çrush-* hear.

clūnis haunch : = **clounis*, **κλοῦνις κλόνις* (cf. *μοῦνος μόνος*) os sacrum, W. *clun* hip, ONor. *hlaunn* haunch, Lit. *szlaunis* hip, Zd. *çraoni* Sk. *çrōnîs*.

clūrīnus apish : *clūra* ape :

co- with (used before vowels or *h* : *comedō* shows 'Recomposition ') : OIr. *co* to, Got. prefix *ga-* E. enough handi*work* : fr. *cu-m*.

†**coccum** scarlet (E. *cochineal* ; and *cock*roach ?) : †*κόκκος* kermes-berry :

†**coclea** snail (E. *coach cockle*shell) : *κοχλίας, κόχλος* :

coepī begin : = **co-îpî*, *co-* + Perf. (un-reduplicated, as usual in Compounds) of *apô*, see *apiscor*.—Lucr.'s *co-ēpî* is from **ēpî* reduplicated Perf. of *apô*.

cōgitô think : *co-* + *agitô* (fr. **agó, agō*).

cohors enclosure (E. *court*) : *co-* + *hortus*.

†colaphus cuff (E. *copse*, Fr. *coup* blow *couper* cut): κόλαφος, cf. κολάπτω peck:

†cōliphia cōlȳphia loin-pieces: Plur. from κωλύφιον ham Phrynichus p. 77 Lobeck, Dimin. of κῶλον leg (as δενδρύφιον of δένδρον).

collis hill: = *colnis*, Ags. *hyll* E., cf. κνοɩɴοs Lit. *kálnas* mountain, κνοɪɴυs Got. *hallus* rock: Nom. κνοLŌN, whence κολωνός hill: 'rise,' fr. *celsus*.

collum neck: = *colsum*, Ags. *heals* E. †*hauberk*.

†collybus agio: †κόλλυβος doit: Phœn.?

†collȳra vermicelli: κολλύρα roll, cf. κόλλαβος κόλλιξ:

colō tend: = *quelō* (see *inquilīnus*), πέλω go, fr. *celer*.

†colocāsium Egyptian bean: κολοκάσιον, fr. κόλος stunted + †*kásiον bean (Egyptian, from its habitat).

color colour: 'covering' (cf. Sk. *várṇas* colour from *var-* cover), κɪ̯- see *cēlō*.

colostra biestings:

coluber colober snake (E. *culverin*): 'turning,' cf. πόλος axis, fr. *colō*.

cōlum strainer (E. *colander culvert* portcullis): = *caulum fr. *caulae*.

†columba dove (E. *culver*): *κολύμβη, κόλυμβος grebe, fr. κολυμβάω dive: 'ducking its head' (of. E. *dove* fr. *dive*).

columen top: 'turning'-point (cf. *vertex* top fr. *vertō*), see *colō coluber*.

colurnus (1) of hazel (Serv.): Metath. for *corul-nus fr. *corulus corylus*.
(2) of cornel (Fest.): Dissim. for *cor-urnus fr. *cor-nus*.

colus distaff:
not 'revolving,' fr. *colō celer*, as the distaff was held stationary.

†coma hair: κόμη:

comes companion: from *com cum.*—Not a compound fr. *eō*.

cōmis kind: from *com cum with vowel lengthened to form Adj. (cf. *cūpēs* fr. *cūpiō*, see *immānis sōpiō* and *suppus*), cf. κοινός kind = *κομ-jós.
Cosmis in the Dvenos inscr. (E. Schneider 19) obscure, sec. Jordan = *cōmis*, sec. Bücheler = *comes*, sec. Bréal = *commissi*.

†cōmissor cōmīsor revel: *κωμίζω fr. κῶμος revel (while κωμάζω is fr. κώμη village).

cōmō arrange: 'put together,' from *com (see *cōmis*).
*co-imō from *emō* take would give *coemō, cf. *coctus* beside *coïtus*: in Plaut. Bacch. 976 Löwe reads *coemptionalem* (oe a diphthong: the reading *comptionalem* is due to Livy's 'contionali seni,' 3. 72. 4).

compēscō confine: *pāscō fix = *pac-scō fr. *paciscor*, cf. Plin. *dispēscō* separate.

compīlô rob:

compitum cross-road: πετῶ 'go'.

con- with (before any cons. but *p, b, m*): OIr. *con-*; = *com, cum*.

†concha shell: κόγχη, see *congius*.

†conchis lentils: *conchus, κόγχος dialectic for *κόγκος, cf. Sk. *kankus* millet.

concinnus neat: 'harmonious,' = *concen-nus from con-cinō sound together.

concipilô finish off (Plaut. uses in the same sense 'offatim conficiam' and 'offatim concipilabo'): dialectic for *concumulô or *concublô fr. *cumulus*.

condālium (in Plaut. prob. trisyllabic) ring: fr. †*condus, Hesych. κόνδος knob, Sk. *kandas* lump.

condiciō agreement: DIK- cf. DEIK- *dīcō*, 'fix'.

condiō preserve: by-form of condō put together (cf. *pinsītum sancītum* from *pinsiō sanciō beside *pistvm sanctum* from pinsō *sancō), see -dō.

confūtô check: *fūtus Part. fr. DHŪ- ONor. *dȳja* shake, Sk. *dhū-*.

†conger sea-eel: *κόγγρος by-form of †γόγγρος (see cōrȳtos).

congerrō playmate: fr. †gerrae.

congius quart: 'shell-full,' KONKHV- κόγχη mussel, Sk. *çankhás* and (with -e-) Lett. *sence*.

congruō meet: 'fall in with,' from *grūō fall, Lit. *griūti* fall down, GVRŪ- cf. GVROU- *gravis*.

cōniveō conniveō cognīveō wink: from *nigveō, see *nictô*.

cōnor attempt:

conquinisco cower: from *qua-n-iscō (cf. *frūniscor* beside *fruor*), *qua-nō, KVA- cf. KVĀ- πεπτη-ώς crouching (for πτ = π cf. πτόλις = πόλις).

Perf. *conquexi* and Part. *quactum* driven together Isid. Orig. 20. 2. 35 are from the fuller KVAK- κατα-πτακών crouching, cf. KVĀK-πτήσσω crouch.

considerô inspect:

hardly (1) fr. *considō* am in session, from *sīdō*, as 'look at' seems the orig. meaning: (2) 'look at something bright,' SVĪD- cf. SVID- Lit. *swidus* shining.

consilium assembly: fr. *sedeō*.

consternāre alarm: by-form of con-sternere overthrow (as *appellāre compellāre* of *appellere compellere*), cf. STRN- OHG. *stornēn* be astounded.

consul chief magistrate: formed from Plur. *consulēs*, fr. *sedeō*.

consulō deliberate: 'sit together,' praeced.

contāminô blend: fr. *tagmen touching, *tangō*.

cōntiō (cōntio late, Diomedes, Keil 1. 433) meeting:=*coventiō dialectic form (see cūria) for *conventiō*.

contumāx insolent, contumēlia insult: *tumeō* swell (with pride).

†contus pole: κοντός, fr. *κέντω κεντέω prick.

†cōnus cone: κῶνος pine-cone:

hardly add (1) ONor. *húnn* knob, on account of the vowel: (2) Sk. *çānas* grindstone, see cōs (no resemblance of meaning).

convexus vaulted: **vaxus* Part. (for the term. see *celsus*) of **vacō* bend, see *vacillō*.

convicium outcry: fr. *vīcus*, 'meeting in the street'.—Also spelt *convitium* as tho' fr. *vīta*, 'meeting of guests'.

†**cophinus** basket: †κόφινος:

coquō cook (E. E. *coke cockney kitchen* apricot *biscuit*): = **quequō*, κνεκν-τέπων ripe, κνοκν- W. *pobi* bake: blending of the forms κνεπ- Lit. *kepù* I bake and πεκν- τέσσω I cook, OSlav. *peką*, Zd. Sk. *pac-* cook.

cor heart: *cord-* = κ*ε*d-, καρδία κραδίη, OIr. *cride*, Lit. *szirdis* OSlav. *srūdīce srīdīce*, Sk. *hṛd*, cf. κεrd- κέρδεα wiles ('intelligence'), MIr. *cerd* art, Got. *hairtō* heart E., Arm. *sirt*, Zd. *zarad-* (in *zaraz-dāiti* devotion), see *cardō*.

†**cōralium** coral: **κωράλιον* Dor. for †κουράλιον:

corbis basket (E. *corbel*): κ*ε*bi- cf. κrebi- ONor. *hrip*.

corbīta hoy (E. *corvette*): praeced., 'carrying a basket full of stones' to serve as an anchor (*εἶναι*).

†**cordāx** a dance: κόρδάξ, see *carduus*.

†**coriandrum** coriander: **κορίανδρον* by-form of †κορίαννον: Semitic?

corium hide (E. *cuirass quarry*[2] *scourge*): = **querium*, κνεr-, cf. Sk. *cárman*.

cornīx crow: fr. **corna* (see *coxendīx*), κοrn- cf. κorn̦- Hesych. κόραφος a bird: Nom. κοrōn (see *collis*), whence κορώνη crow.

cornū horn (MIr. *corn*; E. *corn*[2] *cornelian corner*): κ̣ρn- Galatian κάρνος trumpet (Hesych.), Got. *haurn* horn E., cf. κ̣rn-gvo- Sk. *çŕngam*, see *crambē*.

cornus cornel: κ̣rn-, κράνεια.
Hardly add Lit. *kirna* band of brushwood.

†**corōna** garland (E. *crown*): Fem. (sc. *taenia*) of **corōnus*, χορωνός Simonides 174 Bergk: 'worn by dancers,' see *chorus*.

corpus body (E. *corps corpse*): κνεr- πραπίδες midriff, Zd. *kehrp* body Sk. *kŗp* form, cf. κνεεπ- πρέπω appear, Ags. *hrif* womb E. *midriff*.

cortex bark (E. *cork*): = **quertex*, 'cut off' (cf. E. *bark* fr. *break*), κνεrt- Lit. *kertù* I strike, cf. κνort- OSlav. *kratŭkŭ* short, Zd. *kareṭ-* cut Sk. *kart-*, and κνrent- Ags. *hrendan* cut down (Skeat) E. *rend*.

cortīna curtīna caldron: fr. *curtus*, 'cut down,' not tall like the *amphora*, cf. Lucr. 4. 1026 dolia curta.

cor-ūscus scor-īscus (Probi Appendix, Keil 4. 198: for the term. cf. *labrūscu mollūscus marisca vopiscus*) waving:

corvus raven (MIr. *crū*; E. *cormorant*): κοr- κόρ-αξ:

†**cōrycus** sack: κώρυκος:

corylus (with *y* as tho' Greek!) **corulus corilus** hazel: κosel- Ags. *hässl* E., cf. κosl- OIr. *coll*.

†**corymbus** cluster: κόρυμβος top, κ̣rn-gvo- cf. *crambē*, see *cornū*.

†cōrȳtos quiver: *κωρῡτός by-form (see *conger*) of †γωρῡτός:

cōs flint: KŌ-TIS cf. KŌ-NOS Sk. *çānas* grindstone, *çā* sharpen, see *catus*.

costa rib (E. *accost coast costermonger cutlet*): cf. OSlav. *kostĭ* bone?

†costum a plant: †κόστος, Sk. *kushṭhas*.

†cothurnus boot: κόθορνος:

†cottabus clap: κότταβος a Sicilian game:

†cottana cōtona coctana small figs: †κόττανα, Syrian (Plin. 13. 51), Heb. *qīṭōn* little.

cottī-diē cōtī-diē (cf. Catull. 68. 141 *cōtīdjānā* MSS.: Mart. 11. 1. 2 . *quŏtĭdiānā* quasi fr. *quot*) daily: Loc. of *cōtus *quŏ-tus (correlative of *tŏ-tus*), fr. *quī*, + *diēs*.

cŏturnīx (Ovid, quasi fr. κόθορνος, artificially 'booted' for fighting) cōturnīx (i.e. *cotturnīx) cocturnīx (Caper, Keil 7. 108) quail: fr. *cocl-ur-na (see *cornīx*), KVOKT- OHG. *wahtala* (E.).

†covinnus covīnus car: Belgic (Lucan 1. 426), = *co-veg-nos fr. co- + *vehō*, cf. W. *cy-wain* convey.

coxa hip: 'bend,' KVOKS- OIr. *coss* foot, MHG. *hahse* bend of knee, Zd. *kasha* shoulder Sk. *kákshas* armpit.

coxendīx hip (for term. cf. *clacendix* shell fr. *culx²*): fr. *coxenda (see *cornīx*) 'bending' (for term. cf. *merenda*), fr. praeced.

crābrō hornet: = *crās-rŏn, KĒS- cf. KRS- Lit. *szirszen-* (Nom. *szirszū*) wasp OSlav. *srŭšenĭ* hornet.

†crambē cabbage: κράμβη, KĂN-GVĪ, see *corymbus cornū*.

crāpula intoxication:

not fr. κραιπάλη.

crās to-morrow: = *crāss from *crāssum* 'close' (i.e. 'near'), sq.?

crāssus thick (E. *grease*): 'matted,' = *crāt-tós KVĒT- cf. KVEBT- OIr. *certle* ball of wool, KVORT- κύρτη weel κροτώνη excrescence on trees, Got. *hardus* hard E., Sk. *kathinas* hard *kaṭas* wickerwork *kart-* spin, sq.

crātis wickerwork (E. *grate grill*): KVĒTf- *cartilāgō* gristle ('meshed'), cf. KVRT- κάρταλος basket κρατύς strong, Got. *haurds* door (orig. of wickerwork) E. *hurdle hoarding hurst*, Pruss. *korto* hedge.

crēber thick: 'increasing,' fr. *crē-scō*.

crēdō believe (E. *grant miscreant recreant*):=*cred-dō, KRĒD-DHŌ, OIr. *cretim* I believe, Sk. *çrád-dhā-* believe; 'put the heart to,' from KRED- cf. KERD- under *cor*, + -*dō*. A word of the Ursprache, and so not regarded as a compound (which would be *crēfō from *creffō *cred-fō).

cremō burn:

cremor broth (E. *cream*):

creō make (E. *creole*):

hardly *cre-* Metath. for *cer-* Fest. *cerus* creator, Varr. *cereō* make, cf. KVOR- Zd. Sk. *kar-*.

†creper uncertain: Sabine (Varro): 'dark,' *crepes- fr. *crepusculum*.
crepida slipper:
  not from κρηπίς military boot, see sq.
crepīdō foundation:
  not from κρηπίς basement:
crepô rattle: = *crequô*, KVREKV- κρέκω make a noise by striking,
  OSlav. *krektati* to quack, cf. KVRENKV'- Ags. *hringan* to sound E.
  ring Vb.
†crepusculum twilight: Sabine (Varr.), see *creper*.
crē-scō grow (E. *accrue crew recruit*): fr. *creô*.
crēta chalk (OIr. *crē* clay; E. *crayon*): 'sifted,' *crētus* Part. of *cernô*.
crībrum sieve: MIr. *criathar*, KRĪ-DHRO- cf. KRI-DHLO- Ags. *hriddel* E.
  riddle; from KRĪ- κρίνω separate, cf. KROI- Got. *hrains* clean.
crīmen charge: fr. κρί-νω decide, praeced.
crīnis hair:
  not cf. Lit. *szerȳs* bristle.
crīsô crissô move the haunches:
  not cf. Got. af-*hrisjan* shake off.
crīspus curled (E. *crape*): cf. KRISP- Ags. *hrespan* tear to pieces E. *rasp*
  †*trapier*, and KRIPS- W. *crych* curled (E. *crease*).
crista tuft:
crōciô croak: = *crauciô*, Lit. *kraukti* OSlav. *kruků* raven.
crū-dus raw: KVRŪ- MIr. *crū*, Sk. *krū-rás*, see *crūsta*.
†crumēna crumina purse: cf. (with *ū*) *κρūμέα by-form of †γρūμέα bag
  (see *conger côrȳlos*):
cruor blood: = *crūs-ôr*, cf. MIr. *crū*: 'curdled, thick' (as opp. water),
  fr. *crūs-ta*.
†cruppellāriī champions: Gaulish (Tac.).
crūs leg from knee to ankle: 'hard' (as opp. the thigh), fr. sq., cf.
  Arm. *sru*-n-kh shins.
crūsta crust (E. *custard*): KVRŪS- hard, Ags. *hrūse* earth, cf. KVRUS-
  κρύσταλλος κρύ(σ)ος frost, Lit. *kruszà* hail, Zd. *khrush*- injure; see
  crū-dus.
†crux cross (E. E. *crouch crusty curse*): Punic (as a Carthaginian
  instrument of torture)?
cubitum elbow (Sicil. κύβιτον): KVUB- 'bent,' Got. *hups* hip E. E. *hoop
  hump*, Sk. *kub-jás* humpbacked.
cubô lie (E. *covey*): KVUBH- κύπτω bend, cf. KVŪBH- κūφός bent, by-form
  of praeced.
†cucullus hood (OIr. *cocul*; E. *cowl*): Gaulish (Santonic, Juv. 8. 145).
cucūlus cucullus cuckoo (E.): KVUKV- κόκκυξ, Lit. *kukilti* cry as a
  cuckoo, Assyr. *huuku* cuckoo, cf. KVOUKV- MIr. *cûach*, OSlav. *kuka-
  vica* Sk. *kôkas*, onomatop.

cucumis cucumber (E.): fr. Adj. *cucumus* 'baked, ripe,' fr. *coquō*, cf. πέπων (ripe) 'a kind of gourd not eaten till quite ripe' (Liddell & Scott).

cucurbita gourd (E.): Redupl. of *corbis*, 'shaped like a basket'.

? cucus cuckoo (Plaut. Persa 173 Ritschl, from Gruter; MSS. *cujus*): fr. *cucŭlus*.

cūdō strike: fr. *cūdus* Adj., ΚVOU- cf. ποίη grass (= *πof-ίη, 'struck' by the sithe), Ags. *heā-van* hew E. E. *hay hoe*, Lit. *kauti* fight OSlav. *kovati* strike.

culcita pillow (W. *cylched*, E. *quilt cushion counterpane*): 'rounded,' ΚVULKV- Lit. *kulkà* ball, cf. ΚVŪLKV- Sk. *kūrcás* cushion.

culex gnat (Ir. *cuil*): 'wheeling' in its flight, fr. *colō celer*.

culina colina kitchen (E. *kiln*): fr. *colō*, 'quod ibi colebant ignem' (Varr.).

culleus cūleus: cf. *cōleus* scrotum: fr. *caulae*, 'having a mouth'.

culmus stalk: ΚLMOS *κάλαμος*, cf. ΚOLMOS Ags. *healm* E. *haulm*, OSlav. *slama*.

culpa colpa fault (E. *culprit*):

culter knife (E. *coulter cutlass cutler*): Sk. *kuṭharas* 'axe' seems too late (A.D. 500) to compare.

culullus culūlus culillus sacrificial vessel:

cūlus πυγή: fr. *caulae*, 'opening'.

cum[1] com- with (E. para*gon*): *κοινός* common (= *κομ-jós, see *cōmis*), OIr. *com-* with.

cum[2] quom quum when: from ΚVO- *quī* + a case-ending (see *tam*: but *cume* is only a conjecture for *cuinc* in Terentius Scaurus, Keil 7. 28).

cumera meal-tub:

†cuminum cumin: †κύμῑνον, Heb. *kammōn*.

cumulus heap (E. *cumber*): = *cub-lus*, 'arched,' fr. *cubitum*, cf. ΚVOUB- Ags. *heap* E.

cūnae cradle: = *coinae*, ΚOI- *κοίτη* lair, cf. ΚEI- *κεῖμαι* lie, ΚΙ- Zd. Sk. *çī-*.

cunctor delay: ΚONKV- Sk. *çank-* doubt.

cunctus conctus all: 'inclusive' (see *frequens omnis saepe*), Part. of *congvō* i.e. *cingō*.

cuneus wedge (W. *cyn*, E. *coign coin*): no resemblance of meaning to *κῶνος*, see *cōnus*.

†cuniculus rabbit (Polyb. κύνικλος, W. *cwning*, E. *coney*): Iberian (Aelian N. A. 13. 15); properly 'little dog,' = *caniculus* (whence NHG. *kaninchen* rabbit), fr. *canis*.

†cunila savoury (not *cunīla* in Plaut. Trin. 985): κονίλη:

cunnus: = *cut-nus*, ΚVUT- κύσθος κυσός (= *κυτjós) κύτος a hollow, Lit. *kutys* purse.

cūpa tub (E. *coop cup cupola coif cuff goblet kibe*; OSlav. *kupa* cup):
KVŪP- Sk. *kū̆pas* pit, cf. KVUP- *κύπελλον* cup, Ags. *hyfi* hive E.

cupiō desire (E. *covet*): KVOP- cf. KVEP- *capiō,* 'try to take' (see *amō*).

cuppēs cūpēs dainty: 'greedy,' KVŌP- long form of praeced., cf. Lucr. *cūpēdō* desire Apicius *coppādia* titbits.

†cupressus cypress: *κύπρεσσος by-form of †κυπάρισσος, Heb. *kopher* a tree.

cūr quōr why: = *quŏd Abl. of *quī.*

cūra care (E. *proctor proxy scour sure*): = *coisa, Pælignian *coisatens* curaverunt, KVOIS-, cf. KVIS- τε-τι(σ)-ηώς sorrowing.

curculiō weevil: *curculus thin, KVR̥K- cf. KVORK- Zd. *kareç-* be thin Sk. *karç-,* KVROK- *cracens* (see *gracilis*).

cūria division: = *coviria, *co-* (see *cōntiō*) + *vir,* cf. Volscian *covehriu* conventu.

currō run (E. *corridor corsair*): = *quorsō, KVR̥S- MHG. *hurren* move quickly E. *hurrah.*

curtus mutilated (E. *curtail,* OHG. *kurz* short): KR̥TÓS καρτός sliced, Part. fr. KER- κείρω cut, MIr. *cert* small, Got. *hairus* sword.

curvus bent (E. *curb*):

cuspis point:

cūstōs keeper (E. *accoutre*): KŪZDH- cf. Got. *huzd* hoard E. :

cutis skin: KUT- ἐγ-κυτί close ('on the skin'), cf. KŪTÍ- Ags. *hȳd* hide E.

†cyathus ladle: κύαθος:

†cybaea transport: *κυβαία Adj. Fem. fr. *κύβη by-form of κύμβη, see *cymba.*

†cycnus cygnus swan (E. *cygnet*): κύκνος: KUKV- Sk. *çukrás* bright, white.

†cymba cumba boat (E. *coomb*): κύμβη boat, cup, cf. KHVUMBH- Zd. *khumba* pot Sk. *kumbhás.*

†cymbalum cymbal (E. *chime*): κύμβαλον: 'cup-shaped,' fr. praeced.

†cytisus clover: †κύτισος:

†daedalus variegated: δαίδαλος, DAID- Ags. *tāl* delicate, joyful.

-dam enclitic (in *quīdam quondam*): a case-ending (cf. *jam*) from DO-, see *-de -do -dum.*

damma dāma deer:

damnum loss (E. *damage*): = *dapnum, DAPNO- ONor. *tafn* sacrifice, cf. DAPN̥Ā δαπάνη expense, fr. sq.

daps feast: cf. δάπτω devour.

†dapsilis (term. after *facilis*) sumptuous: δαψιλής, = *δαπ-τι-λ-ής fr. praeced.

-de enclitic (in *inde* &c. *unde quamde*): -δε (in ὅδε τοιόσδε), cf. *-dam.*

dē from (E. *denizen*): OIr. *dī* concerning: = *dvē* a case-form fr. *dvō* two, δῶ- (in δώδεκα twelve), OIr. *dā*, OSlav. *dva*, Sk. *dvā́*, see *duo dis-*.

decem ten (E. *dismal* ?): DEKM̥ Lit. *dészimtis* OSlav. *desętĭ* (*m* for *n* from the ordinal DĒKM̥-MOS, see *novem septem*), for DEKN̥ δέκα, OIr. *deich n-*, Got. *taihun* E. E. *tithe*, Arm. *tasn*, Zd. *daçan-* Sk. *dáça.*

decet befits: DEK- cf. DOK- δοκέω seem.

dē-fendō repel (E. *fend fender*): 'beat off,' cf. *of-fendō* strike against:

dē-frūtum (Plaut.) must boiled down: BHROUTÓM Ags. *brēad* bread E., cf. BHRŬTOM Thracian βρῦτον beer, Parts. fr. BHREU- Ags. *breōvan* brew E. Also **dēfrŭtum** (Verg.) must, BHRŬTOM OIr. *bruth* heat, Ags. *brod* broth E., cf. MIr. *bruith* cookery.

de-inceps next following (orig. Adj.): fr. *dē + incipiō* begin.

dein-de thereafter: *de-im* 'from that,' *dē + *im* Abl. of *is* (cf. *illim istim*).

dē-jerō swear: formed for *dē-jūrō* on anal. of *pējerō* quasi = *per-jūrō*.

dēlēniō dēlīniō (quasi fr. *linum* 'net') charm: fr. *lēnis*.

dē-leō destroy: see *lētum*: not fr. δηλέομαι (Dor. δᾱλέομαι) hurt.

dē-līberō consider: fr. *līber*, 'set free' from extraneous matter.

dē-libūtus anointed: fr. *libuō* anoint, LIBH- cf. LEIBH- ἀλείφω.

†delphīnus dolphin (E.): *δελφῖνος by-form of δελφίς: 'young,' GVELBH- δέλφαξ porker δελφύς womb, cf. GVOLBH- Got. *kalbō* calf E., Zd. *gareua* womb Sk. *gárbhas.*

-dem enclitic (in *ibidem idem identidem itidem prīdem quidem tandem tantundem totidem*): -DM̥, cf. κρύβ-δα secretly, Sk. i-*ddm* it (see *idem*).

dēmō take away: fr. *dēmus* Adj., sq. (see *emō*).

dēmum at length: Neut. of *dēmus* Adj. from *dē.*

dēnī 10: for *dec-nī*, on anal. of *sēnī* 6 = *sex-nī.*

dēni-que at length: fr. *dēne*, *dē + -ne.*

dens tooth: DN̥T- OIr. *dēt*, Got. *tunthus* E. E. *tusk*, Zd. *dañtan* Sk. *dántas*, cf. DONT- Lit. *dantìs* and with copulative prefix ὀ-δούς: Part. (with reduced root) of *edō.*

densus thick: = *dent-tús* Part. fr. DN̥T-, cf. δασύς = δη̄τ-ύς.

√ **depsō** knead: δέψω, cf. DESP- OHG. *zispan* tread on; from DEBH- δέφω knead.

dēsīderō long for: hardly (1) 'miss from the session,' fr. *sīdō*: (2) 'fail to see,' see *considerō.*

dē-stinō make fast: from *stanō *sta-nō set, STA- στάσις standing, MIr. *scssed* (= *si-sta-tu-), cf. Got. *sta-n-dan* stand E., and STĀ- *stō.*

dēterior worse (for term. cf. *exterior interior*): 'degenerate,' *dēterus* from *dē.*

deus god (E. *deuce*): = *dēvus*, *dīvus.*

dexter right: Comparative form, cf. δεξιτερός, from DEKS- δεξιός, OIr. *dess*, Got. *taihs-va*, cf. DÉKSINOS Lit. *deszinè* right hand OSlav. *desĭnŭ* right, Zd. *dashina* Sk. *dákshiṇas*.

†**diaeta** diet (E.): δί-αιτα maintenance, fr. δίδ through + αίνυμαι take, Osc. *aeteis* partis.

†**dica** lawsuit: δίκη, fr. sq.

dicāx witty, **diciō** command, **dicis** (Gen.) form, **dicô** consecrate: DIK- Zd. *diç-* show Sk. *diç-* point, cf. sq.

dīcō deicō say (E. *dight ditty*): DEIK- δείκνῡμι show, Got. ga-*teihaṇ* proclaim E. *token teen tiny*, cf. praeced.

dierectus crucified: pop. etym. (quasi ' dies rectus,' euphemism for ' dies malus '), for *directus* 'cut in pieces' from *dī-rigó*.

diēs diēs day (E. *journey sojourn*): DIĒ- cf. DJĒ- Sk. *dyáus* sky, day, see *diurnus nŭndinae.*—Also DEV-, *biduum* two days.

digitus finger: DEG- cf. DĒG- Got. *tēkan* touch E. *take tack tick* &c. *tickle.*

Osc. *degetasis* (epithet of a magistrate, quasi ' fingering ' the public money !) is obscure.

dīgnus worthy (E. *dainty deign disdain*): 'noticeable,' fr. *dīcô.*

dī-ligō love: from **legô* care for, cf. *intel-legō neg-legô* (all three with Perf. in *-xī*) *relligiō*, ἀ-λέγω care for.

dī-micô fight: 'strike on different sides,' *micô.*

dirus ill-omened: = **dvi-rós* fr. *duo*, 'different' from what should be, cf. Serv. Aen. 3. 235 Sabini et Umbri, quae nos mala, dira appellant.

dis- (Got. *dis*-tairan burst) **dī-** apart: lost cases fr. *duo*, 'in two,' cf. Got. *tvis*-standan to separate.

discipulus pupil: = **disci-blus* Adj. (see *dŭplus*) fr. sq.

discō learn: = **dic-scô* fr. *dīcō*, 'have pointed out to me '.

†**discus** quoit (E. *dish dais desk*): δίσκος, = **δίκ-σκος* fr. δικεῖν throw.

disertus fluent: 'with different accomplishments,' fr. *ars*, with intervocalic *s* preserved as though Deponent Part. of *disserō* discourse.

dis-sipô scatter: from *supô* throw, Lit. *sùpti* swing.

dī-stinguō divide: 'strike asunder,' see *stinguō.*

†**dīthyrambus** hymn to Bacchus: †διθύραμβος (for term. see *iambus triumphus*):

diurnus by day: fr. **dius* day, OIr. *die* (= **di-jos*), cf. *diēs*, with term. of *nocturnus* by night, νύκτωρ.

dīves rich: 'godlike, blest,' fr. *dīvus.*

dī-vidō divide (E. *device devise*): VIDH-, see *viduus.*

dīvus deivos dius god **dīvum** sky (as home of the gods): DEIV- Lit. *diéwas* god, Sk. *dēvăs*, cf. DĪV- δῖος divine, MIr. *dia* god, ONor. *tivi* Ags. *Tíves*-däg Tuesday E.

-do enclitic (in *endo quando*, and see *idōneus*) : DŌ to, Ags. *tō* E., cf. DO OIr. *do*, OSlav. *do*, see *dōnec*.

dô give (E. *dado dice*) : = *da-ō*, cf. *ōd-vos* gift, Arm. *ta-m* I give, DA- weak form of DŌ- *dōnum*.

-dō put (in *crē-dō*) : for *-deō -dēō* (by analogy of *abdō* &c.), DHĒ- τίθημι, Got. ga-*dēds* action E. *deed*, Lit. *dēmi* I place OSlav. *dēja*, Zd. *dā-* put Sk. *dhā-*, cf. DHŌ- θωμός heap, Got. *dōms* judgment E. *doom deem* Ags. *dōn* do E.

But *abdō addō condō dīdō ēdō indō obdō perdō reddō subdō vēndō* are from Adjs. *ab-dus* &c., cf. *condus* ' one who lays up ' from *con-*.

doceō teach :

dōdrans three-fourths : = *dōquadrans* from *dō* by-form of *dē* (see *nōn* and *sōbrius*) + *quadrans* quarter : ' minus a quarter,' as *dēxtans* five-sixths = *dē + sextans*.

doleō suffer : ' am beaten,' fr. *dolō*.

dōlium jar :

dolō pike, studding-sail (triangular, like the head of a pike : Polyb. †δόλων, while Plut.'s δόλων ' stiletto ' is fr. δόλος) : sq., ' striking ' (cf. πελεκάω dolô fr. πέλεκυς battle-axe).

dolô hew : DL- MHG. *zol* log.   ·

dolus guile : δόλος.

domicilium habitation : fr. *domiculus* Dimin. of *domicus* Adj. of *domus*.

dominus domnus dubenus (Fest.) master (E. *dam* &c. *danger demesne domain duenna dungeon monkey*) : = *dob-nos* : foreign ?

domô tame (E. *daunt*) : DOM- W. *dofi*, Got. ga-*tamjan* E., Sk. *dam-* control, cf. DM- δαμάζω, OIr. fo-*daimim* I suffer (' am tamed ').

domus house : δόμος, OIr. *dom*, OSlav. *domŭ*, Zd. *demn* Sk. *damás*, cf. DM- Arm. *tun* house (= *tm-an*) : fr. δέμω build, Got. *timrjan* E. *timber*.

dōnec dōnique (on anal. of *neque* beside *nec*) **dōnicum** till : *dō-* ' to ' (see *-do*) + *-ne + cum* when.

dōnum gift (E. guer*don*) : OIr. *dān*, DŌ- δίδωμι give δῶρον gift, Lit. *dúti* give OSlav. *dati*, Arm. *tur* gift, Zd. Sk. *dā-* give.

dormiō sleep : DR-M- cf. DER-M- OSlav. *drēmati* nod, and DR- δαρθάνω sleep.

dorsum dossum back (E. *reredos*) : = *dort-tum* DRT- cf. DROT- OIr. *druim*.

dōs dower (E.) : DŌ-TI- cf. δωτίνη gift, fr. *dō-num*.

†**drāpeta** runaway : δραπέτης : ' going at a run,' fr. ἀπο-διδράσκω run away, Sk. *drā-* run, + PET- ' go ' see *petō*, cf. ὠκυ-πέτης swift-running.

dubius doubtful (E. *doubt*) : fr. *dubus* (cf. *medius-merus*), Fest. *dubat* dubitat *addubānum* dubium : fr. *duo* + BHO- (see *acerbus*). ·

dūcō doucō draw (E. *douche* re*doubt* sub*due*) : = *deucō*, DEUK- Got. *tiuhan* E. *tow tug tie toil toy tuck* Vb. wan*ton* †*touch*, cf. DUK- *dux* leader, Hesych. δαιδύσσεσθαι be dragged.

dūdum before : ' till now,' *dō-* to (see *dōnec*) + *-dum.*
duellum war (E. *duel*) : = **dvellum*, cf. *bellum* :
dulcis sweet : = **dluquis*, cf. γλυκύς = **δλυκύς :
-dum now (in *dūdum nōndum*) : Acc. Neut., cf. *-dam -de -do* :
dum while : Acc. Neut. from DŌ, see *-do.*
dūmus dūmētum dummētum thicket : **dusm-*, cf. Fest. *dusmō*
dumoso :
duo duō (Ausonius) two (E. *dozen*) : DUVŌ, OUmbr. *tuva* (Neut.),
δύ(F)ω, OSlav. *dŭva*, cf. DUVO *δύo*, DVO Got. *tvai* E. E. *twig* &c., Zd.
dva- Sk. *dvā-*, cf. sq.
dupl-ex duplus double (E.) : DU- two Lit. *dù*, + term. *-blus* for *-bdus* cf.
Umbr. *tribdiçu* trebling (= **tri-plic-iō).
dūrus hard (MIr. *dūr*) :

ēbrius drunk : *ē* (see *ex*) ' very ' + **brius* drunk (see *sō-brius*) :
ebulum danewort :
†ebur ivory (E.) : cf. Egyptian *āb* (Pierret), and perhaps Sk. *ibhas*
elephant.
e-castor O Castor : **e* Interj., cf. *ē ē.*
ecce lo : *et* + *-ce.*—In comedy also declined (on anal. of *ille ipse iste*),
Acc. Sing. *eccum eccam*, Acc. Plur. *eccōs eccās ecca.*
†echinus hedgehog : ἐχῖνος, EGH- cf. OHG. *igil*, Lit. *ežỹs* OSlav. *ježĭ*
(= **j-ez-jŭ), and OGH- Arm. *ozni.*
   Hardly fr. ἔχις viper, Arm. *iž*, Zd. *azhi* snake Sk. *áhis* : no resemblance of meaning.
†ēchō echo : ἠχώ :
ecquis any : *et* + *quis².*
edepol indeed : Osc. **ed* for *et* (cf. Osc. *deded* = dedit), as in late Lat. :
short for ' e Castor ed e Pol-,' O Castor and O Pollux.
edō eat : ἔδω, MIr. *esur* Fut., Got. *itan* E. E. *fret ort*, Sk. *ad-*, see
ēsca.
egeō want : EG- ONor. *ekla* dearth, Zd. *az* to desire.
ego egō I : ἐγώ, Got. *ik* E., Lit. *àsz* OSlav. *azŭ* (the *a* in both obscure),
Arm. *es* ; cf. ἐγών, Zd. *azem* Sk. *ahám.*
ehem Interj. : = *ĕm* (cf. *mehe* = *mē*, see *vehemens*).
ē-heu Interj. : **ē* cf. ἤ + *heu.*
e-hō Interj. : *e-* see *ecastor* + **hō* = *ō.*
ēja hēja Interj. (*e* lengthened by the *j*) : *ela.*
ējerō refuse : formed for *ē-jūrō* on anal. of *pējerō* quasi = *per-jūrō*, see
dējerō.
ējulō hējulō wail : fr. *ēja*, the meaning of Interjs. being indeterminate,
ah and *oh* are used both of joy and of grief.
†ēlectrum amber : †ἤλεκτρον : Prussian (amber from the Baltic) ?

ē-legans ē-ligans luxurious: 'very careful,' *legó by-form of *legō (as lavó sonó of lavó sonó) care for, see dīligó.

†elegī elegy: †ἔλεγοι:

elementum element: = *edementum, ED-, see ās:

†elenchus ear-pendant of tapering pearls (Plin. 9. 113): ἔλεγχος refutation: history of change of meaning unknown.

†elephās elephant: †ἐλέφᾶς, Heb. eleph bull, see alpha.

†elleborus helleborus hellebore: †ἐλλέβορος ἑλλέβορος:

ēllum behold him: = ēm (ī)llum.

†tē-logium inscription: ἔ + λόγιον announcement.

ēm hēm Interj.

ē-mineō project: MŪN- see prōmunturium, cf. ἀ-μύνω ward off.

emō buy (E. ransom redeem): orig. 'take' (Fest.), as in adimō &c., MIr. fo-emaim I take, cf. M- ἀμάω collect, Lit. imti take OSlav. j-ęti.
  Hence adimo coëmo dirimo eximó interimó perimó redimó, Perf. adēmī &c., and *surimó (see sirempsc); but not cómó dēmo promó súmó, Perf. cómpsī &c.

ēmolumentum gain: fr. ē-molō grind out.

ē-mungō wipe the nose: MŪNGV- cf. MŪGV- mūgilis.

ēmūsitātus finished Plaut. Mil. 631: ē + a comic form *mussim for amussim.

ēn lo: ἤν, cf. OIr. ēn-de (Stokes, Remarks), onomatop.

enim indeed: NUmbr. enem then: 'inside,' fr. in + a quasi numeral ending, see autem.

ensis sword: ṇsís, Sk. asís.

eō go (E. issue): = *ejó, EI- εἶμι, Lit. eíti to go OSlav. iti, Sk. ay, cf. I-Got. iddja I went, Ags. gān go (=*ga-i-n; see co-) E., Zd. Sk. i-.

†epirēdium trace: *ἐπι-ρήδιον fr. †*ῥήδη, raeda.

†epops hoopoe (E.): ἔποψ, for *ὄποψ, see upupa.

†epos epic: ἔπος word, VEKV-, see vocó.

epulae feast:

e-quidem indeed: e- pronominal element, cf. ἐ-κεῖνος he?

equus horse: ἔκ-vos, OIr. ech, Got. aihva- (in aihva-tundi bush, quasi 'horse's tooth'), Ags. eoh, Zd. açpa- Sk. ácvas, cf. OK-vos Lit. aszva mare.
  ἵππος ἵκκος horse can hardly be connected.

ergā opposite, ergō because of: = *edgā *edgó, EDH- up see ad- + Adj.-ending -GVO-.

ēricius (from an Adj. *ērūcus) ēr hedgehog (E. urchin): = *hēr, Hesych. χήρ.

errō wander (E. arrant err): = *ersó, of. Got. airzjan mislead OHG. irrón err.

ērūca colewort (E. rocket²): 'like a hedgehog curled up,' ēr see ēricius.

erus herus master: = *esus, Zd. anhus; 'proprietor,' ES- see sum, cf. oùsia (from the same root) property.

ervum pulse (OHG. araweiz pea NHG. erbse); 'of the field,' fr. arvum?

ēsca food: = *ēd-sca, ĒD- Got. uz-ēta crib, Lit. ēdmi I eat OSlav. jadī food, Sk. ādyas edible, cf. ED- edo.

†essedum car: Belgic (Verg. Geo. 3. 204).

et and: = *éti, ἔτι further, Got. ith and, Sk. áti over, cf. ĒTI Zd. āiti.

etiam also: = et + jam, as quoniam since = quom + jam.

†euax Interj.: *εὔαξ from εὐοῖ, sq. (cf. πόπαξ from πόποι).

†euhoe ēvoe Interj.: εὐ(f)οῖ.

†eurus S. E. wind: εὖρος: = *εὖσ-ρος fr. ūrō, 'scorching'?

ex ē (on anal. of dē) out of (E. strange): ἔξ, OIr. ess-, Zd. ash- very: = EK ec-ferō carry out, ἐκ out of, Lit. isz (cf. EG OSlav. izŭ), + s (cf. abs- ōs-).

exāmen exagmen swarm: = ex + agmen train (fr. agō).

†exanclô draw out: ἐξαντλέω, fr. ἄντλος hold of a ship.

†excetra snake: hardly cf. Pruss. esketres sturgeon.

exemplum model (E. sample): = *exem-blum (for term. see duplus) fr. eximō take out.

ex-īlis thin: 'eviscerated,' fr. īlia.

ex-pediō set free: 'unfasten,' PED-, see oppidō.

ex-perior try: see periculum.

ex-plōrô search out: 'strike out,' fr. plōdō (as excutiō examine fr. quatiō shake).

ex-sul ex-sol (Cassiodorus, Keil 7. 152) exile: fr. sedeō, see consul.

exta internal organs: = *enxta ṆKVSTO- Lit. inkstas kidney.—Hardly add ONor. eista testiculus, OSlav. isto, from OISTO- (or OIKVSTO-).

ex-torris banished: TṚS- cf. TERS- terreō.

ex-uō doff: = *exuvō from *avō clothe, NUmbr. an-ovihimu let him assume, Lit. aúti put on shoes, see induō subūcula.

faba haba bean (W. ffäen): BHAB- (or BHABH-) Pruss. babo OSlav. bobŭ.

faber smith (E. forge frigate): 'adapter,' DHABH- Got. ga-daban happen ga-dōbs fitting E. dapper daft deft, Lit. dabinti adorn.

facētus elegant: 'well-made,' fr. *faceō by-form of faciō.

faciēs shape, **faciō** make (E. feat fetish franion surfeit): DHE-K- OIr. dēnim I do, cf. DHĒ-K- ἔθηκα I placed: from DHE- Arm. dnem I place, cf. DHĒ-, see -dō.

faenum fēnum hay (E. fennel):

faenus fēnus interest: fr. praeced. (cf. ēmolumentum).

faex dregs:

fāgus beech : φηγόs oak (see on *frāxinus*), Ags. *bēce* beech E. E. *buck-wheat*.

†**fala** tower : Etrusc., cf. Etrusc. *falandum* sky (Fest.), ' high '.
Hesych. φάλαι· ὔρη is a conjecture for φάλαι· ὄρα.

†**falārica** fiery arrow : Spanish (used by the Saguntines, Liv. 21. 8) ?

fallō deceive (E. *fail falter fuult*) : = *falnō*, DHVĻ̥- MIr. *dall* blind, cf.
DHVOL- θολερόs turbid θολόs mud, Got. *dvals* dull E. E. *dolt* Ags.
drelian mislead.

> Not = *falvō*, BHALV- φαῦλοs slight (= *φάλϝοs*), Got. *balvjan* to
> plague E. *baleful*: which gives too strong a meaning.

falx sickle (E. *falchion*) :

fāma fame : φήμη, fr. *fāri*.

famēs hunger (E. *famine*): ' gaping,' GHVAM- χαίνω yawn (= *χdμjω),
cf. GHVĀM- χαῦνοs gaping (=*χᾶμϝos) χήμη cockle, Ags. *gōma* jaws E.
gums, Lit. *gomurŷs* gum.

†**famulus** slave : Osc. *famel* (Fest.) for *famcd-*, cf. OUmbr. *famedias*
families: ' dweller ' in the house (οἰκέτης), BHAM- cf. BHĀM- Osc. *faamat*
he dwells.

fānum temple : ' sacred,' = *fās-num* fr. *fās*.

far spelt : *farr-* BHAR-S-, Ir. *bar* bread, OSlav. *brašĭno* food, see *farina*.
Hardly add Ags. *bere* barley E. E. *barn*.

farciō cram (E. *farce forcemeat*): BHŖKV- OIr. *bārc* multitude (Stokes
Remarks), cf. BHŖKV- *fortis*, φράσσω fence, BHREKV- see *frequens*.

†**farfarus farferus** coltsfoot : Sabine, cf. the river-name *Farfarus* or
Fabaris: nascitur secundum fluvios Plin. 24. 135.

farīna flour : = *faris-na*, cf. Got. *barizeins* of barley, BHAR-ES- cf.
BHAR-S- *far*.

fārī to speak : BHĀ- φημί I speak, OIr. *adbo* I forbid, OSlav. *bajati* to
converse.

fās religion :

fascinō bewitch : βασκαίνω (for *φασκαίνω : Thracian, see *boreās* ?) :
' bind,' fr. sq.

fascis bundle : BHASK- φάσκωλοs wallet.

fāstidium loathing : = *fāstitĭdium* fr. *fāstus* + *taedium* weariness (fr.
taedet).

fāstīgium top : = *farstī-gvium* fr. BHŖSTÍ- cf. BHRSTÍ- Ags. *byrst* bristle
E., Sk. *bhrshtĭs* point, + term. -GVO-.

fāstus pride : = *farstus*, BHARS- OHG. *parrunga*, *parrēn* be stiff.

fāstus Adj. lawful : *fās*.

fateor own : ' open the mouth,' FET- see *fessus*, sq.

fatīgō fetīgō (Probus, Keil 4. 212) tire (' cause to gape '), **fatiscō** gape :
fr. *fetis* gaping, *fessus*.

fatuus foolish (E. *fade*): ' gaping,' praeced.

fauces pharynx:

not fr. Sk. *bhūkas†* opening.

faveō favour: 'give life to,' = **foveō*, BHOU- cf. BHŪ- *fui*.

favīlla embers: 'glowing,' = **fovīlla* DHOGHV- cf. DHŌGHV- Sk. ni-*dāghās* heat, DHEGHV- τέφρα ashes (= **θέχϝ-ρα*), Lit. *degù* I burn.

favus honeycomb: 'dwelling,' = **fovos*, BHOU- Got. *bauains* dwelling E. *bower booth*, Sk. *bhavanam*, fr. *fui*.

fax torch:

febris hebris fever:

not fr. (1) φέβομαι flee: no similarity of meaning: (2) Ags. *bifian* tremble, BHIBH-.

fēcundus faec- foec- fertile: 'nourishing,' cf. *fēlīx*, DHĒ- suck, see *fellō*.

fel gall: *fell-* GHVEL-N- cf. GHVOL-N- Ags. *gealla* E.; and GHVOL- χόλος, GHVL- OSlav. *žlūtī*: 'yellow,' see *flāvus*.

fēlēs faelēs cat:

fēlīx fertile: 'nourishing,' fr. **fēla* breast, θηλή, DHĒ-L- cf. DHE-L- MIr. *del*, OHG. *tila*, sq.

fellō fēlō suck: DHĒ-L- θῆλυς female, Lit. *dėlė* leech, Sk. *dhārús* suckling: from DHĒ- θῆσθαι suck, OSlav. *dětę* infant, Arm. *diem* I suck, Zd. *dā-* suck Sk. *dhā-*, cf. DHE- OIr. *dith* suxit, DHO- Got. *daddjan* suckle.

fēmina woman (Ags. *faemne* maiden; E. *female*): 'giving suck,' DHĒ-, see praeced.

femur femen thigh:

†fenestra fēstra window:

fērālis funereal: 'solemn,' fr. *fēr-iae.*

ferē nearly: 'brought close to,' fr. *ferō*.

ferentārius lightarmed: 'rushing,' fr. *ferens* Part. of *ferō*, in the sense of *sē ferre*, to rush.

fēriae holydays (E. *fair* Subst.): = **fēsiae*, cf. *fēs-tus*.

feriō strike: BHER- ONor. *berja*, cf. BHOR- Lit. *barù* I scold OSlav. *borja* I fight.

fermē nearly; fr. *ferē* + Adj.-ending -*mo*-.

fermentum yeast: 'causing movement,' fr. sq., cf. Ags. *beorma* and BHOR-MO- E. *barm*.

ferō bear, move: φέρω bear, OIr. *berid* fert, Got. *bairan* E. E. *barrow*[2], OSlav. *berą* I take, Arm. *berem* I bear, Zd. *bar-* bear Sk. *bhar-*.

ferrum iron (E. *farrier*):

not (1) Heb. *barzel*: (2) cf. Ags. *bräs* brass E., ONor. *brasa* harden by fire E. *brazier*.

fertum ferctum cake: Part. Neut. of **fergō* 'bake,' BHERGV- cf. BHR̥GV- OIr. *bairgen* bread, BHR̥GV- Pruss. *birga-karkis* basting-ladle.

ferula fennel-giant: 'light' (gestatu facilis Plin. 13. 123), fr. *ferō*.

ferus wild (E. *fierce*):

    not cf. GH-V-ĒR- φήρ θήρ beast, Lit. *żwiëris* OSlav. *zvĕrĭ*.

ferveō ferbeō boil: BHERV- MIr. *berbaim* I boil.

fessus weary: = *fet-tus* gaping, see *fatiscō*, Part. from FET-:

festīnō hasten:

festūca fistūca stalk: see *fistula*:

fēstus solemn: cf. Osc. *fiisno* temple:

fēteō faeteō foeteō stink:

fētiālēs heralds:

fētus foetus fruitful, newly delivered: 'giving suck,' DHĒ- see *fellō*.

fī Interj.: cf. *fū*.

fibra fibre: = *fis-ra* cf. GHVĪS- *filum*.

fībula buckle: = *fivi-bula* fr. *fivō* (Cato) = *figō*.

fīcēdula (for the term. see *acrēdula*) **fīcēlla** becafico: fr. sq.

fīcus fig (E.): 'shaped like a drone,' *fūcus*[2].

fidēlia pot: BHIDH- πίθος jar.

fidēs faith (E. E. de*fy*): BHIDH-, see *fīdus*.

fidēs[3] lyre:

    not GHIDH- κιθάρα (quasi *χιθ-άρα: rather Semitic).

fīdus trusty: BHEIDH- πείθω persuade, cf. BHOIDH- Got. *baidjan* compel.

fīgō fix: dialectic for *fīvō*, see *fibula*: 'prick,' DĪGV- Lit. *dygus* prickly.

fīlius son: = *fūlius* tribesman, φῦλον tribe, from BHŪ-, see *fui*.

    Rather than = *fēlius* suckling fr. *fellō*, cf. Lit. pirm-*dĕlŷs* firstborn (of animals).

fīlix felix fern:

fīlum thread, thickness (Munro Lucr. 2. 341: E. pro*file*): = *fislum*. Lit. *gýsla* sinew, see *fibra*.

fimbriae fringe (E.): = *finsriae* GHVINS- cf. GHVĪS- praeced.

fimus dung: 'strong-smelling,' = *fumus*, see *suffiō*.

findō split (E. *vent*): cf. BHID- φιτρός (i.e. *φιδ-τρός, see *meditor*) log, Zd. *bid*- split Sk. *bhid*-, and BHEID- φείδομαι spare ('take a bit of'), Got. *beitan* bite E. E. *butt* Vb.

fingō mould (E. *faint feint*): cf. DHIGH- Sk. *dih*- smear, DHEIGH- τεῖχος wall (see *māceria*), Got. *deigan* mould E. *dough dairy* la*dy*.

fīnis limit (E. *finance fine* Subst. and Adj.): 'marked by a rope,' *fūnis*.

fīō become: = *fūō* fr. *fui*.

firmus firm (E. *farm*): = *fĭd-mus* fr. *fīdō*, 'reliable'.

fiscus basket:

fīstūca rammer: fr. *fūstis*.

fistula pipe (E. *fester*): fr. *festūca* (cf. *avēna* stalk, pipe).

flaccus flap-eared (E. *flange flank flunkey*): = *flācus*, BHḶKÓS φολκός bandy-legged, fr. *flectō*.

flāgitium importunity ('demanding'), shameful act: sq.
flāgitō demand: 'press, beat,' long form. fr. *flag-rum*.
flagrō burn: BHLEG- φλέγω, OHG. *blechen* to flash, cf. BHLŌG- Sk. *bhrāj-* shine.
flagrum whip (E. *flail flog*):
flāmen priest: = **flād-men* (for term. cf. ποι-μήν), BHLĀD- Got. *blōtan* to worship.
flamma blaze: = **flāma* fr. *flŏ*.
flāvus yellow (E. *flavour*): GHVĪ̥-VOS cf. *fulvus gilvus*, GHVĪ̥- χλωρός, GHVEL- Lit. *gelsti* grow yellow.
flectō bend (E. *flinch*):
flēmina congestion of blood: = **flēt-mina*, BHLĒT- cf. BHLŌT- Got. *blōth* blood E.: fr. sq., 'flowing'.
fleō weep (E. *feeble foible*): φλέω overflow: see *flōs*.
flīgō strike: BHLĪGV- φλίβω θλίβω, W. *blif* catapult.
Not add Got. *bliggvan* beat, or OSlav. *blizna* scar.
flō blow (E. *flageolet flute flout flue*): = **flā-ō*, BHĪ̥- cf. BHĪ̥- ONor. *bylr* gust.
floccus lock of wool:
flōs flower (E. E. *flour*): BHLŌ-S- Ags. *blōs-ma* E. *blossom*, cf. BHLŌ- MIr. *blā-th*, Got. *blō-ma* E. *bloom* Ags. *blō-ván* to smell E. *blow* Vb.², and BHLĒ- cf. *fleō*.
fluō flow (E. *floss-silk flotilla*; but not *flow*): = **flugvō*, BHLUGV- οἰνό-φλυξ drunken φλύκταινα blister ('discharging').
fōculum fire-pan Plaut. Persa 104: = **foviculum* fr. *foveō*.
focus hearth (E. *fuel fusee*): 'place,' fr. *faciō*.
fodiō dig: BHODH- βόθρος trench (with β, for π, from βαθύς?), Lit. *badaū* I prick OSlav. *bodą*, cf. BHEDH- W. *bedd* grave, Lit. *bedu* I dig.
foedus fīdus (Enn.) **fēdus** Subst. treaty: = **foidos*, see *fīdus*.
foedus fēdus Adj. foul: = **foes-dus* fr. *fūs-cus, fois-*.
folium leaf: φύλλον (for **φόλjον*).
follis bag (E. *fool*): = **fol-nis*, BHOL-N- OHG. *ballo* ball E.
fōmes tinder: = **fovimes* fr. *foveō*.
fōns spring: = **fauns favens* 'blessing,' Part. of *faveō*, cf. NUmbr. *fons* (i.e. **fau-nus*) favens.
forceps pincers: = **formi-ceps* (fr. *capiō*), Fest. *formus* hot, GHVOR-MO- Zd. *garema-* hot Sk. *gharmás* heat, cf. GHVER-MO- θερμός hot, Arm. *Jerm*, GHVB-M- Pruss. *gorme* heat; from GHVOR- Lit. *gáras* steam OSlav. *gorēti* burn, Sk. *ghar-*, cf. GHVER- θέρομαι grow warm.
fore to be about to be: short for 'fore esse,' to be out, abroad, beyond, cf. Hor. Sat. 1. 2. 67 exclusus fore (= *foris* out as *muge potc* = *magis potis*).—From *fore*, taken as Inf., was formed *forem* Subj.

foris door (E. *foreign forest foreclose forfeit*) : DHVṚ-IS OSlav. *dvĭrĭ*, cf. DHUR- θύρα, OIr. *doros*, Got. *daur* E., Lit. *dùrys*, Arm. *duŕn*, DHVOB- Zd. *dvara* ; and DUB- Sk. *dur-*, DVŌR- Sk. *dvĭr*.

fōrma shape :
   not cf. Sk. *dhariman* balance, form†, from *dhar-* hold.

formīca furmīca ant :

fōrmīdō bugbear, fear : 'shape, imaginary shape,' fr. *fōrma*.

fornāx oven, **fornix** arch ('vaulted' like an oven): see *furnus*.

forō bore : BHṚ- φάρος plough, Ags. *borian* bore E., cf. BHER- Zd. *bar-* bore.

fors chance : *forti-* BHṚTÍ- Ags. *ge-byrd* fate, cf. (for the form) Got. *ga-baurths* birth E., Sk. *bhṛtis* maintenance : 'what comes,' fr. *ferō*.

fortāssis fortāsse perhaps : 'you would affirm' (hence in Plaut. and Ter. with Inf.), 2 Sing. Perf. Subj. of **fortŏ* (*=firmŏ*, 'affirm,') fr. sq.

fortis forctis strong (E. *force fort*): fr. *forctus horctus* good (Fest.), BHṚKV- TÓS φρακτός fortified, fr. *farciō*.

forum market-place: DHVOR- Lit. *dwáras* court OSlav. *dvorŭ*, Zd. *dvara* palace : 'place with doors,' see *foris*.

forus gangway : fr. *ferō* (as *via* fr. *vehō*).

fovea pit : GHEVIĀ χε(ϝ)ιά hole.

foveō warm : 'revive,' BHEV- Ags. *beōn* be E. E. *bondage bonds*man *husband husbandman boor bylaw neighbour*, cf. BHĒV- Sk. *bhāvayis* fostering, fr. *fuī*.

frāga strawberries : = **srāqa*, cf. ῥάξ grape.

fragrō fraglō flagrō (Ellis Catull. p. 344 sq.) smell : = *flagrō*, smell being brought out by burning (the 2 first spellings to differentiate the meaning).

†framea spear : German (Tac.) :
   hardly a mistake for **franca*, Ags. *franca*.

frangō break (E. *frail osprey refrain* Subst.) : = **frengō*, cf. BHREG- Got. *brikan* E. E. *brook* Subst. *brake bray* †*bribe*.

frāter brother (E. *friar*): φράτηρ clansman, OIr. *bráthir* brother, Got. *brōthar* E., Lit. *broterélis* (Dimin.) OSlav. *bratrŭ*, Arm. eλbair, Zd. *brātar-* Sk. *bhrātar*.

fraus hurt : BHROUDÍ- cf. BHREUD- Ags. *breōtan* break E. *brittle*.

frāxinus ash : = **frāg-ti-nus*, BHĒG- *farnus* (Vitruvius, = **farg-nus*), Sk. *bhūrjas* birch (for confusion of tree-names see *fāgus*), cf. BHERG- Ags. *beorce* E., Lit. *béržas* OSlav. *bréza*.

fremō roar : GHVREM- χρεμετίζω neigh, Ags. *grim* wild E. *grim grumble*, cf. GHVROM- MIr. *gromma* satire, Got. *gramjan* provoke, OSlav. *gromŭ* thunder.

frendō crush, gnash the teeth : GHRENDH- Ags. *grindan* grind E.

frēnum fraenum bit (E. *refrain* Vb.) :

frequens frequent: BHREKV- see *farciō*, 'crowding' (see *cunctus*).

fretum strait:

frētus relying on: 'borne up by,' Part. of *ferō* (as *crētus* of *cernō*).

fricô rub (E. *fray* Vb.): fr. **fri-cus* Adj. fr. *friō*.

frīgō roast (E. *fritter fry*): = **frūgō*, φρύγω, cf. BHRUG- Ir. *bruighim* I roast (E. *broil*).

frīgus cold (E. *frill*): = **srīgus*, ῥῖγος.

frīguttiō (Plaut.) **fringuttiō** (Varr.) twitter: *frīgv-* cf. *frīgō* squeak (Afranius), *fringv-* cf. *fringuilla* chaffinch (Varr.): not cf. Lit. *brizgéti* bleat.

friô rub: GHRI- cf. GHRĪ- χρίω anoint χρῖμα oil, and GHRĪ-s- χρῖσμα.

fritillus dicebox: Dimin. of **frutus = frutex* (cf. *allus allex*), 'like a small tree'.

frivola lumber: **frī-vus* rubbed, W. *briw* broken, see *friō*.

frōns[1] brow (E. *flounce* Subst.): BHRŌNTĪ- cf. BHRONT'- ONor. *brand* ship's beak (Vigfusson).

frōns[2] leaf: BHRŌNDf- cf. BHREND- Lit. *bréndau* I ripen.

fruor enjoy: = **frūor *frūgvor*, BHRŪGV- Got. *brūkjan* enjoy E. *brook* Vb. *broker*.

frūstrā in error: = **frūd-trā* fr. *fraus*.

frūstum frūstrum bit: DHRAUS- θραύ(σ)ω break.

frutex shrub:

fū Interj.: φῦ, E. *foh.*

†**fūcus**[1] rock-lichen (used as a dye): foreign, cf.† φῦκος seaweed, Heb. *puk* paint.

fūcus[2] drone:

fugiō flee: φυγή flight, Sk. *bhuj-* bend, cf. BHŪGV- Lit. *bügau* am frightened, BHEUGV- φεύγω flee.

fui fū-vī was: BHŪ- φύω produce, Lit. *búti* be OSlav. *byti*, Zd. *bū-* Sk. *bhū-*, cf. BHU- φυτόν plant, MIr. *both* hut ('place to live in'), see *faveō favus fīō foveō.*

fulciō support:

fulgō shine: BHLG- cf. BHLEG- *flagrō.*

fulica coot: = **fuliga* (see *pertica*) BHLI-GVĀ- MHG. *belche* (= **buliche*), cf. BHL̥- φαλαρίς: 'white-headed,' fr. *fullō.*

fūlīgō soot: = **fūvilī-gō* fr. **fūvilis* Adj. (see *ūlīgō*) from DHŪ- *fūmus.*

fullō fuller (E. E. *foil* Vb.): 'whitener,' = **ful-nō*, BHL̥- φαληρίδω whiten φαλακρός bald, cf. BHOL- Lit. *báltas* white, BHĒL- Ags. *bael* fire, OSlav. *bělŭ* white, Sk. *bhālam* brightness.

fulvus yellow: GHVL̥-VOS, cf. *flāvus.*

fūmus smoke: Lit. *dúmas* OSlav. *dymŭ*, Sk. *dhūmás*, from DHŪ- θύω rush.

funda sling: sq., 'striking'.

fundō pour, scatter (E. *foison funnel refuse*): BHUND- cf. BHEUD- *fūdī*
Perf., BHOUD- Ags. *beátan* strike E. *beat* †*butt*, see *fūsus*.
    Rather than GHUND- cf. GHEU-D- Got. *giutan* pour E. *gush gust gut*
ingot, from GHEU- χέ(ϝ)ω, see *gutta*.

fundus bottom (E. *found* Vb. *founder* Vb.): BHUND- πύνδαξ (for *φύνδαξ,
with π- from πυθμήν), OIr. *bond* (E. *bounds bourn*[1]), cf. BHUD- Ags.
botm E.: by-form BHUDH- πυθμήν, Zd. *buna* Sk. *budhnás*.

fungor perform: cf. BHUG- Sk. *bhuj* enjoy, BHOUG- Arm. *boic* food.

†**fungus** mushroom: foreign, cf. †σφόγγος σπόγγος sponge (E. E. *spunk*).

fūnis rope: = *foinis* GHVOINIS cf. GHVEINIS Lit. *geinis*?

fūnus corpse on the pyre (Serv.):

fūr thief: = *fōr* (cf. *fōrcilla* Dimin. of sq., Catull. 105. 2 Ellis), φώρ:

fūrca fork: praeced., 'instrument for punishing thieves'.

furfur bran: 'purgamentum farinae' (Facciolati), cf. NUmbr. *furfant*
they cleanse:

furnus oven: GHVRN6S OSlav. *grŭnŭ* kettle, Sk. *ghṛṇds* heat: from
GHVOR-, see *forceps*.

furō rage: = *fusō* DHUS- θυ(σ)ιds Maenad θυσ-τds (Hesych.), Ags. *dysig*
foolish (Grein) E. *dizzy*.

furvus forvus black:

fuscina trident:

fūs-cus black: see *foedus* Adj.:

fūstis club (E. *fusty*):

fūsus fussus spindle: = *fūd-tus* Part. fr. *fundō*, 'struck' to make it
revolve.

futtilis fūtilis vain: fr. *fūtus*, see *confūtō*, 'shaky'.

futuō: Ir. *both* πέos (O'Donovan).

†**gaesum gēsum** javelin (ONor. *kesja* halberd): Spanish (Athenaeus)
Polyb. †γαῖσos: GHAIS- χαῖ(σ)os shepherd's staff, OIr. *gai* spear, Ags.
gār E. au-*ger* garlic *gore* Vb.

†**galbanum** a gum: *χάλβανον †χαλβάνη, Heb. *ḥelb'nāh*.

galbinus green:

†**galea** helmet (orig. of weasel-skin, Il. 10. 335 κτιδέη κυνεη): γαλέη
weasel.

gallus cock: =‚*gal-nus*, GAL-N- ONor. *kalla* call E.

gāneum underground room (Fest.):

ganniō yelp:
    not = *gangniō* fr. *gang-nus* Adj., GVANGV- OSlav. *gągnati* to murmur,
       cf. GVAGV- MHG. *kach* loud laughter this would only become *gagniō*.

garriō chatter: = *garsiō* GVARS- Hesych. γαρριώμεθα we abuse, OHG.
kerran to cry, Lit. *garsas* noise.

†**garum** caviar: †γάρος:

gaudeō rejoice (E. E. *gaud jewel joy*) : = *gāvidcō* (cf. *gāvīsus* Part.) fr. Adj. *gāvidus* fr. *gā-vus*, ɢᴀ̄- γη-θέω, cf. ɢᴀ- γα-ίων (Part.).

†gaulus pail : †γαυλός : cf. Sk. *gōlā†* jug?

†gausape felt : *γαύσαπι †γαύσαπος :

†gaza treasure (E. *gazelle*?) : †γάζα, cf. Pers. *geng′* Zenker 763 a.

gelus frost (E. *jelly*) : ɢᴠᴇʟ- cf. ɢᴠᴏʟ- Got. *kalds* cold E. E. *cool chill*, OSlav. *golotĭ* ice.

geminī twins : 'fellows,' dialectic by-form of *heminēs fr. *hemō*, see *humo* (for the terminations cf. *terminī* τέρμονες).

gem-ma bud, gem (E. *cameo*) : 'swelling,' fr. sq.

gemō groan (Ital. *gemere* trickle) : 'am sated, oppressed,' ɢᴠᴇᴍ- γέμω am full, cf. ɢᴠᴍ- OSlav. *žĭmǫ* I compress.

gena cheek : OIr. *gen* mouth, Arm. *cnaut* cheek, see *genuīnus*.

gener son-in-law : 'kinsman' by election, fr. *genus*. Not for *gemros* ɢᴍ-ʀᴏ́s cf. ɢᴀᴍ-ʀᴏ́s γαμβρός, fr. γάμος marriage.

genesta genista broom : 'sprouting,' fr. *genus*.

genū knee : ɢɴ̥ᴜ̄ cf. ɢᴏ́ɴᴜ γόνυ, ɢᴏ̃ɴᴜ Sk. *jā́nu*, ɢᴏ̃ɴ- Arm. *cunr*; and ɢɴᴜ γνύ-πετος fallen on the knees, Zd. *zhnu* knee Sk. *jnu*, ɢɴᴇᴜ Got. *kniu* E.

genuīnus grinder : ɢᴇɴᴜ- γένυς jaw, Got. *kinnus* cheek E. *chin*, cf. Sk. *hánus* jawbone, see *gena*.

genus birth (E. *gender jaunty*) : ɢᴇɴ- γένος, MIr. *gein*, Arm. *cin*, Zd. *zan-* give birth to Sk. *jan-*, cf. ɢɴ̥- Got. *kuni* kin E. E. *kind king knave knight*, see *nāscor*.

germānus brother : ɢᴇɴ-ᴍɴ̥-ɴᴏ́s (see *hūmānus*), ɢᴇɴ-ᴍɴ̥- cf. sq.

germen sprig : = *genmen* cf. Late-Lat. *genimen*, fr. *genus*, 'growth'.

gerō carry (E. *jest register*) : = *gesō* :

†gerrae nonsense : γέρρα wickerwork ('flimsy') :

gibbus hump : = *gibbus *gūbus ɢᴠᴜ̄ʙ- (or ɢᴠᴜ̄ʙʜ-) cf. ɢᴠᴜᴍʙ- (or ɢᴠᴜᴍʙʜ-) Lit. *gumbas* excrescence.

gignō produce : cf. γίγνομαι become, Redupl. of ɢɴ- see *genus*.

gilvus gilbus yellow : dialectic by-form of *helvus* light bay, ɢʜᴠᴇʟᴠᴏs Ags. *geolo* yellow E. E. *yolk*, cf. ɢʜᴠʟᴠᴏs *fulvus*, and see *flāvus*.

gingīva (for term. cf. *sal-īva*) gum : Gaulish (as first in Catullus)?

glaber smooth : ɢʜᴠʟᴀᴅʜ- OHG. *glat* smooth, bright, gay Ags. *gläd* gay E. *glad*, cf. ɢʜᴠʟᴀ̄ᴅ - Lit. *glodùs* smooth OSlav. *gladiti* to smooth, see *blandus*.

glaciēs ice :

gladius sword (E. *glaive*) :

glaeba glēba clod :

†glaesum glēsum amber : German (Plin. 37. 42), Ags. *glaere* resin (Kluge); akin to Ags. *gläs* glass E.

glans acorn : 'like a stone,' ɢʜʟᴀɴᴅ- cf. ɢʜʟᴀ̄ᴅ- sq.

glārea gravel : = *glādea,* cf. χλῆδος rubbish.

†**glaucus** bright : γλαυκός :

glīscō spread : GLĪ- cf. GLI- Zd. zri- extend, GLOI- Sk. *jráyas* extent.

globus ball :

glōmus glomus ball : 'bound together,' cf. Ags. *clam* band.

glōria fame : = *glōsia,* OSlav. *glasŭ* voice, 'making a noise in the world '.

glūbō peel : GLEUBH- Ags. *cleōfan* split E. *cleave,* cf. GLUBH- γλύφω carve.

glūten glūtinum glue (E.) : *glūtus* tenacious, GVLOI- γλοιά glue γλοιός oil, Ags. *claeg* clay E., NHG. *klei* slime, OSlav. *glēnŭ* mucus.

glūtio gluttiō swallow (E. *glut glutton*) :

gnārus nārus skilful : GṆ- cf. GṆ- see *ingens.*

†**gōbius** gudgeon (E.) : *γωβιός †κωβιός (see *conger*) :

†**grabātus** couch : *γράβάτος †κράβάτος (cf. praeced.), Macedonian.

gracilis thin :

hardly cf. Enn. *cracens* Part. of *cracēō,* KVROK- see *curculiō.*

gradus step : = *gredús* GHVREDH- OIr. *ingrennat* they follow, Got. *grids* step, cf. GHVRENDH- OSlav. *grędą* I come.

grāmen grass : GHRĀ- Ags. *grōvan̥* grow E., Ags. *grēne* green E., cf. GHRA- Got. *gras* grass E.

grandis large :

grandō hail : GHRAND- cf. GHRĀD- OSlav. *gradŭ* (for the *g* cf. *anser*), Sk. *hrādúnis,* fr. Zd. *zrād*- rattle Sk. *hrād*- to sound.

grānum grain (OIr. *grān* Plur. ; E. E. *garnet granite grange grenade*) : GṆNO- cf. GṆNO- Got. *kaurn* E. *corn churn kernel,* Lit. *žirnis* pea OSlav. *zrŭno* grain : 'ripe,' GṆNÓ- Sk. *jīrnds* worn out, fr. GER- γέρων old man, OSlav. *zrēti* grow ripe, Sk. *jar*- grow old.

grātus pleasant (E. *agree*) : GHṚ-TÓs cf. GHṚ-TÓS see *hortor.*

grāvastellus old man : comic Dimin. Masc. fr. *grāvastra* 'old woman formed from *γραυάζω grow an old woman, γραῦς old woman.

gravis heavy (E. *grief*) : = *grovis* GVROV- of. GVRŪ- βαρύς, Got. *kaurus,* Sk. *gurús* Zd. *gouru*- hard, see *congruō.*

gremium lap :

gressus going : = *gred-tus,* see *gradus.*

grex flock (MIr. *graig* herd of horses) : 'rounded mass' (for the meaning cf. *globus* ball, company), GVREG- cf. GVḄG- *gurges,* γάργ-αρα plenty.

grunniō (dialectic, cf. *mannus*) **grundiō** grunt (E. *gurnard*) : GRUND- cf. GRUD- ONor. *krytja* to murmur (E. *grudge*).

grūs crane : GVRŪ- Arm. *krunk,* cf. GVERV- Lit. *gérwė,* GVERŌV- OSlav. *žeravĭ* ; also GVRON- Ags. *crane* E., GVORN- Lit. *garnỹs* stork, GVERṆ-γέρανος crane, Gaulish tri-*garanus* with 3 cranes W. *garan* crane, shank.

†**grȳps** griffin (E.) : γρΰψ, fr. γρῡπόs hooknosed.

†**gubernō** steer (E. *govern*) : *γυβερνάω κυβερνάω (see *gōbius*), cf. Sk. *kūbaras* pole (so E. *helm* fr. *haulm*), and Lit. *kumbryti* steer.

gula throat (E. *gullet gully*) : GḶ- Ags. *ceole*, cf. GEL- OIr. *gelid* he consumes.

Not GVEL- Arm. *klanem* I devour, GVOL- Sk. *galas* throat.

gumia gourmet (Span. *gomia*) : 'full,' NUmbr. *gomia* gravidas, GVOM- cf. GVEM- *gemō*.

gurges whirlpool (E. *gorge gorgeous gargoyle gurgle*) : 'round,' see *grcx*, cf. OHG. *querca* throat (E. *carcanet*), and GVᴇ̄G- OIr. *brāge* neck.

gurguliō gullet : GVᴙG-ʟ- OHG. *querechela* (= *quur-i-chulja), cf. GVᴙG-ᴙ-γαργαρεών, fr. praeced.

gurguliō² weevil : pop. etym. (quasi fr. praeced., 'quoniam paene nihil est nisi guttur' Varr. ap. Serv. Geo. 1. 186), for *curculiō*.

gurgustium hut : fr. *gurgus* Neut. pit, cf. GVORG- γόργυρα dungeon, GVERG- γέργυρα, GVᴙG- *gurgcs*, 'circular '.

gustō taste (E. *ragout*) : GUS- OIr. to-*gu* I choose, Ags. *cyssan* to kiss E., Zd. *zush*- to love Sk. *jush*- enjoy, cf. GEUS- γεύ(σ)ω give to taste, Got. *kiusan* approve E. *choose*, GOUS- Got. *kausjun* to taste.

gutta drop (E. *gout gutter*), **guttus gūtus** flask : *gūta, dialectic for *hūta Part. Fem. fr. GHEU- χέ(F)ω pour, GHU- Sk. *hu*- pour into the fire, see under *fundō*.

guttur throat : fr. praeced., 'pipe '.

†**gypsum** white lime : †γύψοs, cf. Pers. *ǧibs* gypsum Zenker 348 c.

†**gȳrus** circle : γῦρόs :

habeō hold (Got. *haban* have E. E. *behave havoc hawk* : E. *able binnacle malady pledge*) : GHVABH- Osc. *hafiest* habebit, OIr. *gabāl* to seize, OSlav. *gobino* abundance.

haedus aedus (Roman, Varr. L. L. 5. 97) **hēdus ēdus** (rustic, Varr.) kid : GHAᴀ́DOS OLat. *foedus* (Fest.) Sab. *fēdus* (Varr.), Got. *gaits* goat E.

haereō stick : GHVAIS- Got. us-*gaisjan* frighten (' cause to hesitate ') E. *gaze garish ghastly ghost*, Lit. *gaiszti* tarry.

hahae hahahe ahahe Interjs. of laughter : MHG. *hahā* E. *haha*.

hālō breathe :

†**thama ama** bucket : ἄμη ἄμη, cf. Arm. *aman* vessel, Sk. *amatram*.

hāmus hook :

†**thapalopsis** a spice : *ἀπάλοψιs, fr. ἀπαλῶs ὀπτᾶν roast moderately.

hara pen : = *hesā BHES- cf. συ-φε(σ)όs sty ?

harēna arēna sand : Sab. *fasēna* :

hariolus ariolus soothsayer : BHAR- Ir. *bar* sage.

†**tharmonia** concord : ἀρμονία fastening, fr. *ἅρμων Adj.

†harpē falchion : ἅρπη sickle, ѕʀᴘ- OSlav. *srŭpŭ*, cf. ѕʀ̣ᴘ- *sarpŏ*.

harūndō arūndō reed :

haru-spex aru-spex hari-spex (fr. *speciō*) diviner: 'inspecting entrails,' ɢʜʀ̣- χορ-δή gut (E. *cord*), cf. ɢʜʙ̣- Sk. *hirã* vein, ɢʜᴏʀ-ɴᴏ- ONor. *yarnir* guts Ags. *gearn* yarn E., Lit. *žárna* gut.

hasta spear : ɢʜᴀᴢᴅʜᴀ̄ cf. Got. *gazds* goad OHG. *gart* E. *yard* [2] *gird* at (but not E. *goad*).

hau au Interj.

haud haut hau not := *au-de*, see *au-tem* and *-de*, 'now' (the notion of negation being supplied by gesture).

hauriō draw (E. *oust*) := *ausiō* ᴀᴜѕ- ἐξαυστήρ flesh-hook Hesych. ἐξαῦσαι take out, ONor. *ausa* pump, sprinkle.

†hebenus ebenus ebony (E.) : *ἔβενος †ἔβενος, Heb. *hobnīm*.

hebes blunt :

hedera edera ivy : 'tenacious,' ɢʜᴠᴇᴅ- cf. ɢʜᴠᴇɴᴅ- *prehendō*?

hei ei Interj.

helluō hēluō glutton : foreign?

helvella pot-herb : ' green food,' fr. *helvus*, see *gilvus*.

†hēmicillus (reading doubtful) mule : *ἡμίκιλλος, ἡμι- see *sēmi-* + κίλλος ass.

herba grass : fr. φέρβω feed, cf. *forbea* food (Fest.), φορβή fodder.

herciscō erciscō divide an inheritance :

hērēs ērēs haerēs heir (E.) :

hardly cf. χηρωσταί guardians, fr. χηρόω am bereaved.

herī yesterday : ɢʜᴊᴇѕ- χθές, Sk. *hyds*, cf. Got. *gistra*-dagis to-morrow (see Vigfusson on ONor. *gaer*) E. *yesterday*, cf. ɢʜᴊᴇ̄ѕ- *hēs-ter-nus* Adj.

†hērōs hero : ἥρως : cf. Sk. *sãras* strength ?

heu Interj.

heus Interj.

hībernus wintry := *hībrinus *hīmrinus*, cf. *himerinus* χειμε-ρι-νός, from ɢʜᴇɪᴍ- χεῖμα winter, see *hiems*.

†hibīscus marsh-mallow : †ἰβίσκος (Dioscorides) :

†hibrida offspring of a sow and wild boar (Plin. 8. 213): cf. Hesych. ἰβρί-καλος pig :

hīc hīc this : = *hi-ce* (shortened on anal. of *is*) *h-o-i-ce* from -o- cf. Sk. *n-* this, + -i- Demonstr. cf. δδ-ί, Got. that-*ei* as, + -ce.

hiems hiemps winter : ɢʜɪᴇᴍ- MIr. *gam* (for *giam* on anal. of *sam* summer), cf. ɢʜɪᴏ́ᴍ- χιών snow ; also ɢʜɪᴍ- δύσ-χιμος troublesome, Zd. *zima* winter Sk. *hinás*, and ɢʜᴇɪᴍ- χεῖμα, Lit. *žiéma* OSlav. *zima*, Arm. *jiun* (= *jivan *jiman), Sk. *hēman-*.

†hilaris hilarus gay : ἱλαρός :

hīlum trifle : = *filum*.

hinniō neigh : fr. *hinnus *his-nus* Adj., ɢʜᴇɪѕ- Sk. *hēsh-*?

†hinnuleus fawn: cf. Hesych. †ἔνελος :

hiô gape: = *hī-ô (cf. hī-scō) GHEI- OHG. *gīen*, OSlav. *zijati*, cf. GHOI-N-Ags. *gānian* yawn E.

hīra gut: = *hīsā GHVĪS- see *fibra*.

hircus ircus hirquus goat: Sab. *fircus*:

hirnea jug:

hīrsūtus shaggy: fr. *hīrsus Subst. (as *versūtus* fr. *versus* Subst.), = *hīrt-tus fr. sq.

hīrtus shaggy:

hirūdō leech:

hirūndō swallow: = *hedūndōn as χελιδών = *χεδυδών (with λ for δ cf. 'Ολυτεύς = 'Οδυσσεύς, with ī for ū cf. ī for ū in Lesbian ὕψos = ὕψos) :?

hiscō gape: GHEI- see *hiô*.

hīspidus rough:

†histriō actor (term. from *lūd-iō*) ? Etrusc. *hister* (Liv.).

hodiē to-day: = *odiē, Sk. *adyā*, see *hīc* and *diēs*.

holus olus folus (Fest.) vegetables: GHL̥- cf. GHEL- *helus*, Lit. *želmū* plant *želti* grow OSlav. *zelije* vegetables: 'green,' OSlav. *zelenū* green, Zd. *zairi* yellow Sk. *hdris* green.

homo homō human being (E. *homage*): GHOMŌN cf. GHOMN̥- *hominis* &c. ; also GHMŌN *hemō*, GHMON- Got. *guman*- E. *groom*, GHMN̥- see *geminī*, GHMĀN- Lit. *žmónės* men : 'fellow,' see *geminī*.

honōs dignity:

hardly fr. *onus*, 'responsibility' (Varr.).

†thōra ōra hour (E.): ὥρα season, JŌR- OSlav. *jara* spring, Zd. *yāre* year, cf. JĒR- Got. *jēr* E.

hordeum ordeum fordeum barley: = *horsdeum GHVR̥Z-D- cf. GHVERZ-D-OHG. *gerstā*, and GHVR̥S- Arm. *gari* (= *garsi).

Hardly add κριθή quasi = *χρῑθή *χρεσθή *χερσθή.

hōria ōria fishing-smack: 'coasting-vessel,' fr. *ōra* shore?

hornus this year's: = *ornus *orinus *osinus from *osus year, NUmbr. *osc* Gen.

horreō bristle (E. *ordure*) : = *horseō GHR̥S- cf. GHORS- Sk. *harsh-*.

horreum barn: = *horseum BHR̥S- cf. BHARS- *far*, Fest. *farreum*.

hortor urge: fr. *hortús causing delight, χαρτός, Parts. fr. *horior* urge (Enn.), χαίρω rejoice, GHR̥- cf. GHER- OUmbr. *heris* thou wilt, Got. *gairnjan* desire E. *yearn*, Sk. *har*- be gratified, see *grātus*.

hortus ortus garden (E. *ortolan*): χόρτος straw-yard, OIr. *gort* field. Hardly add Got. *gard* house (GHORTÓS) E. *yard* †*garden*.

hospes guest (E. *host*¹): *hospit- cf. *hospt-, *hostis* :

hostia fostia (Fest.) victim (E. *host*³ = eucharist) : 'return' to the gods (see *victima*), fr. sq.

hostiō requite Plaut. Asin. 377 :

hostis fostis (Fest.) stranger (E. *host*[2] = army): Got. *gasts* guest E., OSlav. *gostĭ*: GHVOSPT- cf. *hospes*:

hūc hōc hither: from **hō* (cf. *hōrsum* = **hō-vorsum*, *illō* thither, *istō*), see *hic*.

hui Interj.

hūmānus human: = **hōmā-nus* GHŌMN̄-NŌS (see *germānus*) cf. GHOMN̄- under *homo*.

humus umus ground: GHOM- Zd. *zem* earth, GHŌM- χθών (= **χώμ*), cf. GHEM- Lit. *žĕmė* OSlav. *zemlja*, GHM̥- χαμαί on the ground.

†**hyacinthus** a flower: ὑάκ-ινθος, ὑακ- 'young' = jυῖακ- JUVN̥K- *juvencus*. (Orig. a proper name, see under *juncus*.)

†**hyalus** glass: ὕαλος, Egyptian (as first made in Egypt).

†**hydrus** watersnake: ὕδρος, UD-R- cf. Ags. *oter* otter E., Zd. *udra* Sk. *udrás*, and ŪD-R- Lit. *udra* OSlav. *vydra*, fr. *unda*.

†**iambus** iamb: ††ἴαμβος satire:

†**iaspis** jasper (E. E. *diaper*): ††ἴασπις, Heb. *yash'pheh*.

†**ībis** a bird: ††ἶβις, cf. Coptic *hippen*.

iciō īce (the latter formed backward from Inf. *icere*, see *sisto*) strike: = **jiciō *jeciō*, see *jaciō* (for the meaning cf. βάλλω throw, strike).— Lucr. *īcit* formed after *eicit* (= *ējicit*), and so *īcimur*.

†**ictis** weasel: ††ἰκτίς:

īdem the same:=**is-dem*, *is* + -*dem*.—With Neut. *i-dem* cf. Sk. *i-dám* it.

identidem repeatedly: = *ĭdem* + *ante* + -*dem*, 'the same before'.

ideō for that reason: = **ed-eō* 'and for that reason,' *et* (see *edepol*) + Abl. of *is*.

idōneus proper: fr. **idō* here, *i*- see *is* + -**dō* see -*do*, with Adj.-ending: 'on the spot'.

†**īdūs eidūs** middle of month: Sab., Etrusc. *itus* (Varr. L L. 6. 28), the Etrusc. alphabet having no *d*.

igitur then: = **jigitur *jūgitur* 'it is added,' Aoristic form of *jungitur* (as *tagō* of *tangō*).—In old Lat. it often begins a clause.

īgnis fire (E. *ingle*): = **ingnis* N̥GVNÍS Lit. *ugnìs* OSlav. *ognĭ*, Sk. *agnís*.

īgnōrō know not: *in-* + **gnō-rus* Adj. fr. *nō-scō*.

īlex holm-oak: = **idex*, ἴδη wood.

īlia entrails, flanks (as enclosing them: E. *jade* a stone): = **hīlia* fr. *fīlum*.

īlicō illicō on the spot: = **i-lucō* from **ī* Loc. of *is* + *locō*.

ille (i.e. **ülle*) **olle** (Fest.) **ollus** (Varr., quasi Noun) he: = **ollo* (a pure stem, like *ŏ*: cf. *ipse*), ŌLO, see *ōlim*:
    hardly = **on-lo* from ON- Lit. *ans* that OSlav. *onŭ* he, Sk. *aná-* this.

imāgo emāgō copy, imitor imitate: 'select,' fr. *emō* take.

im-bēcillus weak (E. *embezzle*): 'disabled,' ɢᴠᴇ̄ᴋ- Hesych. ὁ-ζήκης vigorous, cf. ɢᴠᴀᴋ- *baculum.*
imber rain (OIr. *imrim* storm, Stokes Remarks) : = *ümbri-* ᴏᴍʙʀɪ- cf. ὕμβρος.
imbuō fill : dialectic for *in-fūō,* ἐμ-φύω implant, fr. *fuī.*
im-mānis monstrous : 'un-manageable,' fr. *mānus* good (i.e. 'tractable,' εὐχερής), fr. *manus* (see *cōmis*).
immō īmō certainly : ' at bottom,' Abl. of *īmus.*
im-portūnus unfit : see *op-portūnus.*
impraesentiārum at present: = *in* *praesentiārum locō,* periphrasis for *in praesentiā* ' on the spot '.
īmus lowest : = *ins-mus,* OIr. *īs* below, from *in + s* (see *abs*), cf. *eis* into (= *ἐν-s*).
in in : = *en,* ἐν, OIr. Got. Lit. *in.*
in- Negative : ɴ-, ἀν- ἀ-, MIr. *an-,* Got. *un-* E., Arm. *an-,* Zd. Sk. *an-* before Vowel *a-* before Cons.
inānis empty : *in-āgnis* = *āgnis* (as *in-cānus in-clutus in-columis in-vidus invītus* = *canus clutus columis* *vidus* *vītus* : '*in* enim saepe augendi causa adicimus' Fest.), ᴀɢʜ- ἀχήν poor, cf. ᴀɴɢʜ- *angustus* narrow, see *angō.*
†in-cīlô reproach : *cīlô* grin, χειλόω (surround with a rim), fr. χεῖλος lip.
in-clutus in-clitus famous : = *clutus* (Fest.), κλυτός, MIr. *cloth,* Sk. *çrutás* heard, cf. ᴋʟᴜ̄ᴛós Ags. *hlūd* loud E., Parts. fr. *cluō.*
in-cohô in-choô in-coô begin (verbum sacrorum Serv., see Key) : hardly 'put the pole of the plough into the yoke,' fr. *cohum* 'hole in the yoke' (Varr. L. L. 5. 135) or 'strap uniting pole and yoke' (Fest.).
in-columis in-colomis safe : also *columis* (see *in-ānis*) : = *colu-mus* ' taken care of,' fr. *colō* protect + Adj.-ending *-mos.*
ind-āgô track : = *indu* + ᴀ̄ɢ- in *amb-āg-ēs co-āg-ulum,* cf. ᴀɢ- *agô.*
inde thence : = *im* Abl. of *is* (cf. *illim istim*) + *-de.*
indolēs nature : fr. sq. + *alō,* see *adolescō*[2].
indu endo into, in : *endō,* see *in* and *-do.*
in-dulgeō indulge: fr. *dalgus* = *largus,* ' am bountiful to '.
induō don : *indu* + *avō* see *exuō.*
†indūsium smock : *ἐνδύσιον* fr. *ἔνδυσις* dress.—Varr. L. L. 5. 131 spells it *intusium* quasi fr. *intus,* ' worn inside '.
industria industry : *indu* + *strūa* fr. *struō,* ' heaping up,' cf. *in-struō* build up, furnish.
indūtiae truce : fr. *indu* + *ōtium,* 'interval of quiet '.
infensus hostile : = *infend-tus* Part. of *in-fendō* strike, cf. *dē-fendō.*
inferus below: = *infrus* (cf. *infrā* Adv.) for *ins-rus* from *ins,* see *īmus*: dialectic for *imbrus.*

in-fēstus unsafe: 'un-pleasant,' *in-* +*fēstus* merry, cf. *fēstīvus* agreeable.

infit begins: dialectic for **indit* ṂDH- cf. ṂEDH- *medius*, 'interposes'?·

infula fillet: dialectic for **ingula* ṆGH- cf. ṆEGH- *necto*?

ingens huge: 'un-familiar,' *in-gen-ti-* cf. Ags. *un-cūđ* unknown E. *uncouth*, from *in-* +GṆ- Got. *kunnan* know E. *can* &c. *keen*, Lit. *žinóti*, Arm. *canauth* known, Zd. *zan-* know, see *nōscō*.

ingluviēs maw:

in-gruō attack: 'fall on,' see *con-gruō*.

inguen groin: ṆGV-ÉN- *ἀδέν-* gland (Nom. ἀδήν), cf. (unnasalised) EGV- ONor. *ökvinn* lumpy.

inquam I say: 'I should say,' Subj. of **inquō* cut, clear, clear up, whence *co-inquô* cut off:

inquilīnus tenant: *in* + KVEL- *colō*.

in-quinô pollute: fr. **quenō *conō* (of. *inquilīnus* fr. *colō*), cf. Fest. *cuniō* κακκῶ:

insilia leash-rods (?) Lucr. 5. 1353 Munro:

instar image: 'weight,' formed (like *laquear* from *laqueāre*) from *instāre* Inf. of *in-stô* press on.

in-staurô renew (E. *story*[2]): 'put on,' STAUR- place σταυρός stake, ONor. *staurr*.

in-stīgô incite: STĪGV- cf. STIGV- στίζω prick, Got. *stiks* point E. *stick* &c. †*stucco*, and TIGV- Zd. Sk. *tij-* be sharp.

in-stinctus incited: STINGV- cf. praeced.

insula island (E. *isle*; but for *island* see *aqua*): Dimin. of **insa* ṆS- OIr. *inis*, cf. ṆS- νῆσος.

intellegō intelligō understand: sq. + **legō* care, see *dīligō*.

inter between: Ṇ-TÉB OIr. *etar*, Zd. *añtare* Sk. *antdr*, cf. EN *in*.

inter-prēs agent (orig. a commercial term): *inter-pret-* fr. *pretium*.

†**intibus intubus** endive (E., ἔντυβον Geoponica 12. 1): = **hindubus*, Semitic, Arab. *hindibā* Zenker 943 b, fr. *Hind* India.

intrô enter: fr. **intrus* Adj., cf. *inter*.

intus within: ἐντός, *in* + Adverb-ending *-tos*, cf. *funditus* &o. *penitus*, Sk. *-tas*.

inula elecampane (which = *inula campāna*):

invidus envious: 'keeping aloof, unsympathetic,' VIDH- see *dīvidō viduus*.

in-vītô entertain: 'enliven,' fr. *vīta*, cf. *vītulor*.

in-vītus (see *in-ānis*) loth: = **vī-tus* forced, see *vītô*.

†**iō** Interj.: *ἰώ*.

ipse himself: = **ipso* (see *ille*) **i-pti-so* fr. *i-s* + *-pte* + **so* he, see *sīc*.

īra anger: = *hīra* (for the meaning cf. χόλος bile, anger).

ir-rītô provoke: *in* + **rītô* stir, cf. *prō-rītô* incite, fr. *rītus*.

is he : Hesych. *ἱν* Acc. (Cyprian), Got. *is* OHG. *er*, Lit. j-*is* OSlav. *i-že*,
Zd. Sk. *i-* this, cf. EI- *ea* she (= *ej-a), OIr. *ē* he, Got. *eis* they, Sk.
aydm this.

iste he : = *esto (see *ille*), Umbr. *estu* Acc. :

ita so : = *itā cf. Naev. *itāque*, fr. *et* + Instrum. ending (cf. κρυφᾶ ὅπᾶ
ταυτᾶ Dor., Lat. *quā* where).

item also : 'secondly,' *et* + quasi-numeral ending (see *autem*).

iterum again : = *edrum (dialectic for *ebrum) Adj. Neut. from EDH-
back, Ags. *ed*, Sk. *ádhi* up, see *ergā ad-*.

itidem so : = *eti-dem fr. *et* + -*dem*.

jaceō lie (E. *agistment gist joists*) : Intrans. form (see *paveō*) of sq.

jaciō throw (E. *jet*[1] *jetty jotsam jut pargeted*) : JEKV- cf. JĒKV- *jēci*
Perf., JOKV- ONor. *jaga* move to and fro E. *yacht Yankee* OHG.
jagōn hunt.

jam now : 'at' this time, JE ἔρα-ζε on the ground χαμᾶζε, θύραζε at (i.e.
out of) the door, + a case-sign -*am*, see *tam*.

jānua door, **jānus** passage : JĀ- go, Lit. *jóti* ride OSlav. *jad*, Zd. Sk. *yā*-
go, by-form of I- see *eō*.

jecur liver: JEKV-Ṛ- cf. JĒKV-Ṛ- ἧπαρ, JĒKV-Ḷ- Zd. *yākare* (Fick), JOKV-Ṛ-
Plin. *jocur*, JEKV-Ṛ-T- Sk. *yákṛt*: also with -N ending JEKV-N-
jecin-or-is Gen., JEKV-N- Lit. *jeknos*, JEKV-ÓN- Sk. *yakán-*, JĒKV-N-
ἧπα-τος Gen., JOKV-N- Celsus *jocin-or-is*: shortest form IKV- ἴκτερος
jaundice.

jējūnus fasting : 'bound' (cf. Got. *fastan* φυλάττειν, νηστεύειν, Eng. *fast*
'bound' and *fast* 'abstinence'), = *jĭ-jŭ-nus Redupl. from JŪ- cf. JU-
Zd. Sk. *yu-* bind.

jentô (with *e* from next form) **jējentô** (Redupl.) **jantô** breakfast : eat
'at once' on rising, from *jam*.

jocus jest (E. *jeopardy juggle*) : JOKV- cf. JŌKV- Lit. *jūkas* ridicule,
JEKV- ἰψιά pastime (*jεκϝ-τιά) : 'thrown out,' fr. *jaciō* (as σκώπτω
mock fr. σκήπτω hurl, E. *slang* fr. *sling*).

juba mane :

jubar daystar ; 'crested' with light, fr. praeced.

jubeō order : JU- short form of JŪ- *jūs*[2] (cf. OLat. *joubeō*), + DHĒ- see
-*dō* ; Perf. *jussī joust* from *jŭdeō.

jūgerum half-acre : 'ploughed in one day by a *pair* of oxen,' fr. *jŭgus
pair, ζεῦγος, JEUGV- ζεύγνῡμι yoke, cf. JUGV- *jugum*.

jūgis ever-flowing : 'continuous, connected,' see praeced.

jugum yoke (W. *iau*) : ζυγόν, Got. *juk* E., OSlav. *igo*, Sk. *yugám*, JUGV-
cf. JUNGV- Lit. *jùngas*, fr. *jungō*.

jūmentum carriage, beast of burden : = *juvimentum, fr. *iuvō,
*juvô.

jūncus rush (E. *jonquil junk*[2] *junket*): 'twig' (as in Plin. 26. 72), =
*jūnicus, cf. *jūniculus* old vine-branch (Plin. 17. 182), see *jūni-perus*:
not fr. *juvenis*, if only because this is not used of plants (see
hyacinthus).

jungō join (E.): JUNGV- Lit. *jùngiu* I yoke, see *jugum*, cf. JUGV- Zd.
Sk. *yuj-* join.

jūniperus juniper (E. *gin*): 'twig-bearing,' fr. *jūn-cus* + *pariō*.

jūs[1] broth (E. *juice*): Lit. *júszė*, Sk. *yūsas*, cf. ζύ-μη (= **ζύσ-μη*) leaven,
and JOUS- OSlav. *juha* broth.

jūs[2] **jous** law: Zd. *yaosh* welfare Sk. *yós* (change of meaning obscure).

juvencus young: JUVN-KÓ- *ύάκ-ινθος* (see *hyacinthus*), W. *ieuangc*, Got.
juggs (= **juvungas*), Sk. *yuvaçás* youthful, fr. sq.

juvenis young: JUVN- Sk. *yúvan-*, cf. JOVN- Zd. *yavan*, JOVNO- JOUNO-
Lit. *jaúnas*.

juventa youth: JUVN-TÁ Got. *junda* (= **juvundá*) E., fr. praeced.

juvô help (E. *aid*): = **jovô* (whence *jōcundus* pleasant, = **jovi-cundus*,
cf. Faliscan *jovent* = juvent) from **jevô*:

jūxtā near (E. *adjust jostle*): fr. **jūxtus* Part. of **jūxō* join, JEUGV- (see
jūgerum) + *s*.

lābēs fall, stain ('failure,' cf. *cāsus* fall, disaster): fr. *lābor*.

labium labrum lip (Ir. *lab*): lab- (quasi fr. *lambō*) for LEB- Ags. *lippe* E.,
Pers. *lab* Zenker 790 c.

labô totter: SLAB- OHG. *slaf* loose, Lit. *slābnas* weak, cf. SLĒB- Got.
slēps sleep E., see *lābor*.

labor distress: 'falling, failing,' praeced.

lābor fall: SLĀB- OSlav. *slabŭ* weak, see *labô*.

lābrum tub: LĀB- cf. LAB- λαβεῖν seize (cf. NHG. *fassen* seize, contain)?

labrūsca wild vine: fr. *labrum* edge, 'growing at the *edges* of vineyards'.

†labyrinthus maze: †λαβύρινθος, Egyptian (Jablonski Opuscula 1. 250).

lac lact lacte milk (E. *lettuce*):

lacer torn: VLAKV- λακίς a rent, Zd. *vrac-* to tear.

lacerna cloak; fr. praeced., 'skin torn off an animal' (cf. λώπη robe fr.
λέπω peel, E. *robe* fr. Lat. *rumpō*, shroud fr. *shred*).

lacertus lizard (E. E. *alligator*), upper arm (from some fancied resemblance; cf. μῦς mouse, muscle): 'fragile,' fr. *lacer*.

lacinia lappet: 'torn,' fr. *lacer*.

lacrima lacruma dacrima tear: DAKR- δάκρυ, OW. *dacr* Zeuss 827 b,
Got. *tagr* E. E. †*train*-oil.

lactēs intestines: 'juicy,' fr. *lac*.

lactô allure: fr. *laciō* draw (Fest.), see *laqueus*:

lacūna lucūna cavity (in poetry 'pool,' quasi fr. sq.), **lacūnar** panelled
ceiling: 'space,' fr. *locus*, with pretonic *a*.

lacus vat, tank (E. *lake*, MIr. *loch* lake): λάκκος pit.

laedō hurt: 'strike,' cf. *collīdō* strike together:

†**laena** mantle: pop. etym. (quasi fr. *lāna*) for *claena*, χλαῖνα: which = *χλάμ-ja fr. χλαμύς, *chlamys*.

laetus glad:

laevus left: λαι(ϝ)ός, OSlav. *lēvŭ*.

†**laganum** cake: λάγανον, fr. λαγαρός thin, see *langueō*.

†**lagēna lagoena** flagon: = *lagūna*, *λαγύνη cf. †λάγυῖνος, an Aeol. form (as χελΰνη of χελώνη) of *λαγώνη whence *lagōna*.

lallō sing: = *lālō* LĀL- cf. LAL- λάλος babbling, NHG. *lallen* lisp E. *lull lullaby loll* (W. *lol* prattle), Lit. *lalúti*, onomatop.

lāma slough: 'broken' ground, LĀM- OHG. *luomi* faint ('broken'), cf. LAM- Ags. *lam* lame E. E. *lam* Vb., OSlav. *lomŭ* slough *lomiti* break.

lamberō tear: 'lick up,' fr. sq.

lambō lick (E. *lamprey*): LAMB- cf. LAB- OHG. *laffan*, OSlav. *lobŭzŭ* kiss; also LAP- λάπτω I lick, Arm. *laphem*.

lāmentum wailing: LĀ- Arm. *lal* to lament.

†**lamia** ogress: λάμια, fr. λαμυρός greedy.

lāmina lammina lāmna plate (E. *omelette*): fr. *lā-tus* Adj. + participial ending.

lāna wool: VL̥N- W. *gwlan* (E. *flannel*), Sk. *ūrṇā*, cf. VL̥N- *vellus*.

†**lancea** spear (E. *launch*): Spanish (Varr. ap. Gell. 15. 30 fin.):

lancinō tear: 'divide into pieces, weigh out,' fr. *lanx* scale of a balance.

langueō faint: SLANGV- λαγγάζω slacken, cf. SLAGV- λαγαρός thin, MIr. *lag* weak (E. *lag*), Ags. *släc* slow E. *slack* &c. *slake slouch*; and SLĒGV- λήγω cease.

†**lanista** trainer (Cic.): = †*danista* moneylender (Plaut.), δανειστής: a slang term of gladiators.

   Isid. calls it Etruscan, only because the use of gladiators came from Etruria.

lanius butcher: = *lam-jus* from LAM- see *lāma*, 'breaking up' meat.

†**lanterna lāterna** (quasi fr. *lātus* carried) lamp: = *lamplerna*, λαμπτήρ, with term. of *luc-erna*.

lanx dish:

†**lapathum** sorrel: λάπαθον, fr. λαπάσσω empty (Plin. 20. 235 alvom folia solvont).

lapis stone: *lapid-* = *lepid-* cf. λέπας bare rock, fr. λέπω peel.

lappa burr:

laquear panel: fr. *lacūna*.

laqueus noose (E. *lace lasso latchet*): fr. *laciō* draw, see *lactō*.

largus abundant: = *lalgus* *dalgus* DL̥GHVÓS δολιχός long, Zd. *daregha-* Sk. *dīrghás*, cf. DL̥GHVOS Got. *tulgus* steadfast, Lit. *ilgas* long OSlav. *dlŭgŭ*.

lāridum lārdum bacon (E. *lard*):

lārva lārua ghost, mask:

†**lasanum** pot: †λάσανον:

lascīvus wanton: fr. **lascus*, LAS- λιλαίομαι desire, Sk. *lash-*.

†**lāserpīcium lāserpītium** silphium: African (as first grown near Cyrene Plin. 16. 143)?

lassus weary (E. *alas*): = **lad-tus*, LAD- Got. *lats* slothful, E. *late let*[2] (= hinder), cf. LĒD- Got. *lētan* to leave, E. *let*[1].

lateō lurk: 'efface myself,' LA- cf. LĒ- *dē-leō lētum*?

later brick:

latex liquid: *latic-*, cf. MIr. *laith* ale.

Hardly cf. λάταγες drops.

†**latro** mercenary (E. *larceny*): *λάτρων* by-form of †λάτρις servant: from Heb. *notér* guardian (as λίτρον natron from Heb. *nether*)?

lātrô bark (Hesych. λατρά(ζειν talk gibberish): fr. **lātra* barking dog, LĀ- Lit. *lóti* bark OSlav. *lajati*, Sk. *rā-*.

latus side: LAT- cf. ̣LT- OIr. *leth* half.

lātus stlātus Adj. wide: STĻ-TÓs extended, Part. fr. STEL- OSlav. *stelją* I spread, cf. STOL- Lit. *stálas* table.

lātus Part. borne: TĻ-TÓs, fr. *tollō*.

†**laurus** baytree: = **daurus*, **δαῦρος* **δρῥϜος* tree, OIr. *daur* oak, DRVO- cf. DRU- Zd. *dru* wood Sk. *drus* log, DRŪ- δρῦς oak, DREU- δενδρε(Ϝ)ον tree, Got. *triu* E. E. *tar*; also DERV- Lit. *derwà* pine-wood OSlav. *drēvo* tree, DORU δόρυ beam DŌRU Zd. *dāuru* log Sk. *dầru*.

laus praise: *laudi-*:

lautia dautia (Fest.) banquet, **lautus** splendid: **dautos*:

lavō wash (E. *laundry lava lavender*): = **lovō*, LOV- λούω, Gaul. *lautro* balneō, Ags. *leáh* lye E., Ags. *leáđor* lather E., Arm. *loganam* I bathe.

laxus loose (E. *lazy lease leash*): = **lag-sus* Part. (see *celsus*) from SLAGV- see *langueō*.

†**lebēs** kettle: λέβης:

lectus bed (E. *litter*): = **leg-tus* LEGHV- λέχος λέκτρον, λέξαι to lay, OIr. *lige* bed, Got. *ligan* lie E. E. *lay ledge log low* †*rely*, OSlav. *legnąti*, cf. LOGHV- Lit. at-*lagai* fallow land.

legō gather (E. *cull*): λέγω.

†**lembus** pinnace: †λέμβος, Cyrenaic (Plin. 7. 208).

†**lēmniscus** ribbon: λημνίσκος Polyb.:

lemurēs ghosts:

lēnis soft: Lett. *lēni*, see *lentus*.

lēnō:

lens lentil: *lent-* fr. *lentus*, 'soothing' (Plin. 18. 123 aequanimitatem fieri vescentibus eā).

lentīscus mastic-tree: fr. sq., 'resinous'.

lentus flexible : LEN-TÓS cf. LÉN-T- OHG. *lindi* soft ; Part. from LEN-
Got. af-*linnan* yield, cf. LĒN- *lēnis*.

†**lēnunculus** skiff : Dimin. of **lēnus*, λην*ós* trough :

†**leō** lion (E.) : †λέων : Assyrian *aria*.

W. *llew*, OHG. *lewo* (whence Lit. *liûwas* OSlav. *lĭvŭ*), may go with E.
low Vb.

lepor charm :

lepus hare (Sicil. λέπορις Varr. L. L. 5. 101 ; E. *leverct*) :

lessum (Acc.) wailing :

lētum death : Part. Neut. from LĒ- *dēleō*, see *lateō*.

levis light (E. *carnival leaven lever levy*) : LEGHV- Arm. *arag* quick, Sk.
raghús light, cf. LENGHV- Lit. *leng-wùs*, Zd. *renj-* be light Sk. *langh-*
leap, LĒGHV- Got. *leihts* light E., LGHV- ἐ-λαχύς small ἐλαφρός light,
OSlav. *lĭgŭkŭ*, LOGHV- (?) MIr. *laiget* smallness.

lēvis laevis smooth : = **līvis *līvus* λεῖ(ϝ)*os* : ' beaten,' see *līveō* (cf. E.
smooth fr. *smith*).

lēx law (Osc. *ligud* Abl.) : ' laid down,' LĒGHV- cf. LEGHV- *lcctus*, LOGHV-
Ags. *layu* E.

liber inner bark :

līber leiber free (E. *deliver livery*) : = **lūbcr *lcuber*, Osc. *lùvfreis* Gen.,
ἐ-λεύθερος (dialectic for **ἐλεύφερος*) : ' doing as one likes,' LEUBH-
cf. sq.

libet lubet it pleases : LUBH- Sk. *lubh-* be lustful, cf. LŪBH- Lit. *lùbȳtis*
to love oneself, LEUBH- Got. *liubs* dear E. *love lief believe* †*furlough*
leave Subst. *leman livelong*.

libô take a little of : = **lūbô* taste, fr. praeced. (as Got. *kausjan* taste fr.
kiusan approve, see *gustô*).

lībra pound (E. *level*) : LĪDHRĪ, Sicilian λίτρα (for **λίθρα* as Sicilian
κιτών for χιτών) :

lībum cake : ' taste,' fr. *lībô*.

liceō am for sale, licet is allowed : ' is left,' LIKV- cf. LINKV- *linquo*.
Hesych. λίσσωμεν· ἐάσωμεν is too doubtful to add.

licium thrum (E. *lists*) : fr. ob-*liquus*, ' at right angles ' to the woof (see
trāma).

lictor marshal : ' binding,' fr. **ligô* by-form of *ligô*.

liēn ljēn (Plaut., see Key) spleen : = **spljēn* (no Lat. word begins with
spl-, see †*splendeō*), σπλ(j)ήν :
not related to SPELGH- MIr. *selg*, OSlav. *slēzena*, SPḶGH- Zd. çpereza
(Fick), or PLĪGH-, Sk. *plīhán- plihan-*.

lignum log : = **lic-num* LIKV- see *linquô*, ' remnant, end '.

ligō mattock :

ligô bind (E. *alloy ally league liable rally*) : = **lugô* LŪGV- bend, λυγίζω
twist, Ags. *loc* lock (E.) of hair (' twisted '), Lit. *lugnas* pliant.

ligula shoe-latchet : fr. praeced.

ligustrum privet : fr. *Ligus* Ligurian (as E. *lovage* from Lat. *Ligusticum* Ligurian).

†**lilium** lily : *λείλιον, dissimilated †λείριον : = *λήλιον (with ει from Hom.'s λειρόεις delicate), cf. Pers. *lāle* tulip Zenker 789 c.

lima file : 'fluted across,' from *limus* Adj.

limbus border :

limen threshold : 'at right angles' to the door-posts, fr. *limus* Adj. (as *glūten* fr. *glūtus*).

limes cross-path (E. *lintel*) : fr. *limus* Adj.

limpidus clear : = *dūmpidus* watery, see *lympha*.

limus[1] Subst. mud : = *lūmus* LOIMOS Ags. *lām* loam E., cf. LEIMOS Ags. *lim* lime E.

limus[2] Subst. apron : sq., with a purple stripe 'across' the bottom (Serv.).

limus Adj. sidelong : = *lix-mos* LIKV-S- see *oblīquus*.

linea string (E. *line*) : fr. *līnum*.

lingō linguō (Priscian, as though fr. sq.) lick : LINGH- cf. LIGH- Ags. *liccian* (= *lic-jan*) E., Sk. *lih-*, LĪGH- OIr. *ligim* I lick, LEIGH- λείχω, Lit. *liežiù* OSlav. *lizati* lick, Arm. *lizum* I lick, and LOIGH- Got. bi-*laigōn* lick.

lingua dingua tongue : DNGHVĀ OIr. *tenge* (with *t* from Teut.), Got. *tuggō* E.

linō smear : = *le-nō* LE- cf. LĒ- *lēvī* Perf. :

linquō leave : LINKV- cf. LIKV- Arm. *lkhanem* I leave, Sk. *ric-* leave, LIKV⁻ Lit. *lýkius* remainder, LEIKV- λείπω I leave, OIr. *lēicci* sinit, Got. *leihvan* lend E. E. *loan*, Lit. *liēkù* I leave, and LOIKV- OSlav. otŭ-*lēkŭ* remainder.

But for Got. af-*lifnan* see *lippus*.

linter lunter tub, boat : LUNT- cf. LŪT- ONor. *lúdr* flour-bin ('trough')?

linteum cloth : LINT- cf. LĪT- λῖτα :

līnum flax (Got. *lein* linen E. E. *linseed linnet*) : LIS-NOM λίνον (Lit. *linai* OSlav. *linŭ*: for *λίννον *λίσνον), ONor. *lesni* head-gear, cf. LĪS-NO-λῖν-οπτδομαι watch nets, LĪS-N-ION OIr. *lēine* shirt.

lippus blear-eyed : = *lipus* 'sticky' with rheum, LĪP- cf. LIP- λίπος fat, Got. af-*lifnan* remain ('stick') E. *leave eleven*, Lit. *lipti* to stick OSlav. *lĭpēti*, Sk. *lip-* smear.

liquô liquefy : VLIKV- OIr. *fliuch* wet.

liquor flow : VLĪKV-, cf. praeced.

lira ridge (E. *delirious*) : LĪSĀ Lit. *lýsè* garden-bed, cf. LOISĀ OSlav. *lěha*, LOIS- Got. *laists* track E. *last* Subst. and Vb.

lis leis slis stlis sclis strife : orig. 'division,' cf. *littera littus* :

litô worship successfully : 'pay a debt,' = *lutô* fr. *lutus* Part. of *luō*.

littera lītera leitera letter: 'division, cutting,' see *līs*.

littus lītus shore: 'cut,' see *līs* (cf. E. *shore* fr. *shear*).

†**lituus** trumpet: Etrusc. (as being an Etruscan invention)?

līveō am blue: 'am beaten' (see *lūridus*), fr. *lēvis*.

lixa sutler: 'water-carrier,' *līxa* water (Nonius):

locuplēs trustworthy, substantial: 'of full position,' *locō* *plētō (see *plē-nus*: cf. pleno jure 'with a complete title').

locus stlocus place (E. *couch*): STLOKVOS, see *loquor*:

locusta lucusta lobster (E.):

†**lōdīx** blanket:

lōlīgō lollīgō cuttlefish:

loſium darnel (OHG. *lolli* Graff):

longus long (Got. *laggs* E. E. *lounge lunge* pur*loin*): cf. λογγάζω loiter.

loquor speak: 'put in order, *place* my words,' fr. *locus*, Varr. L. L. 6. 56 is loquitur qui suo loco quodque verbum sciens ponit.

lorea after-wine:

lōrum thong (E. *loriner*):

†**lōtos** a plant: *λωτός, Egyptian (Jablonski Opuscula 1. 250).

lūbricus slippery: fr. *lūb-rus, SLEUB- Got. *sliupan* slip.

lūcar pay of actors: Etrusc. (see *histriō*)?

lucerna lamp: LUKV- ἀμφι-λύκη twilight, Zd. Sk. *ruc-* shine, see *lūx*.

lucrum gain: 'pay,' fr. *luō*.

luctor wrestle: LŪGV- *ligō*, 'twist'.

lūcus loucos grove: LOUKVOS Ags. *leāh* E. *lea* meadow, Lit. *laúkas* field, Sk. *lōkás* space: 'clearing,' fr. *lūx*.

lūdus loidos game:

luēs pestilence ('flood' of corruption), fluid Petronius 123. 192: LU- λύθρον gore, see *lutum*, cf. LŪ- λῦμα filth, ruin.

lūgeō mourn: LEUG- λευγαλέος wretched, cf. LUG- λυγρός sad: 'broken,' Lit. *lúžau* I break, Sk. *ruj-* break.

lumbrīcus worm (W. *llymriad* sand-eel):

lumbus loin (E.): LONDH-, cf. LENDH- Ags. *lenden*, OSlav. *lędvija* loins.

lūmen loumen light (E. *limn loom* Vb.): = *loux-men, see sq.

lūna lōsna (Praenestine, E. Schneider 55) moon: = *louxna, cf. Pruss. *lauxnos* stars, Zd. *raokhshna* shining, LOUKV-s- see *lūstrō*.

luō pay: LU- cf. LŪ- λύω loose, Got. *lūn* ransom, Sk. *lū-* cut, LOU- Lit. *liautis* cease, LOU-s- Got. *lausjan* to loose E. E. *lose*.

lupīnus pulse: 'sharp, bitter' (tristis Verg. Geo. 1. 75), fr. sq.

lupus wolf: dialectic (Umbr.?: Sab. was *hirpus* or *irpus*) for *luquus, λύκος, cf. Praenestine *Luqorcus* Lupercus E. Schneider 48, vĺkvos Got. *vulfs* E., Lit. *wilkas* OSlav. *vlŭkŭ*, Arm. *gail* (= *galy *galg), Zd. *vehrka-* Sk. *vŕkas*.

lurcō lurchō glutton:

lūridus yellow: fr. *leurus 'beaten,' λευρόs smooth (for transition of meaning see līvcō lēvis).

luscinia nightingale:

luscus one-eyed: MIr. losc blind, lame: = luxus Adj., see luxus.

lūstrô illuminate: = *lūxtrô LOUKV-s- see lūna, cf. LUKV-s Zd. rukhsh-shine, fr. LOUKV- see lūx.

lustrum morass: = *lut-trum fr. lutum.

lūstrum purification: 'clearing,' fr. lūstrô (for transition of meaning cf. ONor. skeirr clear, bright, cleansed from guilt).

lutum mud: Part. from LU- see luēs.

lūtum weld:

lūx light: LEUKV- λευκόs white λεύσσω see, Got. liuhath light E., OSlav. luči, cf. LOUKV- OIr. lōche thunderbolt, Lit. laûkas bald-faced, LUKV-see lucerna.

luxus extravagance: 'derangement,' fr. luxus Adj. dislocated, = *loxos, λοξόs slanting, see luscus.—The transcription of luxuria as λειξουρία (Ducange) must be due to popular etymology.

†lychnus lamp: λύχνοs, LUKHV- by-form of LUKV- see lucerna.

lympha water: pop. etym., quasi from *λύμφη (Varr. L. L. 7. 87 λυμφο-λήπτους) by-form of Νύμφη, quasi 'fountain' Nymph: for *dūmpa, Osc. Diumpaís Nymphis, see līmpidus.

†lynx lynx: λύγξ, LUNK- cf. LUK-s- OHG. luhs, Lit. lúszis.

†lyra lyre: †λύρα: Semitic?

†maccis a spice (E. mace): cf. †macir an Indian spice Plin. 12. 32, Diosc. †μάκερ.

†macellum meat-market (NHG. metzger butcher): fr. *macelum railing, Hesych. μάκελος, 'enclosed by a railing'.

macer lean (E. meagre): 'mauled,' fr. macô.

māceria wall: 'moulded' of clay, fr. sq. (see fingô).

mācerô steep (E. macaroni): MĀK- cf. MAK- macô.

†machaera sword: μάχαιρα (Heb. m'kērā): not used in war, so not fr. μάχη battle.

†māchina engine: μάχανά Dor. μηχανή Ion., MĀGHV- cf. MAGHV- OIr. do-for-maig auget, Got. magan be able E. may &c. maw, OSlav. mogą am able.

macô maul:

mactô[1] sacrifice (Ir. mactadh slaughter; E. matador): praeced. Hardly 'offer in honour of a god,' sq.

mactô[2] honour, macte good luck: MAK- μακρόs long, Zd. maç great.

macula spot (E. mackerel mail-clad trammel): 'bruise,' fr. macô. Hardly add Got. mail (quasi *mahil) wrinkle, cf. E. mole[1].

madeô am wet: μαδάω.

†maena mēna sprat: μαίνη:

maereō moereō mourn: MAIS-:

†māgālia huts: Heb. *māgōr* habitation (whence also μέγαρον hall, Μέγαρα a town?).

magmentum offering: fr. *mactō*.[2]

†magnēs magnet: μάγνης, from Magnesia in E. Thessaly.

magnus great (E. *main* Adj. *master mayor merino*): = *meg-nós MEG- μέγας, Got. *mikils* much E., Arm. *mcc* great, Sk. *mahás*.

†magūdaris stalk of silphium: †μαγύδαρις, Syrian (Plin. 19. 46).

†magus magician: †μάγος, Median (the Magi a Median tribe).

mājālis barrow hog: 'offered to the goddess Maia' (Isid.: *Māja* fr. *mājus* great, = *mag-jus* fr. *mag-nus*).

māla jaw: = *max-la*, see *maxilla*.

†malacus soft: μαλακός, = *μαλ-ṇ-κός (see *juvencus*) fr. ἀ-μαλός, see *malus*.

malleus hammer (E. *mallet maul*; OSlav. *malĭ*):

†mālobathrum a plant: Diosc. †μᾱλάβαθρον: Indian (from its habitat).

mālum apple: μῆλον (E. *melon marmalade*):

malus bad: ἀ-μαλός weak, MIr. *maile* malum.

mālus mast: = *mādus MAZDOS, Ags. *mäst* E.

Hesych. μασταλίδες stakes is doubtful: M. Schmidt conj. σταλίδες.

malva mallow (E. E. *mauve*): MAL-VĀ cf. Lucian μάλβαξ (= *μάλϝ-αξ), cf. MAL- μαλάχη:

mamma mother Pers. 3. 18, breast: onomatop., MAMMĀ μάμμη mother, E. *mamma*, cf. MĀMĀ OHG. *muomā*, Lit. *máma* OSlav. *mama*, Pers. *māmā* Zenker 802 a, MAM- *mamilla* breast, W. *mam* mother.

mancus maimed (E. *mangle* Vb. *mullion*): 'tamed,' *manicus fr. *manus* (as χείριος 'in one's power' fr. χείρ hand).

mandō chew (E. *mange manger*): 'moisten,' MAND- cf. MAD- *madeō*.

mandô commit (E. *commodore*): fr. *mandus *manidus Adj. of *manus*, 'hand' a thing to a person.

†mandra pen: μάνδρα: cf. Sk. *mandurā* stall, *mand*- linger?

māne early: 'in manageable time,' see *immānis*.

maneō stay (E. *manor manse menial menagerie messuage*): = *menéō, MEN- μένω, Arm. *mnam* I stay, Zd. *man*- stay.

mangō dealer, furbisher: = *mengŏn, cf. MIr. *meng* craft.

mani-festus manu-festus plain: *manus* + ?

manipulus maniplus handful: fr. *manus* + Adj.-ending, see *disci-pulus*.

†mannus cob: = *mandus (see *grunniō*), Basque *mando* mule (Van Eys).

mānô flow:

†mantēle napkin, mantēlum mantle (E.): 'cloth,' Spanish *mantum* cloak (Isid. Orig. 19. 24. 15).

manubiae booty: fr. sq. + the same term. as *dubius*.

manus hand (E. *maintain manage manner*): MṈ- cf. MṈ- Ags. *mund*.
†**mapālia** huts: Punic (Fest.).
†**mappa** napkin (E. E. *apron map mop*): Punic (Quint.).
marceō droop: fr. **marcus* Adj., MḆ-KVŎs cf. MR- *morior*.
mare sea: = **morî*, OIr. *muir*, Got. *marei* E. *mere marsh*, Lit. *mârés.*—
Sk. *mîras*, MḆ-, is unauthenticated.
†**margarita** pearl: †μαργαρίτης (Got. *marikreitus*; Pers. *merwārîd* Zenker 838 c):
hardly cf. Sk. *manjarî.*†
margō edge: MḆG- Got. *marka* E. *mark marches* †*marquis* †*marquee*,
cf. MROG- MIr. *mruig* boundary.
marîsca fig: ' big,' fr. *mās*.
†**marmor** (term. after *aequ-or*) marble: μάρμαρος, cf. μαρμαίρω shine,
Redupl. of MAR- Sk. *mârîcis* ray.
marra hoe :
†**marsūpium marsuppium marsippium** purse: μαρσύπιον, †μάρσῖπος :
kmarsp-, cf. κράσπεδον border of a cloak (in which the purse was
kept: so †κανδύς †μανδύη from *kmand-*, †κίνδος †μίνδαξ from *kmind-*):
Pers. (as μανδύη is).
mās male (E. E. *mallard marry*): MAS-:
†**massa** lump: μάζα cake, = **μάγ-ja* MAG- μάσσω knead (dialectic for
*μάζω).
†**mastrūca manstrūga** (Plaut. Poen. 1313 Goetz) sheepskin: Sardinian
(Isid. Orig. 19. 23. 5), i.e. prob. Phoen.
māter mother (E. *madrepore*): μήτηρ, OIr. *māthir*, Ags. *mōdor* (with *d*,
for *d*, from *fäder* father, see *pater*) E. (with *th*, for *d*, from the *-er*,
see *pater* and cf. Ags. *veder* = E. *weather*), Lit. *moterà* woman OSlav.
mater- mother, Arm. *mair*, Zd. *mātar-* Sk. *mātár-*.
māteria stuff (E. *Madeira*): ' ready for use,' MĀT- see *mātūrus*.
†**materis matara madaris** pike : Celtic (Hesych. s. v. μαδάρεις) :
mātertera aunt: = *māter* + Comparative-ending as in θηλυτέρη female.
matula pot :
mātūrus ripe, **mātūtīnus** early (E. *matins*): cf. OSlav. *matorŭ* old.
maxilla jaw:
mē mehe (Quint.) me: OIr. *mē* I, Zd. Sk. *mā* me, cf. ME μέ, Got. *mi-k*
E., OSlav. *mę*, Arm. *mekh* we.
†**meddīx mēdix** magistrate: Osc. *meddíss* μεδδειξ *metd(ix)* :
medeor heal: ' stand in the middle, stop the disease,' see *merus*.
mediastinus mediastrinus drudge: fr. **mediaster* formed fr. *medius* (as
surdaster fr. *surdus*, on anal. of Verbs in *-άζω* e.g. μητράζω take after
my mother), ' between childhood and manhood '.
†**medimnum** bushel: μέδιμνος, fr. sq.

meditor consider: μέδομαι think on, OIr. *mess* judgment: 'measure,' cf. praeced., μέτρον (for *μέδτρον, see *findō*) measure, Got. *mitan* to measure E. *mete meet* Adj.

meditullium middle : *medus* (see *merus*) + ?

medius middle (E. *mean* Subst. *mizen*-mast *moiety*): MEDH-J- μέσσος, Got. *midjis* E., OSlav. *mežda* μέσον, Arm. *mēj* μέσον, Zd. *maidhya* Sk. *mádhyas*, see *merus*.

medulla marrow: fr. *medus merus*, ' in the middle' of the bone.

mējō : = *mijō* *mig-jō* MĪGH- ὸ-μῖχέω, Ags. *micgan*, cf. MOIGH- Arm. *mēz* οὖρον, MINGH- *mingō*.

mel honey (E. *molasses*): *mell- *melv-* MÉDHU μέθυ wine, MIr. *mid* mead (E. *metheglin*), Ags. *medu* E., Lit. *medùs* honey OSlav. *medŭ*, Zd. *madhu* Sk. *mádhu* mead.

Not MEL- μέλι honey, MIr. *mil*, Got. *milith* E. *mildew*, Arm. *meλr*.

†**mēlēs maelēs** marten: dialectic for *mālēs* (Caper, Keil 7. 110) i.e. *mūdēs* *mazdēs* Ags. *meard* OHG. *marder* E. †*marten* (Lat. *martēs* in Martial 10. 37. 18 is a figment).

melior better : = *medior* fr. *merus*, 'moderate,' a λιτότης.

†**melos** song : μέλος song ('piece '), limb.

membrum limb: MEMS-BÓM OIr. *mīr* morsel (= *mēs-ro-*), cf. MEMS'- Got. *mimz* flesh, Pruss. *mensā* Lit. *mèsà* (dialectic for *mḗsà*, see *anscr*) OSlav. *męso*, MEM- see *memor*: also MĒMS-BÓ- μηρός thigh (= *μησρός), MĒMS- μῆνιγξ membrane (= *μῆνιγξ), Arm. *mis* flesh, Sk. *māmsám*.

meminī remember: Perf. of *menō*, MEN- μένος force, OIr. *menme* mind, OHG. *minna* remembrance E. †*minion*, Lit. *menù* I remember, Zd. Sk. *man-* think, cf. MṆ- Got. *muns* thought, OSlav. *mĭnēti* think, see *mens moneō*.

memor mindful: ' discriminating' (see *sciō*), MEM- see *membrum* (in MEMS- the *s* is a suffix, cf. *anscr mēnsis*).

menda defect: OIr. *mennair* spot (Stokes), Sk. *mindā* defect.

mendāx lying : ' defective,' fr. praeced., a λιτότης.

mendīcus beggar: fr. *menda*, cf. praeced.

mens mentis mind : MṆTÍ- Got. ga-*munds* memory Ags. *mynde* thought E. *mind*, Lit. isz-*mintìs* reason OSlav. pa-*mętĭ* memory, Sk. *matis* thought, see *meminī*.

mensa table (Got. *mēsa*) : ' flesh-board,' = *memsa*, see *membrum*.

mēnsis month : MĒ-N-S- Dor. μής Ion. μείς (μῆν from the oblique cases), OIr. *mis* Gen. *mī* Nom., OSlav. *mēsęcĭ*, Arm. *amis*, cf. MĒ-N-ES- Lit. *mĕnesis*, MĒ-N- Got. *mĕnōths* Ags. *mōnad* E. *month* (and the words for moon, μήνη, Got. *mĕna* Ags. *mōna* E., and the Lit. and OSlav. words), MĒ-S- Zd. *māonh-* Sk. *mās*, from MĒ- measure *mēta*.

mensus measuring : = *ment-tús*, MṆT- cf. *mens*, ' thinking over '.

†**menta** mint (E.) : *μένθα †μίνθα :

mentiō mention: 'thinking,' fr. *mens*.

mentior lie: 'devise,' fr. *mens*, cf. *com-mentum* fiction.

mēntula: = *mehentula*, *mehens* Part. of *mehō* MEIGH- cf. MĪGH-, see *mējo*.

mentum chin: MN̥TO- Got. *munths* mouth E.

meô go (Fr. *congé* leave): 'take my way,' fr. *meus* mine (cf. *suescō* fr. *suus* his).

†**mephitis** exhalation: *μεφῖτις*:

mercēs hire (E. *amerce mercy*): fr. *merx*.

merda dung: 'pungent,' SMERD- cf. SMR̥D- Lit. *smirdéti* to stink, see *mordeō*.

merenda lunch: 'portion,' fr. sq.

mereō earn (E. turm*eric*): fr. *meriō* (see *jaccō paveō*) pay, = *mediō* see *meditor*, 'measure out to'.

mergae pitchfork: fr. sq., 'dipping' into the corn.

mergō dip, **mergus** diver: MEDGV- Sk. *madgús* a water-fowl *majj-* (the final *j* = GV palatilised before original *e*) sink, cf. MODGV- Lit. *mazgóti* wash.

merīdiēs noon: formed from *merī-diē* Loc. of *merus + diēs*.

†**merops** bee-eater: *μέροψ*: formed from *μέροπες* men, 'humane' (genitores suos reconditos pascens Plin. 10. 99).

merula medula (Isid. Orig. 12. 7. 69) blackbird (E. *merlin*):

merus unadulterated: 'central, essential,' = *medus* MEDH- Μεθώνη a town, OIr. *medōn μέσον*, cf. MEDH-J- *medius*.

merx wares (E. *market*): MERKV- cf. MR̥KV- *μάρπτω* seize, Hesych. *βράψαι βράξαι* Inf.

-met self: Abl.-ending, cf. -SMĒT Sk. *-smāt* (see *tam*).

mēta moeta goal: 'measured point.' MĒ- *μῆτις* counsel ('measuring, estimating'), Got. *mēl* season E. *meal*, Lit. *miérà* measure OSlav. *měra*, Zd. Sk. *mā-* to measure.

†**metallum** mine (E. *medal mettle* black*mail*): †*μέταλλον*:

metō reap: MIr. *methel* reapers.

mētô measure: fr. *mēta*.

metus fear: METU- cf. MTU- *ἀτύζομαι* am dismayed.

mīca morsel: SMĪK- *σμῖκρός μῖκρός* little.

micō quiver: = *mucō* 'strike,' MÜK- Lit. *múszti* strike.

migrô remove: MEIGV- *ἀ-μείβω* change, OSlav. *miglivŭ* mobile.

mīles soldier:

milium millet (E.): MEL- cf. *μελίνη*: hardly 'honey-fruit' (mel frugum Plin. 22. 131), fr. *mel*, and *μελίνη* fr. *μέλι*.

mille mīle meile thousand (OIr. *mīle*; E. *mile*):

mīluus mīlvus kite: SMĪD- Ags. *smītan* smite E.?

†mīmus actor: †μῖμος:

†mina pound: †μνᾶ, Heb. *mānēh.*

minae threats (the sense 'battlements' is a figment): 'pressure' (cf. E. *threat* fr. Lat. *trūdō* push), MIN- Low-Lat. *mināre* drive (Ducange) Ital. *menare* (E. *mince²*), MIr. *menad* awl ('pressing'), Lit. *minù* I tread, from SMIN- σμινύη mattock.

mingō: MINGH- Lit. *mįzaů*, cf. MIGH- Zd. *miz-* Sk. *mih-*, see *mējō mēntula.*

†minium vermilion (E. *miniature*): Spanish (Propertius 2. 3. 11), cf. the river-name *Minius* (now *Minho*) in N. W. Spain.

minor less (E. *minstrel mischief mystery*-play): MIN- Got. *mins* E. †*mince,* OSlav. *mĭnij*, cf. MĪN- MIr. *mīn* little: 'pressed down,' fr. *minae.*

minuō diminish (E. *minnow minuet*): μινύθω: 'press down,' fr. *minae.*

minus smooth: MIN- cf. MĪN- MIr. *mīn*: 'pressed down,' see *minor.*

†mirmillō a gladiator: = *murmurulō fr. *murmurulus Dimin. of *murmurus, μορμύρος a fish (as his crest).

mīrus wonderful (E. *marvel mirage mirror*): = *mūsus 'dazzling,' MŪS- μύω shut the eyes.

misceō mix (E. *meddle medley* pell*mell*): MI(K)-SK- MIr. *mescaim* I mix, OHG. *miscan* mix E. E. *mash mess*, from MIK- Lit. su-*miszti* get mixt, Sk. *miçrás* mixt, cf. MIK-S- Sk. *miksh-* mix.—A word of the Ursprache, and so without compensatory lengthening of the -*i*-.

miser wretched (E. *miser*): MŪS- μύσος defilement.

mītis mild: = *mūtis 'quiet' fr. *mūtus.*

†mitra turban: †μίτρα, Phrygian (Aen. 9. 616-617).

mittō send (E. *mass² mess*-room *message*): = *smitō (cf. Fest. *cosmittere* committere):

mītulus mūtulus mussel (E. *niche*):

modus measure (OIr. *mod* mode ; E. *model modern mould* Vb.): MOD- cf. MED- *meditor.*

†moechus: μοιχός, fr. *μείχω = mingō.*

moenia walls:

mōlēs mass (E. *mole³*): μῶλος struggle?

molestus troublesome: 'crushing,' fr. *molō.*

mollis soft (E. *moil*): = *molvis, MOLV- Got. ga-*malvjan* crush E. *mellow.* —Not = *mold-vis MLD- Hesych. ἀβλαδέως sweetly, Sk. *mṛdús* soft, cf. MĮD- ἀ-μαλδύνω destroy, and MOLD- Got. ga-*malteins* dissolution E. *melt,* OSlav. *mladŭ* soft, Sk. *mard-* rub.

molō grind (E. *mill*): MOL- μύλη mill, Got. *malan* grind E. *meal mould,* Lit. *malù* I grind, Arm. *malem* I pound, cf. MEL- OIr. *melim* I grind, OSlav. *meljǫ*, Sk. *mar-* crush.

monēdula (for term. see *acr-ēdula*) daw: 'bird of omen,' fr. sq.

moneō warn (E. *mint money summon*): MON- Ags. *manian* exhort, cf. MEN- *meminī.*

monīle necklace: MON- μάννος (dialectic for *μόννος), OIr. *muin,* Ags. *mene,* OSlav. *monisto:* 'worn on the neck,' cf. OHG. *mana* mane E., Sk. *mányā* neck.

mōns mountain (E. E. marm*ot*): MŌNTÍ- cf. M̥NTÍ- Ags. *mund* protection E. *mound:* 'refuge'.

monstrum prodigy (E. *muster*): = *mond-trum* 'sign,' MONDH- OSlav. *mądrŭ* wise, cf. MENDH- μενθήρη thought, M̥NDH- μαθεῖν learn, Got. *mundōn* consider, MODH- Zd. *mad-* know (Spiegel).

mora delay (E. *demur*): MB̥- cf. MḖ- OIr. *marait* they stay, see *mōrus.*

morbus disease: MR̥-BHOS cf. MḖ-BHOS OIr. *marb* mortuum, fr. *morior* + -BHO- (see *acerbus*).

mordeō bite (E. *morsel muse* Vb. *muzzle*): SMR̥D- cf. SMERD- σμερδαλέος terrible, OHG. *smerzan* feel pain E. *smart* Vb., see *merda.*

morētum salad: fr. *moreō* I pound, cf. *morō* whence *mortārium.*

morior die (E. *murrain*): MB̥- μαραίνω destroy, Lit. *mirti* die, cf. MER- OSlav. *mrēti,* Arm. *meranim* I die, Zd. Sk. *mar-* die, and MOR- Ags. *mearian* weaken E. *mar moor* Vb. *marline* night*mare* †*moraine,* Lit. *marinti* cause to die.

mōrōsus peevish: 'stickling for etiquette,' fr. *mōs.*

mors death: MR̥TÍ- Lit. *mirtis* OSlav. *sŭ-mrŭtĭ,* Sk. *mr̥tis,* cf. MR̥T- Got. *maurthr* murder E., fr. *morior.*

mortārium mortar: see *morētum:*

†**mōrum** mulberry (E. *mul-berry murrey,* Lit. *mōras*): *μῶρον by-form of †μόρον:

†**mōrus** foolish: μωρός: MŌR- cf. MḖ- Sk. *mūrás,* and MR̥- *mora* (as E. *dull* fr. *dwell*), 'halting'.

mōs measure, custom (E. *demure*):

moveō move (E. *mob meeting*): MEV- MEU- ἀ-μενόμαι, surpass, cf. MŪ- Sk. *mū-* push.

mox soon: MOK-SÚ MIr. *mos,* Zd. *moshu,* cf. MOK-SÚ Sk. *makshū,* from MOK- OIr. *moch* early + a case-sign -SŬ.

mūcrō point: MŪK- cf. MUK- *micó.* Rather than MŌK- cf. MOK- Hesych. μόκρων sharp.

mūcus muccus mucus: MOUKV- Lit. *maūkti* let slide, cf. MUKV- ἀπο-μύσσω wipe the nose μύξα (= *μύκτja) phlegm (E. *match*), OIr. *mucc* pig, Zd. Sk. *muc-* release, from SMUKV- Hesych. σμυκτήρ nose σμύξων a fish (cf. sq.).

mūgilis mullet: 'slimy,' MOUGV- by-form of MOUKV-, praeced.

mūginor (sec. Nonius) murmur (E. cur*mudgeon miching*): fr. sq., cf. NUmbr. *mugatu* let him speak.

mūgiō bellow: MOUG- cf. MUG- μύζω groan, OHG. ir-*muccazan* mutter.

mulceō stroke, **mulcō** beat: MELK- Sk. *març-* touch.

mulgeō milk: MᴌG- OSlav. *mlŭzą* I milk, cf. MELG- ἀ-μέλγω, MIr. *melg* Subst., Got. *miluks* Subst. E., Lit. *mélžu* I milk.

mulier woman: 'giving suck,' MUD- μύζω suck, MIr. *muimme* nurse (= *mud-mia).

mūllus mullet (E.): cf. (with ŭ) μύλλος σμύλλα a fish.

mulsus honied: 'softened,' Part. of *mulceō.*

†**multa mulcta** fine: Osc. (Fest.):

multĭcia silks: = *multi-lĭcia,* 'of many threads'.

multus much: = *mulctus Part. of *mulgō swell, see *prōmulgō.*

mūlus mule (E. *mulatto*):

mundus Subst. enclosure, sky, world, equipment, Adj. equipt, neat: ᴍᴜɴᴅ- cf. MUD- MHG. *mutzen* adorn?

mūnis obliging, **mūnus** service: MOI-N- OIr. *māini* gifts, Got. ga-*mains* common E. *mean*[1] Adj., Lit. *maĩnas* exchange; from MOI-, see *mūtó.*

†**mūraena mūrēna** lamprey: μύραινα, SMŪR- σμύρος eel:

mūrex purple-fish: fr. *mūs* sea-mussel, as μύαξ purple-fish fr. μῦς seamussel.

muria brine: MUD- μύδος slime, cf. MOUD- Lit. *máudau* I bathe?

murmur roar (OHG. *murmurōn murmulōn,* Lit. *murmḗti* grumble): MORM- μορμ-ύρω boil, Sk. *marmaras* rustling.

†**murra**[1] **myrrha** myrrh: †μύρρα (also σμύρνα, see *smyrna*), Heb. *mōr.*

†**murra**[2] agate or porcelain: *μόρρα, †μόρρια Paus.: Pers. (from Parthia and Carmania, Plin. 37. 21).

mūrus moerus moiros wall:

mūs mouse (E. *marmot muscle mussel*): μῦς Hesych. σμῦς, Ags. *mūs* E., OSlav. *myst,* Arm. *mukn,* Sk. *mūsh:* 'thievish,' cf. Sk. *mush-* steal?

musca fly (E. *mosquito musket*): MUS- μυῖα (= *μύσ-ja), Lit. *musė,* cf. OSlav. *muha:* 'greedy,' Sk. *mush-* steal, see praeced.

mūscus moss: MŪS- Ags. *mōs* E. E. *mushroom,* Lit. *mūsas* mould, cf. MUS- OSlav. *mŭhŭ* moss.

†**mussô** mutter: μύζω, see *mūgiō.*

mustāceum bride-cake: 'baked on bay-leaves' Plin. 15. 127, fr. *mustāx* bay Plin., from *mustus.*

mŭstēla mŭstella weasel:

mustus fresh (E. *moist mustard*):

mutilus maimed: MUT- *muticus* docked, Theocr. μίτυλος hornless (Dissim. for *μύτυλος).

mūtiō muttiō mutter (E. *motto*): formed fr. †*muttum* a grunt (Lucil.), = *mūtum, μῦθος word.

mūtô change (E. *mews moult*), **mūtuus** lent: MOI-T- Sicil. μοῖτος thanks, Got. *maithms* gift, Lett. *meetōt* to exchange; from MOI-, see *mūnus.*

mūtō muttō Subst.: ᴍᴏɪᴛ-, cf. Lucil. ap. Non. p. 15 Müller *Moetīnus,* MHG. *meidem* stallion. (Mart.'s *mŭtoniatus* a popular corruption.)

mūtus dumb : MŪT- OIr. *mōeth* tender, cf. MUT- Hesych. μύτης μυττός dumb : 'subdued,' cf. *mutilus*, and see *mītis*.

†**myoparō** corsair : μυοπάρων, fr. μῦς see *mūs* + παρών a light ship, 'mouse (i.e. thief) of Paros'.

†**myrica** tamarisk : †μυρίκη = *τμυρίκη TMOR- cf. †*tamarīx* :

†**myrtus** myrtle : †μύρτος, cf. Pers. *mūrd* Zenker 892 a.

†**nablium naulium** harp : *νάβλιον *ναύλιον fr. †νάβλα ναῦλα, Heb. *nebhel* flute.

naevus mole :

nam for, **-nam** Enclitic : =*nām *nā-me (see *tam*), from NO-, see -ne -num.

nanciscor obtain : 'carry off,' NENK- ἐ-νεγκεῖν bring, cf. NEK- MIr. cōemnacar potui, Lit. *nèszti* carry OSlav. *nesti*, Zd. Sk. *naç-* attain.

†**nānus** dwarf : νᾶνος : 'father,' a euphemism, NĀN- cf. NAN- W. *nain* grandmother, Sk. *nanā* mother.

†**narcissus** daffodil : νάρκισσος : hardly fr. νάρκη numbness Plin. 21. 128, quasi 'narcotic'.

†**nardus** nard : †νάρδος, Heb. *nerd*.

nāris nostril : NĀS- Lit. *nósis*, Zd. *nāonha* Sk. *nãs-*, cf. NAS- Ags. *nasu* E.. OSlav. *nosŭ*, Sk. *nãs-*.

narrō nārō gnarrō relate : = *gnārô, fr. *gnārus*.

nāscor am born : = *gnā-scor cf. *gnā-tus* Part., GN̄-, see *genus*.

nassa naxa weel :

nāsus nassus nose : dialectic for *nārus, see *nāris*.

natis (E. *aitch*-bone) : = *notis NOT- cf. NŌT- νῶτον back ?

†**nauclērus** skipper : ναύ-κληρος : 'whose ship is his estate,' κλῆρος estate.

naucum trifle :

†**nausea** seasickness (E. *noise*) : *ναυσία Ion. form of ναυτία, fr. ναύτης sailor, sq.

nāvis ship (MHG. *nâwe*, E. *nave* of a church) : NĀV- NĀU- ναῦς, OIr. *nau*, ONor. *nōr*, Arm. *nav*, OPers. *nāvi* Sk. *nāús*.

nāvus gnāvus active : GN̄-vós, cf. GN- see *ingens*: so ONor. *knâr* vigorous fr. *knā* know.

ne- not : OIr. *ni*, Got. *ni* E. E. *nay no naught*, Lit. OSlav. *ne*, Zd. *na* Sk. *nd*, cf. *nē*[1].

-ne Enclitic (in *dēnique pōne superne*) : see -nam -num, cf. *nē*[2].

nē[1] not : OIr. *nī*, Sk. *nă* : = sq. (see *haud*) ?

nē[2] **nae** truly : νή, cf. *vai*.

nebula mist : νεφέλη cloud, W. *nifwl* mist, OHG. *nebul*; from NEBH-νέφος cloud, W. *nef* sky, OSlav. *nebo*, Sk. *nábhas* mist, cf. ṆBH- Arm. *amb* cloud.

nebulō worthless fellow : fr. praeced., 'Child of the Mist,' obscure skulking.

ne-cesse necessary: 'infallible,' fr. *ne-* + *cassus.*
necô kill: NEK- *νέκυς* corpse, Zd. *naç-* disappear Sk. *naç-* be lost, cf. ṆK-
OIr. *ēc* death.
†**nectar** nectar: †*νέκταρ* :
nectō tie (Hesych. *νέξας* bedding) : NEGH- Zd. *naz-* Sk. *nah-.*
nē-cubī lest anywhere: *nē* + **quobī cubē* (Probi Appendix, Keil 4. 199),
Umbr. *pufe* where, fr. *quis*[2] + a case-sign as in *ibī ubī.*
neglegō neglect (for the latter element see *dīligō*) : **ne-ge* from *ne-* + GE
γέ at least, Got. mi-*k* me, see *negōtium.*
negô deny (E. E. *renegade runagate*) : from **nege,* praeced.
negōtium business : **nege* (see *negligō*) + *ōtium.*
nēmō no one : *ne-* + *hemō* (see *homo*).
nempe certainly : NM̩- cf. *ʔ-va* where, see *nam,* + *-pe.*
nemus grove : *νέμος,* Gaul. *νεμητον* temple OIr. *'nemed* : 'portion' of
ground, fr. *νέμω* distribute.
†**nēnia** naenia dirge : **νηνία,* †*νηνίᾱτον* Hipponax 129 Bergk, Phrygian
(Pollux 4. 79).
neō spin : NĒ- *νέω,* Got. *nēthla* needle E., OHG. *nāwan* sew.
Not add SNĒ- Zd. *çnā-* stretch, cf. SNŌ- OIr. *snāthe* thread, Got. *snōrjō*
basket, for SN- would remain in Gothic.
†**nepa** crab, scorpion : African (Fest.).
nepōs grandson (E. *nephew*) : NEPŌT- Zd. *napāt-* Sk. *nápāt-,* cf. NEPOT-
νέποδες children Odyss. 4. 404 (with *δ* from **νήποδες* footless), OIr.
niath nephew's, Zd. *napat-* grandson, see sq. So *nepōs* spendthrift,
opposite of *patruus* uncle, the model of severity : not Etrusc. (as
Fest.).
neptis granddaughter (E. *niece*) : NEPTÍ- *ἀ-νεψιός* cousin (from **νέψα* for
*νέπτja), Got. *ni(f)thjis* kinsman, OSlav. *ne(p)tij* nephew, Zd. *napti-*
relationship Sk. *naptī* daughter, cf. NEPT- OIr. *necht,* OHG. *nift,* and
NEP- Ags. *nefa* nephew, see praeced.
nēquam worthless : *nē* + *-quam* 'anyhow' fr. *quis*[2], 'naughty' : orig.
Adv., cf. *per-quam* extremely.
nervus sinew : NERV- *νεῦρον,* cf. NORV- Ags. *nearu* narrow E.
('bound').
nī unless : = **ne-ī, ne-* + -Ī Demonstr. see *hīc;* 'not,' cf. *nī-mīrum* ('not
wonderful') certainly, see *nihilum.*
nictô wink : GNĪGV- cf. *cōnīveō* :
nidor vapor :
not cf. *κνίση* fat, smell of fat, quasi **χνίθ-jη* from GHNĪDH-.
nīdus nest : NIZDÓS MIr. *net,* Ags. *nest* E., Arm. *nist* situation, Sk. *nīḍás*
nest.
Hardly fr. Sk. *nī-* down + ZD- cf. SED- *sedeō.*
niger black : NEGRO-, Fest. *negritu* grief ('gloom') :

nihilum nīlum nihil nīl nothing: *nī* not, see *nī*, + Adj.-ending -ŪLO-.— Ovid has *nihil* through a popular connection with *hilum.*

nimbus storm : NŪMBH- Νύμφη Nymph ('spirit'), cf. NŪBH- *nūbēs.*

nimis exceedingly, too much (cf. the two senses of ἄγαν) : = **numesum* Acc. of **numesus numerus* (thus *nimis altum* = a quantity high, as Fr. *trop haut* = a crowd high, Lat. *turbam altum*).

ninguit ningit it snows: SNINGHV- Lit. *sninga*, cf. SNIGHV- Pacuv. *nivit*, see *nix.*

nisī nesei (E. Schneider 95. 5) unless: = Fest. *nesī* without, *ne-* + *sī.*

nītēdula (for term. see *acr-ēdula*) **nītēla nītella** dormouse :

niteō shine (E. *neat*) : = **gneteō* 'am polished, rubbed,' GVNET- Ags. *cnedan* knead E., OSlav. *gnetǫ* I press, see *nota.*

nītor lean, strain: = **gnivitor* GNĪGV-, cf. Fest. *gnīxus* Part. (which = **gnīct-tus* as *nīsus* = **gnīt-tus*) :

nix snow: SNIGHV- νίφα Acc., OIr. *snechti* Plur., W. *nyf*, Zd. *çnizh-* to snow, cf. SNOIGHV- Got. *snaivs* snow E., Lit. *snaigýti* to snow OSlav. *sněgŭ* snow.

nô swim (E. *alley andiron*): SNĀ- νάω flow, MIr. *snāim* I swim, Zd. *çnā-* wash Sk. *snā-.*

By-form SNEU- νέ(F)ω swim, MIr. *snūad* river, cf. SNU- Zd. *çnu-* flow Sk. *snu-* distil.

noceō hurt (E. *nuisance*) : NOK- cf. NEK- *necô.*

nōdus knot: NOZDOS, OHG. *nestila* band.

nōmen -gnōmen name (E. *noun renown*; but not *name*): OSlav. *znamę* sign, from GNO- *nôscô.*

nōmenclātor nōmenculātor usher: fr. **nōmenculô* call by name, praeced. + *calô.*

nōn not: = *nonne* (used as Interrog.) i. e. **nō-ne*, from *nō-* by-form (see *dōdrans*) of *nē*, + *-ne.*

Not connected with *noenum*, which = *nē* + *oinom ūnum.*

nōnus 9th : = **novin-us* from **noven*, see *novem.*

nōrma square : = **nōnma* fr. *nōna* ninth, 'shaped like L,' the 9th letter in the Etruscan (*a c e f z h θ i l*) and Faliscan (*a c d e f z h i l*) alphabets; cf. Rev. 22. 13 ἐγὼ τὸ ἄλφα καὶ τὸ ὦ, πρῶτος καὶ ἔσχατος.

nōs we: NŌ- νώ Dual, OSlav. *na* Acc. Dual, Zd. *nāo* Acc. Plur. (Spiegel), cf. NĀU Sk. *nāu* Acc. Dual, NI OIr. *ni* Acc. Plur.

nōscō gnōscō recognise: GNO- γιγνώσκω, OIr. *gnāth* accustomed, OSlav. *znati* know, Zd. *zhnā-* (Spiegel) Sk. *jnā-*, cf. GNĒ- Ags. *cnāvan* recognise E. *know*; and GNA- *agnitus*, GN- *ingens*, GN̄- *nāvus.*

nōster our: NOS, Sk. *nas* us, cf. NS ἄμμες we (= **ns-mes*), Got. *uns* us E. E. *our*, Sk. *as-mān*, see *nōs.*

nota mark: 'rubbing,' GVNOT- cf. GVNET- *niteō.*

†**nothus** spurious: νόθος: 'obscure,' see *umbra.*

†notus south wind : νότος :

novem 9 (E. *noon*) : NEVM (-*m* for -*n* from the ordinal NÉVM-MOS, see *decem*) for NEVN (see *nõnus*) *ἐν-νέα* ('up to 9,' *ἐν* Aeol. and Dor. for *ἐς*), OIr. *nõi* n-, Got. *niun* E., Pruss. *newints* 9th Lit. *dewyni* 9 OSlav. *devęti* (both with *de*- from the words for 10), Arm. *inn* (= *e-nen*), Zd. *navan*- Sk. *náva* : 'the new number' after 2 quaternions, fr. *novus* ?

noverca stepmother : = *nov-ri-ca* fr. sq. with double Adj.-ending, cf. *vit-ri-cus.*

novus new : NÉVOS *νέ(F)ος*, OIr. *nūe*, Lit. *nawas* OSlav. *novŭ*, Zd. *nava* Sk. *návas*, cf. NEV-JOS Ags. *neove* E., NEV-I- Got. *niujis*, NEVO-R- Arm. *nor.*

nox night : NOKVT- *νύξ*, MIr. *nocht*, Got. *nahts* E., Zd. *nakhturu* nocturnal, cf. NOKVTÍ- *noctium* Gen. Plur., Lit. *naktis* night OSlav. *noštĭ*, Sk. *náktis.*

noxa imprisonment, injury : NOGH- cf. NEGH- *nectō*, 'bonds'.

nūbēs cloud : NŪBH- cf. NŪMBH- *nimbus.*

nūbō marry : 'cover my face,' cf. *obnūbō* veil, NŪBH- cf. NUMBH- *νύμφη* bride.

nūdius ago : NŪ *νῦν* now, Got. *nū* E., OSlav. *ny*-nē, Zd. *nŭ* Sk. *nú*, cf. NU Lit. *nù*, Sk. *nú* ; + DIŪ- by-form (see *diurnus*) of DIĒ- *diēs.*

nūdus naked : = *nŏdus* *nŏvi-dus* NŌGV- Lit. *nŭgas*, cf. NÓGVO-TO- MIr. *nocht*, Got. *naqaths* E., NOGV-NÓ- Zd. *maghna* (*m*- a mistake for *n*-) Sk. *nagnás.*

nūgae nōgae naugae trifles : NAUG- :

num whether : = *nu-me* (see *ta-m*) from NU OIr. *nu* Verbal-Particle, see *nūdius*, + a case-ending.

-num now (in *etiam-num*) : cf. *νῦν* (in *τοίνυν*), praeced.

numella tether : 'limit,' = *numerula* Adj. Fem. fr. sq.

numerus number (E.) : = *numesus* (cf. *Numisius* for *Numerius*) :

nūmmus nūmus coin (Sicil. *νοῦμμος*) : = *nūmsus* (cf. Osc. *Niumsieis* = Lat. *Numerii* Gen.), NŪMS- cf. NUMES- praeced. : hardly add NOMS- MIr. *nōs* custom.

nunc now : = *num-ce*, *num* 'now' (see -*num*) + -*ce.*

nūncupō name : = *nōm(e)n-cupō* (cf. *oc-cupō*) fr. *nōmen + capiō.*

nūndinum nōndinum noundinum 8th day : fr. *novem* + DÍN- day, OIr. trē-*denus* 9 days, OSlav. *dĭnĭ* day, Sk. *dínam*, cf. DĪN- Got. sin-*teins* daily (see *semper*).

nūntius nountios messenger : = *noventios* fr. *novens* Part. of *noveō* 'am new,' fr. *novus.*

nūper lately, nūperus fresh : = *novi-perus* fr. *novus + parō.*

nurus daughter-in-law : SNUS- *νυ(σ)ός*, OHG. *snur*, OSlav. *snŭha*, Arm. *nu*, Sk. *snushā.*

nūtō nod : = *neu-tō*, *νεύω.*

nūtriō nourish (E. E. *nurse*) : = *nōtriō*, Quint. 1. 4. 16 *nōtrix* = *nūtrix* nurse : fr. *nōt-rus Adj., NŌD- cf. NĒD- *νήδυμος* refreshing.

nux nut (E. *newel*; but not *nut*) : NUK- :

†**nympha** bride : *νύμφη*, see *nūbō*.

ō oh Interj. : *ὤ*, Got. *ō*, OSlav. *o*.

ob around (sec. Fest. and Serv.), before : Osc. *op* apud : = *όpi, *ὸπι-σθεν* behind, Lit. *api-* around, Zd. *aipi* Sk. *ápi* by.

†**obba ubba obua** (i.e. *obva*) cup for libation to the dead : cf. Etrusc. *uflea* (Bugge B. B. 10. 111).

ob-līquus slanting : LEIKV- cf. LIKV- *licinus* (Serv. Geo. 3. 55) with upturned horns, LINKV- Lit. *linkiu* I bend.

ob-līviscor forget : 'smooth down, repress,' LEIV- see *lēvis līveō*.

oboediō obēdiō obey (E.) : = *ob-ūdiō* from *audiō*.

†**obrussa** assay : *ὸβρύζη fr. †*ὸβρυζος* pure (of gold).

obscēnus obscaenus obscoenus ominous :

ob-scūrus dark : SKVŪ- Ags. *scūa* shade ONor. *skȳ* cloud E. *sky*, cf. SKVU Zd. *çku-* be blind Sk. *sku-* cover.

obs-olescō decay : *obs-* fr. *ob* (see *abs*), and see *ad-olescō* [2].

†**obsōnō** (quasi fr. *ob*) cater : *ὸψωνέω*, fr. *ὄψον* meat, *ἕψω* boil, *ἕπω* prepare see *sequor*, + *ὠνέομαι* buy, see *vēnum*.

ob-tūrō stop up : fr. *taurus*, 'put a bull (i.e. a heavy weight, stopper) on,' cf. *βοῦς ἐπὶ γλώσσῃ* Aesch. Agam. 36.

occō harrow : = *ŏcŏ ŌKV- cf. OKV'- W. *og* Subst., MHG. *ege*, Lit. *akéti* Vb.

oc-culō hide : *celō, see *cēlō*.

†**ōcimum** basil : *ὤκιμον* :

ōcior swifter : ŌK- *ὠκύς* swift, OW. *di-auc* slow Zeuss[2] 894 a, Zd. *āçus* swift Sk. *āçús*; cf. OK- Zd. Sk. *aç-* attain.

ocrea greave : foreign ?

octāvus 8th : = *octŏv-os from OKTŌU Got. *ahtau* 8, Sk. *ashtā́u*, by-form of *octō*.

octingentī 800 : for *octō-centī, sq. + *centum*; with *-in-* from *septingentī* (= *septem-centī) 700, and *-g-* from *vīgintī*, see *quadringentī*.

octō 8 : *ὀκτώ*, OIr. *ocht*, Ags. *eahta* E., Lit. *asztù-*nì OSlav. *os(t)-*mì, Arm. *uth*, Zd. *asta* Sk. *ashtā́*, see *octāvus*.

oculus eye (E. *antler inveigle*) : OKV- *ὄσσε* Dual (= *ŏκ-je) *ὄμμα* (= *ὐπ-μα), Lit. *akis* OSlav. *oko*, Arm. *akn*, Zd. *ak-* see (Spiegel).

odium hatred (E. *annoy noisome*) : OD- *ὀδύσσομαι* am angry *ἰπ-όδ-ρα* fiercely, Ags. *atol* horrible, Arm. *ateam* I hate.

odor smell : OD- *ὀδμή*, Arm. *hot*, cf. ŌD- Lit. *ìdžiu* I smell.

†**oestrus** gadfly : *οἶστρος* :

†**oesypum** unwashed wool : *οἴσυπον cf. †*οἰσύπη* :

offa ball : = *ŏfa*, cf. *ŏfella* :

officīna workshop, **officium** observance : fr. *ob* around + *faciō*, 'complete doing'.

ōhē Interj. : cf. *ō* + *hei*.

†**oiei** Interj. : *oiĕî* cf. *oioî*.

oleō smell : OD- *odor*.

ōlim at that time : Abl. (see *inde*) of *ŏlo*, see *ille*.

†**olīvum** oil (whence *olēvum oleum*, and from this W. *olew*, Got. *alev* E., Lit. *aliējus* OSlav. *olēj*) : ἕλαι(ϝ)ον (unaccented *ai* becoming *ī* as in *Achīvī* from Ἀχαι(ϝ)οί), with *o-* quasi from *olīvus* 'fragrant' Adj. of *oleō*.

ōlla aula pot (E. *olio*) : = *aux-la*, cf. *auxilla* Fest. :

†**olor** swan :

†**omāsum** tripe : Gaulish (Gloss. Philox.) :

ōmen ōsmen (Varr. L. L. 6. 76) sign : = *aux-men* 'authorisation,' from *aux-* see *auxilium*, and cf. the meaning of *augur*.

ōmentum adipose membrane : = *obs-mentnm* (see *ā-mentum*), from obs- ob 'around'.

omittō give up : = *ŏmittŏ* (*ŏ-* as in Plaut. Trin. 712 nihil ego in ŏculto) *obs-mittŏ*.

omnis all (E. *bus*) : = *op-nis* 'comprehensive' (see *cunctus*), fr. *ob* 'around'.

onus honus burden :

†**onyx** onyx : †ŏνυξ, Egyptian, cf. Coptic *ankoki* ring-finger (Peyron).

op-ācus (for term. cf. *mer-ācus*) shady : 'covered,' fr. *ob* 'around'.

op-eriō cover : *ob* 'around' + ER-, see *aperiō*.

ōpīliō (Plaut. Asin. 540) **ūpīljō** (Verg. Buc. 10. 19) shepherd :

opīmus rich : 'well covered,' fr. *ob* 'around' + Adj.-ending (cf. *patrimus*, prob. with -*ī*-).

opīnor think : 'put before myself,' fr. *opīnus* (cf. *nec-opīnus*) Adj. of *ob* 'before' (as *supīnus* of *sub*).

oportet is necessary : 'rises up,' fr. *op-ortum* Part. Neut. of *op-orior ob-orior* spring up.

op-perior wait : see *ex-perior*.

op-pidō exceedingly : 'fitly,' fr. *ob* + PED- seize, hold, see *ex-pediō*, cf. ἕμ-πεδος fixt, and POD- Ags. *fätian* seize E. *fit vat*.

op-pidum town : 'hold, stronghold,' fr. praeced., cf. Sk. *pat-tanam*.

op-port-ūnus fit : 'conducive,' fr. *portŏ* (as σύμφορος conducive fr. φέρω carry).

ops power : 'circumstance,' fr. *ob* 'around' ?

optimus opitumus best : 'complete, perfect,' fr. *ob* (i.e. *opi*) 'around'.

optŏ choose : 'put before myself,' fr. *optum* Part. fr. *ob* before.

opus work (E. *inure manœuvre manure, use* (Subst.) in law): ὄπ- Sk. *ápas*, cf. ὄπ- OHG. *uoba* festival, Sk. *ápas* a religious work.

ōra extremity, rope-end, coast (E. *ullage*):

orbis circle:

orbus bereft: ORBH- ὀρφανός, MIr. *orbe* inheritance (of an orphan), Got. *arbi*, Arm. *orb* orphan.

    Hardly add Sk. *arbhás* small.

ōrca jar:

†**orchas** an olive: ὀρχάς (Nicander): fr. ὄρχις testis, from its shape.

ordō row (OIr. *ordd* order):

orior rise: R- αἴρω raise, Arm. y-*ar*-nem I rise, *cf.* ER- Zd. *ar-* go Sk. *ar-* raise, and OR- ὄρνῦμι stir.

ōrnô furnish: *ōs-nô* Varr. L. L. 6. 76, = *ōsi-nô*:

ornus mountain-ash:

    not Sk. *áṛṇas* stream, teak.†

†**oryx** gazelle: †ὄρυξ ὄρυς, Semitic, Assyrian t-*urahu* antelope.

†**oryza** rice: †ὔ-ρυζα, cf. †ὀ-ριυὄής Adj., VRIND- VRĪD-, OPers., from Sk. *vrīhís* (as OPers. *d* = Zd. *z* = Sk. *h*).

os bone (E. *osprey*): = *ost* (*ossis* &c. formed from Nom. *os* on anal. of *assis* &c. from *ās*) OST- ὀστέον, Zd. *açta* Sk. *asthán-*: 'refuse, not eaten,' fr. Sk. *as-* throw (cf. E. *pluck*, 'heart, liver, and lights of an animal, as *plucked* out after killing' Skeat)?

ōs mouth: = *aus*, cf. Plaut. *ausculum* Dimin. : 'orifice,' see *auris*.

ōstium austium door (E. *usher*): 'opening,' AUS-T- OSlav. *usta* mouth, Sk. *ôshṭhas* lip, fr. praeced.

†**ostreum** sea-snail (E. *oyster*): ὄστρεον oyster, purple made from the sea-snail, OSTR- cf. ὄστρακον shell, potsherd.

†**ostrum austrum** (Priscian, on anal. of *plaustrum*) purple: = *ostrūm* *ὀστροῦν* (cf. for the termination *hēdychrum* = ἡδύχρουν and see *remulcum*) contracted form of ὄστρεον, praeced.

ōtium rest: AUT- Got. *auths* deserted Ags. *cādc* empty, easy OE. *eath* easy (but not E. *easy*).

†**ovis** sheep: Osc. (the Rom. form would be *avis*), ὄVI- ὄ(F)ις, OIr. *ói*, Lit. *avis* OSlav. *ovĭca*, Sk. *ávis*, cf. Got. *avēthi* flock Ags. *eāvu* ewe E.

ovô exult: = *evô* EV- EU- εὐάζω shout εὐαί εὐοῖ Interj.

ōvum egg: Ō-VOM ὠ(F)όν cf. Ō-V-EOM ὤ(F)εον ὤβεον; also ŌI- ᾤον φόν, OSlav. *aje*.

paciscor agree: PEK- Zd. *paç-* bind, see *pecū*, cf. POK- Got. *fahan* seize *faginôn* rejoice *fagrs* fit E. *fain fair* Adj. *fadge*, and PŌK- Sk. *pâças* knot.

†**paeān** hymn: †παιάν, see *paēon*.

†**paedicô**: fr. *paed-īcus* (formed after *am-īca*) Adj. of *παες*, παῖς boy.

paedor pēdor filth :

†**paelex pēlex pellex** (quasi fr. *pelliciō* allure) : *ᵖηλαξ Ion. form of Dor. πάλλαξ boy, cf. προ-πηλακ-ίζω abuse.

paene pēne poene nearly : 'within a little,' *paenus* little, see *pēnūria* : **paenitet poenitet** grieves : fr. praeced., 'does not satisfy, seems too little'.

†**paenula pēnula** cloak : †φαινόλης :

†**paeōn** a metrical foot : †παιών, see *paeān*.

paetus pētus blink-eyed :

pāgina page ('joined' to the other pages : E. *page*³), **pāgus** district ('station' : E. *peasant*) : PĀG- πήγνῡμι fix, cf. PAG- Ags. *fäc* interval *feccan* fetch E., and PANG- *pangō*.

pāla spade (E. *paletic pell*mell) : hardly = *pas-la* fr. *pastinum* dibble, on account of the difference of meaning.

palam openly : 'in the hand,' = *palā-m* *palā-me* (for the term. see *tam*) from *pala* 'hand,' PĻ-, see *palma*¹. .

palātum vault, palate :

palea chaff (E. *pallet*) : PEL'- Lit. *pelat*, Sk. *palāvas*.

palear dewlap : fr. *palea* wattles of a cock, as resembling short straws, praeced.

†**paliūrus** Christ's-thorn : παλίουρος :

palla robe (E. *pall* tar*paulin*) :

palleō am pale (E. *pale* Adj. *pall* Vb. *appal*) : dialectic for *palveō* fr. *palvus* Adj., Ags. *fealu* yellow E. *fallow*, Lit. *palwas* OSlav. *plavŭ* white.

pallium Greek cloak :

palma¹ palm of hand : PĻ-MĀ OIr. *lām* hand, cf. PĻ-MĀ παλάμη palm of hand, Ags. *folmc* E. *fumble* : from PĻ-, cf. PŌL- Sk. *pāṇís*.

†**palma**² palm-tree : Heb. †*tamar* (E. *tamar*-ind).—With *p* for *t*, cf. *pāvō* ; *lm* for *m*, cf. σαλαμάνδρα salamander Pers. *semender* Zenker 519 a, Italian *calamandrea* germander from χαμαί-δρυς, and see *balsamum*.

pālor wander :

palpô stroke : dialectic for *palquô* PĻKV- OSlav. *plakati* mourn ('strike' the breast).

palūdāmentum general's cloak : fr. *palūdô* Vb. cloak :

palumbēs ringdove :

palūs marsh :

pālus stake (E. *pale* Subst. *pole*) : = *pax-lus* cf. *paxillus* peg, PAG-S- cf. *pangô*.

pampinus vinebranch : Lit. *pampti* swell.

pandō spread (E. *spawn*) : not = *pat-nô* fr. *pateō*.

pandus curved: 'hanging by the two ends,' = *pendós* fr. *pendeō*? Hardly cf. ONor. *fetta* bend back.

pangō fix: PANG- cf. PĀG- *pāgina.*

pānicula tuft: 'meshed,' Dimin. of *pāna*, πήνη thread on the bobbin, see *pannus.*

pānicum panic-grass: 'swelling,' fr. *pānus* tumor, ear of panic-grass Plin. 18. 54, = *pannus*, 'meshed'.

Not fr. sq., cf. Plin. 18. 54 panis . . . e panico rarus.

pānis bread (E. *appanage company pannier pantry*): fr. *pānus*, Messapian πάνός Athenaeus 111 c : = *pas-nus* fr. *pastillus*?

pannus cloth (E. *pane panel ραωn[1] penny*): = *pānus* see *pānicum*, πῆνος thread on the bobbin, PAN- cf. PAN- Got. *fana* cloth E. †gon-*fanon vane fond fun*, OSlav. *ponjava.*

†**pantex** paunch (E., NHG. *panzer* coat of mail):

†**panthēra** panther: †πάνθηρ:
hardly cf. Sk. *puṇḍárīkas* a proper name, tiger.†

†**papae** Interj.: παπαί, cf. πόποι.

†**pāpās** tutor: πάπας πάππας father, onomatop., see *pappus*, cf. Late— Lat. *papa* bishop (E. *pope*), E. *papa.*

papāver poppy (E.): fr. *papó* swell (for term. see *cadāver*), *papula*, 'with globular capsules'.

pāpiliō (for term. cf. *pūmiliō* fr. *pūmilus* dwarf) butterfly (E. *pavilion*): fr. *pāpulus *pappulus* Dimin. of *pappus* grandfather (cf. *lūc-avus* stag-beetle, 'grandfather of the grove,' Plin. 11. 97, τέττιξ grasshopper fr. τέττα father, and Eng. 'daddy longlegs').

pappô pāpô eat: fr. *pāpa* food Varro (E. *pap*[1] *pamper*), onomatop.

pappus thistledown: πάππος: 'greybeard,' πάππος grandfather, see *pāpās.*

papula pimple (E. E. *pebble*): PAP- cf. PAMP- *pampinus*, 'swelling'.

†**papȳrus** papyrus (E. *paper*): †πάπῡρος, Egyptian (as growing in Egypt).

pār equal (E. *apparel pair peer* um*pire*): *pari-* fr. *pars*, 'sharing'.

parcus sparing: cf. SPAR- Ags. *spär* E. *spare*, see *parum parvus.*

†**pardus** panther: †πάρδος: cf. Sk. *pŕdākus* snake, panther†?

pāreō parreō obey: 'seem, appear (cf. *up-pāreō*), offer oneself,' = *parseō*, NUmbr. *parsest* will be seemly, PĔ-S- πορσαίνω offer, cf. PĔ- *parō.*

pariēs wall (E. *pellitory*[1]): 'boundary,' cf. πεῖραρ πέρας end.

pariō bring forth: PER'- Lit. *peréti* to brood, cf. POR- πόρις calf, Ags. *fear* ox E. hei*fer*, and PĔ- *parō.*

†**parma palma** target: Polyb. †πάρμη *πάλμη, Thracian (Fest. s. v. *Thraeces*).

parô provide (E. *parachute parade parasol pare parry* ram*part*): PĔ- πορεῖν to offer.

parra a bird: = *parsa*, 'companion,' sq.

parri-cīda pāri-cīda murderer : fr. **parrus *parsus* companion, 'offering himself,' see *pāreō,* + *caedō.*

pars part (E. E. *parcel parse*) : *par-ti-* fr. *parō,* 'what one gets'.

parum but little : Neut. of **parus* Adj., cf. sq.

parvus small : παῦρος (= **πᾰρ-ϝος*) : cf. SPAR-, see *parcus.*

†**pasceolus** purse : **φασκίολος* by-form of φάσκωλος (as φασίολος of φάσηλος), see *fascis.*

pā-scō feed (E. *pastern pester*) : PĀ- Zd. Sk. *pā-* protect.

passer sparrow :

passus step (E. *pace pass*) : = **pat-tus,* PAT- πάτος path, Zd. *pathan* Sk. *páth-,* cf. PĀT- MIr. *āth* ford.

pastillus loaf :

pāstor paastor shepherd : PĀS- fr. *pā-scō* + *s.*

†**patagīum** gold edging : †**παταγεῖον* :

pateō am open (E. *pail*) : PET'- πετάννῦμι stretch, OW. *etem* flounce Zeuss[2] 148 b, cf. POT- Ags. *fäðm* fathom E., Zd. *pathana* broad.

pater father (E. *patois pattern*) : PATĒR PATR- πατήρ Nom. πατρός Gen., OIr. *athir,* Got. *fadar* E., Arm. *hair,* Zd. *patar-* *pitar-* Sk. *pitár-.*

patina dish (πατάνη ; E. *pan*) : fr. *pateō,* as πέταχνον saucer fr. πετάννῦμι.

patior suffer : 'lie open to,' fr. *pateō.*

patrô bring to pass : fr. *pater,* 'act as father,' i.e., as head of a legation, *pater patratus* ('the father who acts as such,' from **patror* Middle).

paucus few : PAU- PAV- Got. *favai* E.

paulus paullus little : = **paux-lus,* cf. *pauxillus.*

pauper poor (E.) : PAU- (see *paucus*) + *parō,* 'provided with little'.

†**pausa** stop (with term. on anal. of *causa*) : παῦσις, fr. παύω cause to stop.

pauxillus pausillus little :
hardly fr. *paucus.*

paveō am afraid : 'am struck' (cf. ἐξεπλάγην fr. πλήσσω strike), fr. sq. (see *jaceō*), cf. *pavitō* shake with ague.

paviō beat (E. *pave*) : = **poviō,* Fest. *puviō* (dialectic), POV- πο(ϝ)ίη grass (cf. E. *hay* fr. *hew*), Lit. *piauti* cut, bite, Sk. *paviram* spear.

In παίω strike, Boeotian πήω (cf. Boeotian κή for καί), the *ai* is original, not for *avi.*

†**pāvō** peacock (E.) : †ταώς (for the *p-* see *palma*[2]), cf. Arab. *tāūs* Zenker 593 a.

pāx peace (E. E. *pay*) : 'arrangement,' PĀK- cf. PĀG- *pāgina.*

-pe enclitic (in *nempe prope quippe, quispiam* = **quis-pe-jam, uspiam* = **us-pe-jam*) : dialectic for *-que.*

peccô err :
hardly = **ped-cô* fr. *pēs,* 'get entangled'.

pectō comb: PEK- πέκω, Lit. *pèszti* pluck, cf. POK- Ags. *feax* (i.e. *feah-s) hair E. Fair-*fax* †*pax*-wax.

pectus breast (E. para*pet*): 'framework, fastening,' from PEK- *paciscor*.— Not cf. Sk. *pakshás* wing, side of the body, which would give *pexus* (see *texō ursus*).

pecū pecus cattle (Lit. *pekus*): Got. *faihu* property E. *fee fellow feud*[2] *fief*, Zd. *paçu* cattle Sk. *páçus*: 'appropriated,' fr. *paciscor* (as E. *farm* fr. *firm*).

pedis louse: 'many-footed,' fr. *pēs*.

pēdō (E. *petard*): PEZD- MHG. *fist* wind E. *foist*, Pruss. *peisda* podex, cf. BZD- βδέω pedo, Lit. *bezdéti* (for *bzdéti) pedere.

pedum crook to catch sheep with: PED- seize, see *oppidō*.

pējerô swear falsely: 'make worse, alter, violate,' fr. *pējes*- properly stem of oblique cases of sq. (cf. *mājes-tās* beside *mājor*).

pējor worse: = *pec-jor* fr. *peccô*.

†pelagus sea: πέλαγος:

pellāx deceitful: 'affecting,' fr. *pellō* move.

pellis hide (E. *peel*[1] &c. *pillion plaid*; W. *pilen* rind): PEL-N- πέλλα pail (orig. of leather), Got. *filleins* of leather E. *fell*[2].

pellō strike (E. *pelt pursy push*): = *pel-nô, PEL-, πέλας near.

†pelta target: †πέλτη, Thracian (Hdt. 7. 75).

pēlvis pēluïs (Nonius 543) **pelluis** (Velius Longus, Keil. 7. 65) basin: = *pēlovis, Sk. *pálavī* vessel.

pendeō hang (E. *pent*house), **pendō** weigh (E. avoirdu*pois pansy poise spend*; NHG. *speise* food = Lat. *expensa*): 'swing,' cf. SPEND- Sk. *spand*- quiver.

penes with (properly proclitic before a consonant, *penes mē, tē, vōs, quem*, or it would become *penis), **penitus** (for term. see *in-tus*) inwardly, **penetrô** (cf. *intrô* beside *intus*) enter: fr. *penus* in the sense of 'closet,' Fest. penus locus in aede Vestae intimus (*penes* Loc. like *alés*).

pēnis tail (E. *pencil*): 'waving,' fr. sq.

penna pesna (Fest.: *petna* is a mere conjecture for *pecna* i.e. *pēna, penna) wing (E. *pen* Subst. *pennou*): = *pet-na from PET- πέτομαι fly, MIr. *ete* wing, Ags. *feder* E. *feather*, Sk. *pát-tram*; 'go,' see *petō*.

†pentethrōnica Plaut. Poen. 471, Ritschl conj. *ptēnanthrōpica* *πτην-ανθρωπική* 'of birds and men,' Goetz *ptēnothērica* *πτηνο-θηρική* 'of birds and beasts'.

pēnūria paenūria want: *paenūrus (for term. cf. *māt-ū-rus*) Adj. from *paenus little, see *pacne*.

penus store: Lit. *pénas* food.

†peplum robe: πέπλος:

per through: Got. *fair*- Verbal-Prefix, Lit. *per*.

per- very: PERI πέρι around, Zd. *pairi* Sk. *pári*.

-per enclitic (in *nūper parumper paulisper semper*): πὲρ altogether, cf. praeced.

†**pēra** bag: πήρᾱ:

per-cellō overthrow: from *cel-nō*, KVEL-, cf. KVOL- Lit. *kálti* strike OSlav. *klati* prick.

per-contor per-cunctor enquire: 'linger over,' from *cunctor*.
Not fr. *contus* pole (first in Verg., while *percontor* is in Plaut.), quasi 'explore'.

per-eg-rē abroad: fr. *per* + *agō*.

peren-diē day after to-morrow:

pergula booth: formed quasi fr. *pergō* go on ('projection'), for *precula* (with -*ē*-?) Quint. 1. 5. 12:
hardly cf. NUmbr. *praco* bulwark.

perīculum danger (E. *peril*): 'experience,' see *perītus*.

perinde equally: = *perim* Abl. (see *inde*) fr. *per-* 'around,' + -*de*.

perītus experienced: PER- πεῖρα attempt περάω go through, MIr. *erud* fear, Zd. *par-* go over (Spiegel) Sk. *par-* pass, cf. PĒR- Ags. *faer* danger E. *fear*, see *portō*.

per-mitiēs ruin: fr. *meto*, 'being cut down, reduced'.

perna ham (E. *prawn*): PERSNĀ πτέρνη heel, cf. PERSN'- Got. *fairzna*, from PĒRSN- Zd. *pāshna* heel Sk. *pắrshnis*.

pernīx (for term. cf. *fēl-īx*) swift: fr. praeced., 'strong in the ham'.

†**pērō** boot: *πήρων*, 'of leather,' fr. πήρᾱ leather pouch, see *pēra*.

perperam wrongly (Polyb. πέρπερος vainglorious): fr. *per-* + *parum*, 'insufficiently, unsatisfactorily'. For term. see *tam*.

persōna mask (E. *parson*): fr. *persōnus* Adj. (with vowel lengthened, see *cōmis*) of *per-sonô* sound through.

pertica pole (E. *perch*[1]): = *pertiga* (Lat. having no ending -*ga*, see *praefica sublica, amurca spēlunca*), fr. *per-tingō* reach, from *tangō*.

pēs foot (E. *pawn*[2] *pioneer trivet vamp*): PED- πέζα, Arm. *het* track, cf. POD- ποδός Gen. foot, Lit. *pắdas* sole, Arm. *otn* foot, Zd. Sk. *pad-*, and PŌD- Dor. πώς, Got. *fōtus* E. E. *fetter*, Zd. *pād-* Sk. *pắd-*.

pessimus worst: dialectic for *peximus*, PEK-, see *pējor peccô*.

pessulus pexulus pestulus (Caper, Keil. 7. 111) bolt: = *ped-tlus* fr. *pēs*, 'foot' of the door (see *assula*).

pessum down: = *persum*, Plaut. Pers. 737 Persa me pessum (i.e. *persum*) dedit:

pestis plague:
hardly cf. πῆμα woe quasi *πῆσ-μα; or Fest.'s *pescstās* plague.

†**petaurum** trapèze: πέταυρον perch, fr. πέτομαι fly, see *penna*.

petō fall on: PET- 'go,' εὐ-πετής easy, Zd. *pat-* fall, run, Sk. *pat-* fall, fly, see *penna*, cf. PT- πί-πτω fall (with ī from πίπτω?).

†petōritum petorritum four-wheeled carriage : Gaulish (Quint.), from
PETOR W. *pedwar* four, see *quattuor*, + RIT- OIr. *rith* course, see *rītus*.

†phaecasium shoe : †φαικάσιον, φαικάς : Egyptian (as worn by Egyptian
priests).

†phalanx host, phalangae (formed from Acc. φάλαγγα) rollers : φάλαγξ
battle-array, log ('bar,' and so 'line '), for *φάλγξ BHĻNG-, cf. BHĻG-
sufflāmen, BHOLG- Ags. *balc* beam E. *baulk bulk*head †*balcony* †cata-
falque †*scaffold*, Lit. *balžiēna* cross-piece.

†phalerae bosses : φάλαρα cheek-pieces, fr. φάλος boss.

†phasēlus bean : †φάσηλος, Pamphylian (cf. the town-name Φασηλίς).

†phiala saucer (E. *vial*) : φιάλη :

†philyra limetree : φιλύρα :

†phimus dicebox : φῖμός cup :

†phōca seal : φώκη :

†phoenix a bird : †φοῖνιξ (formed after Φοῖνιξ Phoenician), fr. Egyptian
bennu (Pierret).

†phū phȳ Interj. : φῦ, cf. ONor. *fȳ* E. *foh phew*.

picus woodpecker (NUmbr. *peiqu* Abl. ; E. *pic*[1], whence W. *pi* magpie) :
PĪKV- cf. PIKV- Sk. *pikas* Indian cuckoo.

But OHG. *speh* magpie goes rather with *speciō*.

piger slow ('irksome '), piget irks : 'pricks,' PUG- cf. PUNG- *pungō*.

pignus pledge : 'handsel,' fr. *pugnus*.

pila ball (E. *pellet pile*[1] *pill platoon*) :
hardly cf. Sk. *pindas* quasi *pil-ndas*.

pila mortar, pillar ('shaft,' see *pīlum*) : = *pis-la* fr. *pinsō*.

†pīlentum chariot : Spanish (Diefenbach Origines Europaeae p. 399) ?

pilleus pīleus felt hat : πῖλος felt ; 'compressed,' fr. sq.

pilō ram down, pīlātus dense Aen. 12. 121 : cf. SPIL- Lett. *špīlēt* squeeze.

pilum pestle, javelin (from its shape) : = *pis-lum* fr. *pinsō*.

pilus hair (E. cater*pillar plush wig*) :
hardly cf. πτίλον down, on account of the difference of meaning.

†pina pinna mussel (E. *periwinkle*[2]) : †πῖνα πίννα :

pingō paint (E. E. *pimento pint*) : 'stipple,' *pungō*.

pinguis thick : = *penguis*, PNGH-V- παχύς.

pinna wing (E. *pin pinion*) : = *penna*.

Hardly add Ags. E. *fin*.

pinsō pīsō pound (E. *piston*) : PINS- cf. PIS- πίσος pea πτίσσω winnow,
OHG. *fesā* hush, OSlav. *plhati* strike, Zd. *pish-* rub Sk. *pish-* crush.

pinus fir (E. *pinnace*) :

†piper pepper (E.) : = *pipere* *πίπερι* (cf. Sk. *pippalī*) †πέπερι.

pīpilō chirp, pīpulum outcry : fr. *pīpō* chirp (OHG. *fīfā* fife E.), PĪP-
onomatop., Ags. *pīpe* pipe E. (W. *pib*) E. *peep*[1] †*pibroch* †*pigeon* †*pimp*
†*pivot*, Lit. *pypti* to pipe, cf. PIPP- πιππίζω chirp, Sk. *pippakā* a bird.

pirum pear (E. E. *pearl perry*):

piscis fish (E. gram*pus*): PISK- Got. *fisks* E., cf. PĪSK- OIr. *īasc*.

†pistris pistrīx (both quasi 'pounding,' fr. *pinsō*) pristis pristīx sea-monster: †*πρίστις*:

pītuita slime (E. *pip*[1] in fowls): formed (like Substs. *dīra noxia satura* from Adjs. *dīrus* &c.) from Adj. **pītuītus* (for term. cf. *fortu-ītus grātu-ītus*) **pūtus* fr. *pūteō*.

pius pīus holy (E. *pity*):

pix pitch (E. E. *pay*[2] a ship): PIKV- *πίσσα*, Lit. *pikis* OSlav. *pĭklŭ*, Arm. †*phiči*.

†placenta cake: formed quasi fr. *placens*, for **placūnta*, *πλακοῦς*: 'flat,' PLAK- *πλάξ* plain, Lit. *plasztakà* hand-breadth.

placeō please (E. *plea plead*): 'stroke' (cf. *mulceō mulcō*), PLOKV- Lit. *plàkti* strike.

plācō appease: PLŌKV- cf. praeced.

plaga net, region: orig. 'rope' Serv. Aen. 4. 131, hence 'net of cords' or 'belt of country' (Nettleship), cf. *plagula* curtain ('hanging on a cord'):

plāga blow (E. *plague play*): PLĀG- *πληγή*, Got. *flōkan* lament ('beat' the breast), cf. PLAG- OHG. *flah* flat ('beaten down') E. *flake* &c. *fleck*.

plagiārius plunderer: fr. †*plagium* kidnapping, *πλάγιος* crooked.

†plagūsia a fish: for **placūsia* (-*g*- from *plaga* 'hunting-net'), **πλακου-σία* fr. *πλακόεις* flat, see *placenta*.

plangō beat (E. *complain*): PLANG- cf. PLĀG- *plāga*.

planguncula doll: Dimin. of †**plangō*, *πλαγγών* Callimachus:

planta sprout ('spreading': OIr. *cland* offspring, whence E. *clan*), sole of the foot: = **plontā* PLONT-, cf. PLOT- Zd. *frath-* spread Sk. *prath-*, PLOT-Ŭ- Lit. *platùs* broad, PLOT-NŌ- Arm. *lain*, PLT-Ŭ- *πλατύς*, Zd. *perethu* Sk. *pṛthús*, PLT-NŌ- OIr. *lethan*.

†planus cheat: *πλάνος*, *πλάνη* wandering.

plānus flat (E. *plain plan*): Lit. *plónas* thin, from PLĀ- Lit. *plóti* beat out.

†platalea spoonbill: **πλαταλέα* Fem. of Adj. **πλαταλέος* fr. *πλατύς*, see *planta*.

plaudō beat:

†plaustrum plōstrum wagon: = **plaux-trum*, see *plōxenum*.

plēbēs people:

not cf. *πλῆθος* multitude, Dor. *πλᾶθος*.

plectō plait: PLEK- *πλέκω*, cf. PLOK- Got. *flahta* plaiting E. *flax*, Sk. *praçnas* basket.

plector am punished:

plēnus full: PLĒ-NŌ- MIr. *līn* number, from PLĒ- *pleō* fill (Fest.), *πλε-ῖος* full, Arm. *li*, Sk. *prā-* fill, cf. PEL- Zd. Sk. *par-*, PḶ-NŌ- *polleō*.

plē-rus most : fr. praeced.

plicô fold (E. *plait plight*[2] *ply* &c. *plot splay supple*) : = *plecô*, see *plectō*.

plōrô cry out : = *plaudô* fr. *plaudō*, ' beat ' the breast. .

†plŏxenum plŏxemum wagon-box: Gaulish (Quint.), ΚVLAUG-S-, ΚVLAUG- = Celt. PLŌG-, whence OHG. †*phluog* plough E., Lit. †*pliŭgas*.

pluit rains (E. *plover*) : = *pluv-it* cf. *pluv-ius* rainy, *plovit*, Fest. *per-plovō* leak, PLEV- ' flow, float,' πλέ(ϝ)ω sail, cf. PLOV- πλό(ϝ)os voyage, OHG. *flawen* wash, Lit. *pláuti* OSlav. *pluti* flow, sail, and PLU- OIr. *luam* yacht, Sk. *plu-* float *pru-* flow.

plūma feather: ' means for floating,' PLŪ- cf. praeced.—Not PLEUGH-, Ags. *fleōgan* fly E. E. †*fili*buster †*fugleman*.

†plumbum lead (E. *plump* Vb. *plunge pump*): MLŪMB- cf. MLŪB- †*μόλυβδos μόλιβos*.

plūs more : = *plūs*, cf. *plūrima plouruma plīsima ploirumē ploera*, *pleus* from *plē-us* *plē-jus*, i.e. PLĒ- *plēnus* with Comparat.-ending, cf. ONor. *fleiri* (= *flā-is-i) and πλε-ίων, OIr. *lia*, Zd. *fráyāo*.

pluteus shed: ' defence from rain ' i.e. from missiles, *plutós* ' rained on,' Part. from PLU-, see *pluit*.

pōdex: POZD- cf. PEZD- *pēdō* (for the sense cf. χόδανos beside χέζω cacô).

†podium wall round the arena : ' foot ' (i.e. lowest part) of the amphi-theatre, πόδιον little foot, see *pēs*.

†poena punishment (E. *pain pine* Vb. *punch*[2] *repine*): ποινή fine, ΚVOI-NÁ OSlav. *cēna* price, Zd. *kaēna* punishment, from ΚVOI- cf. ΚVĪ- τίω value, ΚVI- Sk. *ci-* observe.

†poēta maker, poet : *ποητής* dialectic for ποιητής, as ποέω for ποιέω make.

†polenta pulenta pearl-barley (a Greek preparation, Plin. 18. 72, 84) formed (quasi fr. *pollen*) from *παλυντή Part. Fem. of παλύνω sprinkle.

poliō polish : ' rub,' cf. SPOD- σποδέω beat, see *pudet*.

pollen fine flour : = *pōlen* :

polleō prevail : = *polneō* ' am full,' PḶ-NO- Got. *fulls* full E., Lit. *pìlnas* OSlav. *plŭnŭ*, Zd. *perena*, cf. PḶ-NÓ- πολλοί many, OIr. *lān* full, Sk. *pŭrṇás*, see *plēnus*.

pollex thumb: fr. *pollus* (cf. *allex* fr. *allus*) ' projecting,' = *por-lus* from *por-*.

pol-lingō dress a corpse :

pollūceō offer in sacrifice (esp. to Hercules) : properly ' offer to Pollux,' fr. *Pollūx* (from *Πολυλεύκης by-form), Etrusc. *Pultuke* (from Πολυ-δεύκης), whence Etrusc. *pultace* he sacrificed Bugge B. B. 11. 43.

pōmum fruit (E. *pomade pommel*) :

pondus weight (E. *pound*[1]): MIr. *onn* stone, POND cf. PEND- *pendō*.

pōne behind : = *pos-ne, pos-* see *post + -ne*.

pōnō put (E. *post*[2] *provost*; but *pose* Subst. and *compose* &c. are from *pausa*) : = *posno *po-sinō, po (see *post*) + sinō.

pōns bridge: 'passage,' *pōnti-* cf. OSlav. pątí way (see *saeta*), Sk. *pán-than-* road.

†pontō punt (E. E. *pontoon*): Gaulish (Caes. B. C. 3. 29).

†pontus sea : πόντος :

popa priest's assistant:

popīna cookshop: Oscan form of *coquīna* kitchen, fr. *coquō*.

poples ham of the knee: 'rounded' (whence called in OHG. *knie-rado* 'knee-wheel'), see *populus*.

populor ravage : 'enring,' fr. sq.

populus people (E.): Umbr. *puplum* Acc. : dialectic for *quoclus, ĸvo-ĸvlos 'ring' of people, κύκλος circle, cf. ĸveĸvlos Ags. *hveohl* (Skeat) wheel E., Zd. *cakhra* Sk. *cakrás*.

pōpulus poplar (E.) :

por- forth : pr-, πάρα beside.

porcus pig (E. *pork* &c. *porcelain porpoise*): πόρκος, MIr. *orc*, Ags. *fearh* porker E. *farrow*, Lit. *parszas* pig OSlav. *prasę*.

porricio pōriciō offer: = *por-jiciō from por- + jaciō (j lengthening the preceding syllable and then dropping, cf. ōbiciō from objiciō).

porrigō scurf (for the term. cf. *mcnt-igō ost-igō pct-igō* scab): fr. *porrum* 'head' in the slang dialect, cf. Moretum 74 capiti nomen debentia porra.

porrō forward : Abl. Neut. of *por-rus Adj. from por-.

porrum leek : pásom πράσον.

porta gate : 'passage,' Fem. Part. from pr-, see *portō*.

porticus colonnade (E. *porch*): fr. *portus* 'passage'.

portiō share : prti- cf. prti- *pars*.

portisculus baton:

portō carry (E. *disport sport*): fr. *portús Part., pr- cf. por- Got. *faran* go E. *fare ferry*, see *perītus*.

portōrium toll: = *portitōrium fr. *portitōr* douanier, = *portu-tor fr. sq.

portus harbour ('passage' to land), house (which one enters): pr-t'- Ags. E. *ford*, Zd. hu-*peretu* with a good ford, see *portō*.

pō-sca pū-sca vinegar: fr. *pō-tō* + term. of *ē-sca*.

pōscō ask : = *porc-scō prk-sk- OHG. *forscōn*, Arm. *harths* enquiry, cf. pāk-sk- Zd. *pares-* ask, prek-sk- Sk. *prach-*, see *precor*.

post poste behind (E. *puny*): formed (on anal. of *antc* quasi *an-tc*) from *po-s, i.e. po after (Quint.), πύ-ματος last, Lit. *pa-* under OSlav. *po* about, + -s (see *abs*).

postis doorpost (E. *post*[1]): Sk. *pastyā* dwelling: 'strong,' cf. Got. *fastan* hold fast E. *fast*.

pōstulô demand : = *pōscitulô* fr. *pōscitus* Part. of *pōscō* (as *ūstulô* fr. *ūstus*).

potis able (E. *power puissant*) : PÓTIS πόσις husband, Lit. *pàts* (from *patis*), Zd. *paiti* lord Sk. *pátis*, cf. PÓT- πότνια lady, Got. bruth-*faths* bridegroom, POT'- Ags. *fadian* arrange E. *fad*.

pōtô drink, **pōtus** drunk (E. *pot porridge*) : PŌ- πέπωκα have drunk, Sk. *pā-* drink.

prae before : Loc. of *prā* (as *Rōmae* of *Rōmā*), see *pro-*.

praecō crier : = *praevicō* fr. *prae + vocô* (cf. *calcitrō epulō errō incubō manducō paedīcō palpō praedō* Substs. from Verbs in -*ô*).

praeda booty (E. *prey*) : = *praehida* from *prac* + GHED- Got. bi-*gitan* find E. *get gait gate guess*.

praedium estate : fr. *praes*.

praefica hired mourner : = *praefiga* (see *pertica*) fr. *prae + fingō*, ‘simulating’ grief.

praemium profit : = *prae-imium* ‘what one takes before others,’ fr. *prae + emo*.

praepūtium : = *prae-poutium* fr. *prae + paviō*, cf. Lit. ap-*piau*-klas.

praes surety : = *prae-vis*, OLat. *praevidēs* Plur., from *prae + vas*.

praestigiae praestrīgiae tricks (E. *prestige*) : ‘enchantment, glamour,’ fr. *prae + strīga* witch, see *strix*.

prae-stinô buy : ‘set before other things, choose,’ see *dē-stinô*.

praestō praestū ready : Abl. of *praestus* = *praesitus* (cf. *postus* = *positus*) Part. of *prae-sinō* ‘set before’.—Hence *praestô* warrant, exhibit (opp. *prae-stô* excel).

praestōlor praestūlor wait : ‘set oneself by,’ STŌL- Got. *stōls* seat E. *stall stale still stool*, cf. STEL- στέλλω place, Lit. *steliúti* order, STL- *stolidus*.

prandium lunch :

prātum meadow (E. *prairie*) : = *partum* acquired, PERŌ- Part. fr. *parô*.

prāvus crooked : ‘perverted,’ PR̥-VÓS, cf. PR̥- *por-*, and παρα-βαίνω transgress.

preciae praeciae (vocalic relation obscure) a grape-vine :

precor pray (E.) : PREK- Got. *fraihnan* ask, cf. PERK-S- Umbr. *persnimu* let him pray, see *procāx pōscō*.

prehendo prēndō seize : from *prae-* + GHVEND- W. *genni* be held, cf. GHVN̥D- ἔχαδον I contained.

prēlum praelum press-beam : = *pres-lum* PRE-S- *pressī* have pressed, from PRE- sq. (cf. τρέ(σ)ω beside τρέμω).

premō press (E. E. *print sprain*) : PRE-, cf. *praeced.* :

pretium price (E. E. *praise prize* Vb.) :

prīdem long ago : = *prīs-dem*, see sq. + -*dem*.

primus first (E. *prim primrose privet*): Paelignian *prismu* Abl., from **prĭs*, = **pro-is* fr. *pro-* + the same term. as *bis*.

prior former: Dissim. for **prĭr-or *prĭs-or* fr. praeced.

prĭs-cus prĭs-tinus old: *prĭs-* see *primus*.

prīvignus stepson: 'born before the second marriage,' fr. sq. (in the orig. sense of 'before') + GN- see *gignō*.

prīvus single: 'put in front, selected,' Dissim. for **prĭr-vus *prĭs-vus*, see *primus*.

pro- Prefix: πρό before, OIr. *ro-* Prefix, Got. *fra-* Prefix, Lit. *pra-* Prefix OSlav. *pro* before, Zd. *fra-* Sk. *prd-*.

prō before (E. *pur*lieu): OSlav. *pra-*, long form of praeced.

prō² proh Interj.

probrum disgrace:

probus good (E. *prove reprieve*): *pro-* + -BHO- see *acerbus*.

procāx shameless: 'importunate,' fr. *procó* demand (Fest.), PROK-θεοπρόπος priest (= **θεο-πρόκ-Fος), Lit. *praszýti* beg OSlav. *prositi*, Sk. *praçnas* question, cf. Pn̥K- MIr. com-*aircim* I ask, see *precor*.

procella storm: = **pro-cel-na*, see *percellō*.

procerēs chiefs:

prōc-ērus tall: fr. **prō-cus* Adj. of *prō* (see *sinc-ērus*), 'advanced'.

procul far: = **proculum* Neut. Dimin. fr. **procus* forward, fr. *pro-*.

procus suitor: 'demanding,' see *procāx*.

prŏd-eō go forth: from **prō-du* (see *in-du*) + *eō*.

prŏd-igium portent: **prōdu* praeced. + AGH- *ājō*, cf. the deity *Ajus Locūtius* 'the voice that spoke'.

proelium praelium battle:

proin-de just so: **prō-im* 'according to that,' see *deinde*.

prōlēs offspring: = **pro-olēs*, see *adolescō*³.

prō-līxus stretched out: 'flowing forth,' Part. of **prō-liquor*.

prōmō bring out: fr. *prōmus* cellarer, *prō* + Adj.-ending (see *emō dēmō*).

prō-mulgó publish: 'cause to swell forth,' Ml̥G- Lett. *milst* swell Lit. *milžinas* giant, see *multus*.

prōmuntūrium prōmontōrium (quasi fr. *mons*) headland: fr. *prŏ-mineō* jut out, MŬN-, see *ēmineō*.

prope near (E. *approach reproach*): *pro-* + -*pe*.

pro-perus quick: fr. *parō*, 'ready'.

pro-pitius favourable: fr. *petō* in the orig. meaning of 'go'.

proprius special: = **proprius* Dissim. for **pro-prĭr-us *pro-prĭs-us*, see *primus*.

prō-sāpia race:

prōsper prosperous: = **prō-spĕr* (-ĕ- shortened before final *r*), *prŏ* + *spĕrō* hope, fr. *spēs*.

prō-tēlum row: fr. *tēla*, 'series of threads'.

6

prōtervus (Plaut.) **protervus** wanton: 'trampling down,' fr. *prō* (*pro*-) + *terō*.

Plaut. Truc. 256 *proptervē* is either a mis-reading or from a different word.

prōvincia province: 'governorship,' fr. **prōvinquus* Adj. fr. **prōvus* (as *longinquus* fr. *longus*), cf. OSlav. *praviti* lead; from *prō*.

prōx Interj. (for term. of. *euax*): from *prō*[2].

proximus next: = **proc-simus* fr. **pro-que* Rom. form of *pro-pe*.

pruīna rime: Dissim. for **prurīna *prūsīna*, PREUS- Got. *frius* frost E. E. *freeze*; fr. sq. (cf. Verg. Geo. 1. 93 frigus adurit).

prūna live coal: = **prūs-na* PREUS- cf. PRUS- Sk. *plush*- burn.

†**prūnus** plum-tree (E. *plum*): **προῦνος* cf. **προῦμνος* †*προύμνη*: Syrian (from Damascus Plin. 13. 51).

prūriō itch: 'burn,' PREUS- see *prūna*.

†**prytanis** chief magistrate: *πρύτανις*, from **πρύ* dialectic for *πρό* before, see *pro-*.

†**psallō** play (MIr. *salland* sing): *ψάλλω* pluck (i.e. the strings).

†**psittacus** parrot: †*ψίττακος*, also *βίττακος σιττάκη*, Indian *siptacē* Plin. 10. 117.

†**psythia psithia** a vine: *ψύθιος ψίθιος* a vine:

-**pte** self: PT- *τί-πτε* why, cf. POT- Lit. *pàts* self, see *potis*.

pūbēs adult:

pūblicus pōblicus poublicos public: = **poubdicos*, Umbr. *pupḍike* Dat.: fr. praeced.?—*Poplicus*, fr. *populus*, is a different word.

pudeō am ashamed: 'am stricken,' cf. SPOD- see *poliō*.

puer pover (Corssen Aussprache[2] 1. 362) boy: PEV- cf. PU- W. *w-yr* grandson.

pugil boxer: fr. *pug-nus*.

pugna battle:

pugnus fist: PUG- *πυγμή*.

pulcer pulcher polcer beautiful: PLKV- cf. PLOKV- *placeō*.

pūlējum pūlegium fleabane (E. *penny*-royal): = **pūlec-jum* (see *bājulus*), fr. sq.

pūlex flea (E. *puce*): = **pōlex* fr. *πῶλος* see sq., 'young'.

Not (1) PŪL- cf. PUL- Sk. *pulakas* a kind of grain, vermint: (2) cf. *ψύλλα* flea, or Ags. *fleāh* E., or Lit. *blusà* OSlav. *blicha*, or Arm. *lu*.

pullus Subst. foal, chicken (E. *pool*[2] *poultry polecat pulley Punch*): = **pul-nus* PL- Got. *fula* foal E. E. *filly*, cf. PŌL- *πῶλος* young animal.

pullus Adj. dark: PL-NÓS cf. PEL-NÓS *πελλός* dusky, Cyprian *τιλνός* (Hesych.).

pulmentum relish: 'affecting' the appetite, see *pellāx*, PL- cf. PEL- *pellō*.

pulmō lung: 'beating, pumping,' fr. *pellō pulsō*; pop. etym. for *plūmō* PLEÚ-MŌN πλεύμων, cf. PLEU-TJI- Lit. *plaučiai* lungs OSlav. *plušta*lung: 'floating,' fr. *pluit* (as Ags. *lunge* fr. *lungre* light, and E. *lights* = lungs).

pulpa solid flesh : 'tangible,' PĻKV- cf. PĻKV- *palpó*.

pulpitum stage:

puls pottage (E. *poultice pulse*[2]): POLTI- cf. PÓLTO- πόλτος.

.pulvīnus bank, cushion (E. *pillow*):
    hardly cf. SPĻV- Lett. *ŝpilwens* cushion, fr. *ŝpilwa* marsh-grass.

pulvis dust (E. *powder*):

pūmex pumice (E. *pounce* Subst.): 'like foam' (as E. *meerschaum* = 'sea foam'), POIM- Ags. *fām* foam E.

pungō prick (E. *point pounce* Vb. *punch* Vb. *puncheon*):

pūniceus purple: fr. *Pūnicus* (Carthaginian) in its proper sense of 'Phoenician,' purple coming from Tyre.

†puppis stern: = *pūpis* (quasi fr. sq., 'the boy's' i.e. the steersman's 'place') for *epōpis, *ἐπωπίς fr. ἐπωπή lookout-place.

pūpus boy (E. *puppet puppy*):

†purpura purple: †πορφύρα: Phoenician?

pūrus clean (E. *spurge*): PŪ- Sk. *pū-* cleanse, cf. PU- *putus* Adj.

pūs matter: PŪ-s *pūstula* blister, cf. PU-s πύ(σ)ος matter; from PŪ-, cf. PŪI- Sk. *pūyas*, see *pūteō.*

pūsus boy, pusillus petty : PŪS- PUS-:

pūteō stink: fr. *pūtis* Part. from PŪ- πύθω make to rot, MIr. *ūr* mould, ONor. *fūi* rottenness Got. *fūls* rotten E. *foul,* Lit. *pūti* rot, Zd. *pū-* stink, cf. PŪI- Sk. *pūy-*.

puter rotten: PU-, cf. PŪ- praeced.

puteus dungeon, pit, well (E. *pit*):

putō cleanse, think ('sift' my thoughts): fr. *putus* Adj.

putus Subst. boy: 'young,' PUT- Lit. *putýtis* chick OSlav. *pŭta* bird, Zd. *puthra* son Sk. *putrás.*

putus Adj. pure: Part. from PU- πτύον winnowing-fan, OHG. *fowen* sift, cf. PŪ- *pūrus.*

†pyelus bath: †πύελος trough:

†pȳga: πῡγή:

†pȳramis pyramid: πῡραμίς wheaten cake, pyramid (from its shape), fr. πῡρός wheat.

†pȳtissō spit out: πῡτίζω, Dissim. for *πτῡτίζω SPJŪ- see *spuō.*

quadra square (E. E. *quarry*[1] *squad squadron*): for *quat-ra (with *d* from *quadru-*), cf. *triquetrus,* KVAD-, 'pointed' (i.e. at each corner), Ags. *hvät* keen E. *whet.*

quadringentī 400: for *quadru-centī, sq. + *centum,* on anal. of *septingentī* (see *octingentī*).

quadru- four- (E. *carillon quarantine*) : for **quetru-* (with *d* from some Celtic dialect, cf. the Belgic town-name *Quadri-burgium*?), Zd. *cathru-*, ΚΥΕΤΥΒ̣- see *quattuor*.

quaerō seek (E. *query*) : ΚΥΑΙS- :

quaesō ask : = **quaes-sō* (for term. cf. *capessō* &c.), fr. praeced.

quālis of what kind : fr. **quālus* Adj. of *quā* where, case-form from *quī*, see *tālis*.

quālum basket : = **quas-lum*, see *quasillum*.

quam how : = **quām* **quā-me* from *quā* see *quālis*, and see *tam*.

quantus how great : formed from *quan-tum* (taken as Adj. Neut.) i.e. *quam tum* correlative of *tantum* (see *tantus*), cf. Verg. Geo. 4. 101 nec tantum dulcia quantum et liquida.

quartus fourth (E. *quart*) : = **ctvar-tos* ΚΥΤΥΒ̣- cf. ΚΥΤΥΒ̣- (π)τρά-πεζα 'four-footed' table, and ΚΥΕΤΥΒ̣-ΤΟS τέτρατος fourth, Lit. *ketwirtas* OSlav. *četvrŭtĭ* quarter, Sk. *caturthás* fourth, see *quattuor*.

quasi quasī quasei as if : from the phrase 'tam quam sī' (cf. 'tam qua sei sei': old form *quansei*, Key), with Dissim. of *-m*.

quasillum basket : ΚΥΑS- Lit. *kászius* OSlav. *koša* (= **kos-ja*).

quater four times : = **quetrú*, Zd. *cathrus*, see *quattuor*.

quatiō shake (E. *cask casque fracas quash rescue*) : ΚΥΑΤ- πατάσσω strike.

quattuor quātuor quattor quātor four : ΚΥΕΤΥΒ̣ cf. ΚΥΕΤΥΒ Osc. *petor*, τέσσαρες (= **κϝέτϝαρες*), ΚΥΕΤΥΕR OIr. *cethir*, Lit. *ketweri* OSlav. *četverŭ* Zd. *cathware-*, ΚΥΕΤΎOR Got. *fidvōr* Ags. *feóver* E., Zd. *cathwāro* Sk. *catvāras*, ΚΥ(ΤΥ)OR Arm. *thǰor-kh*.

-que -quē (Attius) and : -ΚΥΟ -ΚΥΕ̄ fr. *quī*, cf. -ΚΥΕ τέ, Zd. Sk. *ca*, and Got. ni-*h* neque.

queō am able : = **quej-ō* ΚΥΕΙ- cf. ΚΥΙ- W. *piau* to own.

quercus oak : = **querquus* cf. Fest. *querquētum* oakwood, = **quorquus* ΚΥΒ̣ΚΥ- Ags. *furh-* fir E. (for confusion of tree-names see *fāgus frāxinus*).

queror complain (E. *quarrel*) : 'sigh,' Κ-ΥΕS- Sk. *çvas-* blow, cf. Κ-ΥΕ̄S- ONor. *hvaesa* hiss E. *wheeze weasand whizz whistle*, Κ-ΥŌS- MIr. *cái* lamentation.

quī who : = **quo-ī* (for term. see *hīc*) NUmbr. *poei* Osc. *pui*, ΚΥΟ- ποῦ where, W. *pwy* who, Got. *hvas* E., Lit. *kàs* quis [1;2]. OSlav. *kova* quando Zd. *ka* quis, Sk. *kás* quis.

quia because : = **quiā* **quo-ī-jā* fr. praeced. + Instrum. ending, cf. (without the *-ī-*) Sk. *ká-yā* πῶς;

quidem indeed : 'somewhat,' fr. *quid* Acc. Neut. of *quis* + Μ̣ see *autem*.

quiēs rest (E. *coy decoy quit quite*) : = **quī-ēs* ΚΥῙ- OSlav. po-*čiti* to rest.

quin but that : = **quī-num*, *quī* Abl. of *quis* + *-num*.

quīnī 5 : for **quīnc-nī* fr. sq., on anal. of *bīnī* 2 = **bis-nī*.

quīnque 5: = *quénque*, cf. OIr. *cōic* (*kvē-* becoming *kō-*), ᴋᴠᴇ́ɴᴋᴠᴇ (with ᴋᴠ- from the word for 4) for ᴘᴇ́ɴᴋᴠᴇ *πέντε*, Got. *fimf* (-*f* by assimilation) E., Lit. *penki* OSlav. *pęti* (for *penk-ti), Arm. *hing*, Zd. *pancan-* Sk. *pánca*.

quippe certainly: = *quī-pe*, *quī* Abl. of *quis* + -*pe*.

quirītō wail (E. *cry*): fr. *Quiris*, 'demand the rights of a Roman citizen'.

quis[1] who Interrog.: ᴋᴠɪ- *τίς*, OIr. *cia*, OSlav. *čito* Neut., Zd. *cis* Sk. *kím* Neut. (with *k*, for *c*, from *kás*, see *quī*), cf. ᴋᴠᴏ- *quī*.

quis[2] anyone: NUmbr. *pis*, *τίς*, OSlav. *čito* Neut., Zd. *mā-cis* nē quis Sk. *mā-kis* nē quis, fr. praeced.

quispiam anyone: see -*pe*.

quisquiliae droppings of trees: = *quesqueliae *quosquoliae cf. *cuscolium* scab on ilex Plin. 16. 32, κοσκυλμάτια shreds of leather fr. *κοσκύλλω tear, ᴋᴠᴏsᴋᴠ- cf. ᴋᴠᴇsᴋᴠ- *κεσκίον* tow.

quo-que also: for *quoquo* Redupl., see -*que*.

quot how many (E. *quote*): = *quoti* Sk. *káti*, cf. ᴋᴠᴇ-ᴛɪ Zd. *caiti*; Loc. of sq.

quo-tus which: from ᴋᴠᴏ- see *quī* + a term. -ᴛᴏ-.

rabiēs rage (E. E. *rave reverie*):

rabula brawling advocate: 'mad dog,' fr. praeced. (cf. Quint. 12. 9. 12 rabulam latratoremque).

racēmus bunch of grapes (E. *raisin*):

radius staff (E. *ray*): 'scraped,' = *rodiós* ʀᴏᴅ- see *rōdō*.

rādīx root (E. *radish*): ᴠʀᴅ-, cf. ᴠʀᴅ- W. *gwreiddyn*, Got. *vaurts* E. E. *orchard wort whortle*berry.

rādō scrape (E. *rack*[3] rail Vb. *rascal rash* Subst. *raze* &c. *graze*[1]): ʀᴅ-, cf. ʀᴏᴅ- *rōdō*.

†**traeda rēda rhēda** (the last from †*ῥήδη, see *epirēdium*) coach: Gaulish (Quint.), ʀᴇɪᴅʜ- OIr. *riad* journeying, Ags. *rīdan* ride E. E. *raid road*.

rāmex hernia, **rāmicēs** blood-vessels of the lungs: 'branching out,' fr. sq.

rāmus branch: 'arm,' ʀᴍᴏ́s *armus*.

rāna frog:

rancens putrid (E. *rankle*; but for *rank* Adj. see *regō*):

†**traphanus** radish: *ῥάφανος: by-form of *ῥάπυς, see *rāpum* ?

rapiō seize (E. *ravage raven* Vb. *ravine ravish*):

rāpum turnip (E. *rape*[2]): ʀᴀᴘ- OHG. *ruobā*, Lit. *rópė*, cf. ʀᴀᴘ- *ῥάπυς*, OHG. *raba*; by-form ʀᴇ́ᴘ- OSlav. *rěpa*.

rā-rus thin: ʀ̥-, cf. ʀ- Lit. *irti* to separate; by-form ʀᴇ̄- see *rēte*.

ratis raft: = *retis*, ʀᴇᴛ-, see *rēmus*.

raucus hoarse : = *ravi-cus* fr. *ravim.*

raudus rōdus rūdus roudus piece of brass :
not fr. *rūfus.*

ravim Acc. hoarseness :

rāvus grey (between yellow and blue Fest.) :

re- back, up (Verg. Geo. 3. 76 crura reponit = lifts his legs ; so ἄνα = back, up.—E. *rear*) :

re-cellō spring back : 'strike back,' see *per-cellō.*

recens fresh : 'coming up,' Part. of *receō* Vb. fr. *re-cus* Adj. of *re-.*

reciperō recuperō regain (E. *recover*) : fr. *recus,* see praeced., + *parō,* cf. Varr. se quiete reciperare 'recruit'.

reci-procus returning : 'demanded back,' fr. *recus,* see *recens,* + *procō,* see *procāx.*

red- back (whence *reccidī reppertī reppulī rettulī* Peris., *reddūcō rellātum relligiō relliquiae, redeō* &c.) : = *re-du *re-do* (see *indu*), from *re-* + *-do.*

red-imiō bind round :

redi-vīvus used again : = *redu-vīvus* 'alive again,' see *red-* and *vīvus.*

reduvia reluvium (Fest.) whitlow : 'shed off,' *red-* + *avō* see *exuō induō.*

rē-fert profits : meā rēfert = mea rēs fert 'my interest tends,' *meā* archaic Nom. (with *-ā* preserved because *rē-* was taken as Abl.).

re-frāgor oppose : cf. *suf-frāgor.*

regō direct (E. *escort rule source surge*) : 'stretch,' cf. *regiō* tract, REG- ὀ-ρέγω stretch, cf. ROG- Got. uf-*rakjan* lift up E. *reach rich right rank* Adj., RG- MIr. *rigim* I stretch, Zd. *erezu* straight Sk. *ṛj-* direct, stretch, attain, ṚG- Zd. *arez-* be straight, see *rēx.*

relligiō rēligiō religion : = *red-ligiō,* fr. *red-* + *legō* care, see *dīligō.*

remeligo hinderer : = *re-medīgo* fr. *re-* + Sk. *mad-* linger *mand-* (see *mandra*) ?

†remulcum tow-rope : formed as tho' from *re-,* for *rūmūlcum,* ῥυμουλ- κοῦν Part. Neut. of ῥυμουλκέω tow, fr. ῥῦμα tow-rope + ἕλκω drag.

rēmus oar : = *resmos* (cf. *triresmōs,* Duilian inscr.) *ret-mós, ἐ-ρετ-μόν,* MIr. *rām,* from RET- *ratis.*

rēnēs kidneys (Plaut. *riēn* Sing. on anal. of *liēn.*—OE. *reins*) :

re-nīdeō smile : fr. *nūdus,* 'show the teeth,' cf. Catull. 39. 1 quod can- didos habet dentes renidet.

†rēnō fur pelisse : Gaulish (Varr.).

reor reckon (E. *arraign rate reason*) : = *reor,* RĒ-, cf. RA- *ratiō* reckon- ing, Got. *rathjō* number.

repens sudden : VREP- ῥέπω fall, cf. VṚP- Lit. *wirpēti* shake.

rēpō creep : RĒP- Lit. *replióti,* cf. REP- Zd. *rap-* go.

re-pudium divorce : 'beating back,' see *tri-pudium.*

rēs thing (E. *rebus*) : Sk. *rās* property.

†rēsina resin : *ῥησίνη* Ion. form of *†ῥητίνη* :

restis rope :

rēte net : Lit. *rėtis* sieve, RĒ- see *rārus*.

reus disputant : = *rēvus *rīvus (see *deus dīvus*) = *rīvālis* (for the terminations cf. *aequus aequālis*).

rēx king : OIr. *rīg* Gen., Got. *reiks* rule E. *drake* (see *anās*), Sk. *rājā* ruler (E. *rajah*) *rāj-* to rule, RĒG-, cf. REG- *regō*.

†**rhētor** rhetorician : ῥήτωρ speaker, VRĒ- OIr. *briathar* word, cf. VER- εἴρω (= *Fέρ-jω) say.

†**rhō** R. : †ῥῶ, for *ῥῶς from Heb. *rēsh* (with -ω- from ὃ μέγα?).

†**rhomphaea** spear : †ῥομφαία sword (used as a missile?), Thracian (Gellius).

†**rhythmus** harmony : ῥυ-θ-μός, fr. ῥέω flow.

rīca veil : 'torn' (see *lacerna*), REIK- ἐ-ρείκω tear.

ricinium recinium a square garment :

rīdeō laugh :

rigeō stiffen : 'stretch,' fr. *regō*?

rigô moisten :

rīma crack : 'running along,' RĪ- see *rītus*.

ringor show the teeth :

rīpa bank (E. *arrive river*) : 'torn' (see *littus*), REIP- ἐ-ρείπω tear down, ONor. *rifa* to tear E. *reef rift rifle* Subst. *rive*, cf. RIP- ἐ-ρίπνη cliff.

†**triscus** chest : †θρίσκος, Phrygian (Donatus on Ter. Eun. 754).

rītus ceremony : 'course,' RĪ- ὀ-ρίνω stir, cf. RI- OIr. *rith* course (see *petorritum*), Got. *rinnan* run E.

rīvālis rīvīnus rival : RĪV- see *reus*, cf. RIV- OSlav. *rīvīnŭ*.

rīvus brook : = *rū-vus *rur-vus fr. *ruō*[1].

rīxa brawl : REIK-S- cf. REIK- *rīca*, 'split'.

rōbīgō rūbīgō rust : 'red,' ROUDH- see *rūfus*, cf. BŪDH- Lit. *rūdìs*, RUDH- ἐ-ρυσίβη mildew, Ags. *rust* E. *rust*, OSlav. *rŭzda* rust.

rōbur strength : MIr. *rūad* : ROUDH- see *rūfus*, 'red' as the sign of 'freshness,' cf. *rudis* Adj. So **rōbur** oak, from its buds and young leaves being red.

rōbus Juv. 8. 155 Schol. red : see *rūfus*.

rōdō gnaw : RŌD- cf. ROD- Ags. *rät* rat E., see *radius rādō*.

rogô ask : ROG- cf. REG- *regō*, 'try to attain'.

rogus pyre : ROG- cf. REG- Got. *rikan* to heap E. *rake*. Not from ῥογός silo.

rōrāriī skirmishers : 'rushing,' ROUS- ὀ-ρού(σ)ω rush, see *ruō*[1].

rōs dew (E. *rosemary*) : RŌS- cf. ROS- Lit. *rasa* OSlav. *rosa*, Sk. *rásas* sap.

†**rosa** rose (E. E. *copperas*) : dialectic for *rossa, Osc. (cf. Verg. Geo. 4. 119 rosaria Paesti, Paestum in Lucania where Oscan was spoken) for *rodia (cf. Sabine *Clausus* for *Claudius*), *ῥοδία Adj. Fem. fr. †ῥόδον, *Fρόδον, cf. Arab. *werd* Zenker 930 b.

rota wheel (E. *barouche rile roll rout round*): BOT- OIr. *roth*, OHG. *rad*, Lit. *rãtas*, Zd. *ratha-* chariot Sk. *rãthas* wagon.

rubeō blush: fr. sq.

ruber red (E. *rouge ruby*): RUDH-R- *ἐ-ρυθρός*, OSlav. *rŭdrŭ*, cf. RUDH-R- Sk. *rudhiras*: RUDH-, cf. BOUDH- *rūfus*.

rubus bramble: 'with red berries,' cf. praeced.

rūctô: REUGV- *ἐ-ρεύγομαι*, cf. RŪGV- Lit. *rúgiu* OSlav. *rygaję*, RUGV- Ags. *rocetan* Inf., Arm. *orcam* vomo.

rudens rope: 'rattling' in the wind, Part. fr. *rudō* (Nonius, cf. Ov. Trist. 1. 713 stridunt aquilone rudentes).

rudis Subst. rod: RUDH- cf. RŪDH- Ags. *rōd* E. E. *rood*.

rudis Adj. raw: 'red,' and so applied to earth, metal, meat (cf. E. brannew 'fire-new,' fresh and bright), BUDH- see *ruber*.

rŭdō roar: RUD- Zd. Sk. *rud-* weep, RŪD- OSlav. *rydati*, REUD- Ags. *reōtan*, cf. ROUD- Lit. *raudà* wailing.

rūdus broken stones: 'fresh,' cf. *rudis* Adj.

rūfus red (E. *roan*): dialectic for **rūbus*, *rōbus*, NUmbr. *rofu* rubros, BOUDH- MIr. *rūad*, Got. *rauds* E. E. *ruddy*, cf. BUDH- Lit. *rùdas*, see *ruber*.

rūga wrinkle:

rūmen throat:

rumex spear, sorrel ('with hastate leaves'):

rumis breast:

rūmor (for term. cf. *clāmor*) talk: RŪ- *ὡ-ρύομαι* howl, Ags. *rūnian*, cf. REU- OSlav. *ruti*, RU- Lit. *rujà* rutting, Sk. *ru-* cry.

rumpō break (E. *rout route rote rut*): RUMP- cf. RŪP- *rūpēs*, Lit. *rŭpéti* to trouble, BUP- Lit. *rupas* rough, Sk. *rup-* break, REUP- Ags. bereōfan be broken off E. be*reave rove rob ruff rubbish rubble gruff*.

rūna dart:

runcina plane (*ρυκάνη*): fr. sq., twigs being compared to hairs.

runcô deprive of hair (Pers. 4. 36), weed out: Sk. *lunc-* tear.

ruō [1] fall, rush; **rūō* Dissim. for **rūrō *rūsō*, ROUS- see *rōrārii*: hence *irruô obruô* [1] *prōruô* [1].

ruō [2] demolish: Sk. *ru-* break to pieces, cf. REU- Got. *riurs* corruptible: hence *dēruô dīruô ēruô* [1] *prōruo* [2] *subruô* [1] *semirutus*.

ruō [3] heap up: hence *adruō obruō* [2]:

ruō [4] dig up: RŪ- OSlav. *ryti* dig, cf. ROU- Lit. *ráuti* dig up: hence *rūta* 'minerals' *ēruō* [2] *subruō* [2].

rūpēs rock: 'broken,' see *rumpō*.

rūs country (E. *roistering*): RŪ-s MIr. *rōe* plain, cf. RŪ-M- Got. *rūms* room E.

rūscum rūstum butcher's broom (E. *rush* Subst.): 'used in the country to make brooms' Plin. 23. 166, fr. praeced.

russus rūsus red (E. *russet*) : = *rūd-tus*, cf. RUDH- *rudis* Adj.

†trūta rue (E.) : ῥυτή : 'curative,' Part. Fem. from ῥύομαι cure Hdt. 4. 187 fin.

rutilus red : RUDH-ḶOS, see *rudis* Adj.

†sabbata sabbath : †σάββατα, Heb. *shabbāth*.

sabulum saburra sand : PSABH- cf. PSĀBH- ψῆφος pebble? Not = *samudum* SAMADH- ἄμαθος sand cf. SAMDH- Ags. E. *sand*.

†saccus bag (E. *sack*) : †σάκκος, Heb. †*saq* : Egyptian, cf. Coptic *sok*.

sacer consecrated : = *sec-ró-* fr. *sequor*, 'followed,' i.e. regarded, by the gods, cf. *secundus* propitious, ὅτις retribution.

saeculum sēculum saeclum sēclum race : SAI-TLOM W. *hoedl* life : 'connexion,' SAI- see *saeta*.

saepe often : short for *saepe-numerō* 'with the tale inclusive,' *saepe* Abl. (cf. Ov. perenne Abl.) of *saepis* Adj. fr. sq., 'crammed, fenced in' (see *cunctus*).

saepēs sēpēs hedge (E. *transept*) : 'enclosure,' dialectic for *saequēs* SAIKV- OSlav. *sěkŭ* sheepfold.

saeta sēta bristle (E. *satin seton*) : 'bound together' to make a brush or line, SAI-T'- Ags. *sād* noose, Lit. *saitai* prison ('place of binding') OSlav. *sětl* noose, Zd. *haětu-* bridge, road ('connecting') Sk. *sětus* binding, from SAI- see *saeculum*.

saevus sēvus fierce :

sagāx acute : 'pointing out the way,' SAG- OIr. *saigim* I visit, Got. *sakan* contend ('point out' the adversary) E. *sake*, cf. SĀG- *sāgiō*.

sagīna cramming : SVAGV- σάττω (dialectic for *σάζω *σϜάγ-jω) load, Zd. *qaj-* surround Sk. *svaj-* embrace.

sāgiō am keen : 'find the way,' ἡγέομαι lead, Got. *sōkjan* seek E., see *sagāx*.

†sagitta arrow :

sagmen sacred herbs :

†sagum cloak (E. *sail*?) : Gaulish (Varr. L. L. 5. 167).

sāl salt (E. *salad* salt-*cellar*) : SAL- ἅλς Masc., OIr. *salann*, Lit. *salunka* salt-box OSlav. *solĭ* salt, Arm. *aλ*, cf. SAL-DO- Got. E. *salt*.

†salacō braggart : σαλάκων ; fr. σάλος tossing, see *salum*.

†salapūtium mannikin : 'deserving a slap,' cf. †*salapitta* (= *salapīta* *sulæpūta*) box on the ear :

saliō leap (E. *sally*) : SAL- ἅλλομαι, MIr. tui-*sel* fall.

†saliunca Celtic nard : Gaulish (to judge by its botanical name).

†salīva (for term. cf. *ging-iva*) : MIr. *saile* : Gaulish (as first in Catullus)?

salix willow : SALIK- Arcadian ἑλίκη (for *ἁλίκη, cf. Arcadian ζέρεθρον for βάραθρον), MIr. *sail*, cf. SALK- Ags. *scalh* E. *sallow* Subst.

salsus salted : Part. of *sallō* (as *falsus* of *fallō*) I salt, = *sal-nō* fr. *sal*.

saltem at least: 'swiftly, without difficulty,' fr. *saltus* leaping, *saliō*, + M see *autem*.

saltus woodland: 'running-ground' for cattle (see *ager*), Zd. *har*- go Sk. *sar*- run.

†**salum** sea: σάλος tossing, SVAL- Ags. *svellan* swell E. E. *swallow* Subst.

salūs safety: *salūt-* = *salūvi-t-* fr. *sal-ūvus* = sq.

salvus safe: sᴜ̣- OIr. *slán* sound, cf. sᴜ̣- *solidus*.

†**sambūca** harp: †σαμβύκη, Aramaic *sabb'kā*.

sanciō ordain: SENKV- cf. SEKV- *sacer*.

†**sandalium** slipper: σανδάλιον Dimin. of †σάνδαλον, Pers. *sendel* Zenker 521 a.

†**sandapila** bier:

†**sandīx sandȳx** vermilion: †σάνδῑξ σάνδῡξ, Lydian (Lydus de Magistratibus 3. 64).

sanguis sanguen blood: SANGVN̄ cf. SAGVN- ἀμνίον (for *ἀβνίον) bowl to catch the victim's blood:

saniēs matter:

†**sanna** grimace (not E. *zany*): *σάννη fr. †σάννας buffoon.

sānus sound: OHG. *suona* expiation ('making whole').

sapa must: dialectic for *saqua*, Lit. *sakaí* resin OSlav. *sokŭ* juice.

†**sāperda** a fish: †σαπέρδης, Pontic (as coming from Pontus).

sapiō taste, understand (E. *savour*): SEP- Ags. *sefan* understand, cf. SOP- ὀπός juice.

sarciō mend: SARKV- Lit. *szarkas* garment (ONor. *serkr* shirt Scotch *sark*) OSlav. *sraka*.

†**sarisa sarissa** spear: †σάρῑσα σάρισσα, Macedonian.

sarpō prune: SᴀRP- cf. SᴀRP- *harpē*.

✓†**sarrācum serrācum** wagon: Gaulish, like other names of wheeled vehicles (*carpentum carrus petorritum raeda, covinnus essedum*)?

sarrapis in Plaut. Poen. 1312 (Goetz) deglupta mena, sarrapis sementium:

sarriō sāriō weed (E. *assart*):

sartāgō frying-pan: fr. *sartum* 'in good repair,' Part. of *sarciō*; 'putting the ingredients in good order, making them serviceable'.

†**satelles** attendant: Etrusc. *zatlaθ* Bugge B. B. 11. 1: a bodyguard of *satellites* first introduced by Tarquinius Superbus, an Etruscan by origin.

satis enough (E. *assets sate*): SAT- MIr. *sathach* satisfied, Got. *saths* full E. *sad* OHG. *sat* satisfied, cf. sᴀ̄T- Lit. *sotùs* satisfying.

†**satrapa** viceroy: †σατράπης ἐξατράπης, OPers. *khshatrapāvā* fr. *khshatram* dominion + *pā*- protect.

saturēja savory: 'satisfying,' fr. *satur* full, see *satis*.

satus sown (E. *season*): = *setós SE-, cf. Sᴇ̄- *sēmen*.

†saucaptis a spice : †*σαύκαπτις :

saucius wounded : fr. *savicus, Chian σαβακός rotten (Hesych.).

sāvium suāvium kiss : from *vāsium, bāsium, quasi fr. suāvis.

saxum stone (E. *sassafras*) : sakso- OHG. *sahs* knife (orig. of flint).

scabellum scabillum scamillum (Terentius Scaurus, Keil 7. 14) castanet : from *scab-lum skvabh- scamnum (the castanet, inserted in the performer's shoe, being compared to a bed-step).

scaber rough, scabō scrape (Nonius' *scapres pro scabres* should perhaps be ' scabres pro scabra es ') : skvabh- σκάπτω dig, Got. *skaban* shave E. E. *shaft shabby scab*, Lit. *skabéti* cut OSlav. *skoblı* scraping-iron.

†scaena scēna stage : σκηνή booth :

scaeva omen : ' seen on the left,' *scaevus* left, σκαιός (for *σκαιϜός), ONor. *skeika* to swerve (for the second -k- see on *vīvus*).

scālae steps : ⹀ *scādae skvād- cf. skvand- scandō.

†scalmus thole : σκαλμός : ' pointed stick,' cf. σκῶλος stake and σκάλλω I hoe.

scalpō carve : skl̩p-, cf. sklp- *sculpō.

†scammōnea scammony : †σκαμμωνία, coming from Mysia (Dioso. 4. 168).

scamnum stool (E. *shambles*) : = *scab-num ' support,' skvabh- Lit. *skaba* horseshoe OSlav. *skoba* buckle, cf. skvambh- Zd. çkemb- to prop Sk. *skambh-*.

scandō climb (E. *scan*) : ' jump up,' skvand- σκανδάληθρον springe (E. *slander*), OIr. *ro-sescaind* he leapt forth, Sk. *skand-* leap, see *scālae*.

†scapha boat : σκάφη trough ; ' scraped out, hollowed,' fr. *scabō*.

scapulae shoulderblades : ' bearers ' on which to carry a burden, skvabh- *scamnum*.

scāpus yarn-beam : ' supporter,' skvāp- σκῆπτρον staff σκήπτομαι support myself, by-form of skvabh- *scamnum*.

†scarus wrasse : σκάρος ; fr. σκαίρω skip.

scateō gush : skvat- Lit. *skatau* I leap.

scaurus large-ankled (σκαῦρος, 10th century A.D.) :

scelus crime : ' debt, requiring expiation,' skvel- cf. skvol- Got. *skal* I must E. *shall*, skvl̩- Lit. *skilti* become indebted.

scheda sheet of paper (σχέδη, 12th century A.D., so *scheda* cannot be borrowed from it : E. *sketch*) : pop. etym. (quasi fr. σχέδιος common) for *scida*, see *scindo*.

†schoenus rush : σχοῖνος :

scindo split : skhvind- cf. skhvid- σχίζω, Zd. çcid- break Sk. *chid-* cut off.

scintilla spark (E. *stencil tinsel*) : fr. *scintus Part. of *scinō shine, skin- cf. skīn- Got. *skeinan* shine E.

sciō know (E. *nice*): 'discern,' = *sciō* SKEI- 'separate,' MIr. *scian* knife, cf. KEI- κείω split.

scīpiō staff: σκίπων: 'for throwing,' SKVĪP- OHG. *scībā* ball, cf. KVSIP- Sk. *kship-* throw.

scirpus sirpus rush (OHG. *sciluf?*), **surpiculus** rush-basket:

scobis sawdust:

†**scomber** mackerel: σκόμβρος:

scōpae twigs (E. *scullion*):

†**scopulus** rock: σκόπελος; 'place of observation,' fr. σκοπέω see *speciō*.

†**scorpius** scorpion: σκορπίος:

scortum hide: 'cut off,' SKVᴙTÓM Part. Neut., see *cernō*.

screô hawk: = *scrējō* SKREI- cf. SKRĪ- OHG. *scrian* cry, SKRI- MIr. *scret* a cry, cf. E. *scream screech shriek*, onomatop.

†**scrīblīta** cheesecake: pop. etym. (quasi fr. sq., 'marked' with notches) for *streblīta*, *στρεβλίτης* fr. στρεβλός twisted (cf. στρεπτός cracknel fr. στρέφω turn, E. *tart* Subst. from Lat. *tortus* twisted).

scrībō write (OHG. *scriban*, E. *descry scribble scrivener shrive*): SKRIBH- cf. SKᴙIBH- σκαρίφδομαι scratch.

scrinium chest (Ags. *scrīn* ark E. *shrine*; OSlav. *skrina* chest): = *scrī- n-ium* fr. *scrū-ta*, 'place for keeping odds and ends'.

scrobis ditch (E. *screw*): 'dug out,' SKVBOBH- Lett. *škrabt* scrape.

scrōfa sow: dialectic for *scrōba*, SKVBŌBH- cf. praeced., 'scratching up the ground'.

scrūpus sharp stone: = *scrōpus* SKRŌP- cf. SKᴙP- Ags. *sceorfan* scrape E. *scurf scurvy*.

scrūta trash: Ags. *scrūd* garment E. *shroud*, SKRŪTÓ- Part. of *scruō*.

scrūtor examine (OIr. ara-*scrūta* ut scrutetur, OHG. *scruton* explore): 'cut up,' fr. praeced.

sculpō carve: SKᴌP- see *scalpō*, cf. SKOLP- σκόλοψ stake.

sculpōneae wooden shoes:

†**scurra** buffoon: = *scūra* *scōra*, *σκωρᾶs* (cf. the slave-names 'Αλεξᾶς Δημᾶς 'Επαφρᾶς 'Ερμᾶς) from *σκωρ-φάγος* 'dirt-eater' (cf. E. toad-eater).

scūtāle thong: 'strip of hide,' fr. *scūtum*.

scutica lash: 'strip of hide,' SKUT- cf. SKŪT- *scūtum*.

scutra square tray (E. *scuttle* Subst. *skillet*):

†**scutula** roller: σκυτάλη staff:

scūtum oblong leather shield (E. *escutcheon squire*): cf. σκῦτος hide.

†**scymnus** whelp: σκύμνος:

†**scyphus** cup: σκύφος:

sē Acc. himself: svĒ (see *mē*), cf. SVE †, Got. *si*-k E. ba*sk* bu*sk*, OSlav. *sę*, see *suus*.

sē- apart: 'by oneself,' Abl. fr. praeced.

sēbum sēvum tallow: = *saebum* SAIB- Ags. *sāp* red antimony E. *soap* (Gaulish *sāpō* pomade Plin. 28. 191 from Teutonic).

secô cut (E. *risk scion sickle*): SEKV- OHG. *seh* coulter ONor. *sigde* sickle E. *sithe sedge* †*hassock*, cf. SOKV'- Ags. *saga* saw E., SĒKV- OSlav. *sēkǫ* I cut.

secô² follow Aen. 10. 407, Hor. Epp. 1. 16. 42: fr. *sequor*.

secta path (E. *sept suit suite*): fr. praeced.

sectius (Gell. 18. 9) **sētius** less:

hardly cf. Got. *seithus* late, which will not account for *sectius*.

secus otherwise, **sequius** worse: SEK- *ĕkds* apart, OIr. *sech* beyond.

Enn.'s Prep. *secus* 'by,' Sk. *sácā* with, is fr. *sequor*: from it come *altrinsecus extrinsecus intrinsecus*.

sed set without (Fest.), but: = *sĕd*, OLat. *sē-dum*, see *sĕ-* and *-dum*.

sedeō sit (E. *assize hostage see* Subst. *siege size* surcease): SED- *ĕdos* seat *ἕζομαι* sit, Got. *sitan* E. E. *seat set* †*seize*, OSlav. *sedlo* saddle, Zd. *had-sit* Sk. *sad-*, cf. SOD- (?) MIr. *saidim* I settle, see *sīdō*.

sēd-itiō discord: fr. *sē-du* (see *in-du*), see *sĕ-*, + *eō*.

sēdō settle: SĒD- OIr. *sīd* peace, Lit. *sėdė́ti* sit, cf. SED- *sedeō*.

sēdulō diligently (whence *sēdulus* diligent): 'without deceit,' *sĕ* without (Fest.), see *sĕ-* and *sed*, + *dolus*.

seges cornfield: SEG- cf. SOG- W. *hau* sow.

segnis slow: cf. Sk. *saj-* hang?

sella sedda (Terentius Scaurus, Keil 7. 13) seat: = *sēda*, see *sēdō*.

semel once: Oscan (see *famulus*) for *semul* *semulum* Adj. Acc. Neut. from SEM- *ἕν* one Neut., see *simul*.

sēmen seed: SĒ-MN̥ cf. OHG. *sāmo*, Lit. *sė́menys* OSlav. *sěmę*, from SĒ- OIr. *sīl* (E. *shillelagh*), Got. *saian* sow Ags. *saed* seed E., Lit. *sė́ti* sow: 'throw,' cf. *ἵημι* (= *σί-ση-μι*) send.

sēmi- half: *ἡμι-*, Sk. *sāmi-*, cf. SĒM- OW. *hanther* Zeuss² 149 b, Ags. *sām* E. *sand-*blind.

sēmis half-as: from *sēmissis* = *sēm(i)-issis* *sēm(i)-essis* (cf. *quinquessis* five asses), fr. praeced. + *ās*.

sēmita footpath (E. *sentinel*): fr. *sēmi-*, 'half the width of the road'.

semper always: SEN- Got. *sinteinō*, Arm. *hanapaz*, Sk. *sanūt*, + *-per*: 'as of old,' fr. *senex*.

sempiternus eternal: for *semper-nus* fr. praeced., on anal. of *aeviternus* (fr. *aevitās*).

senex old (E. *sir sirrah surly*): SEN- *ἕνος*, OIr. *sen*, Got. *sineigs* E. †*seneschal*, Lit. *sénas*, Arm. *hin*, Zd. *hana-* Sk. *sánas*.

senticētum thorn-brake: fr. *sentex* formed from *sentis* on anal. of *frutex ilex*.

sentina bilgewater: SN̥TI- *ἄσις* mud for *ἅτις*?

sentiō perceive (E. *scent*): 'recognise as being, realise,' fr. **sens* Part. (cf. *prae-sens*) of *sum*.

sentis thorn:

sentus rough:

sepeliō bury:

†**sēpia** cuttlefish: σηπία, fr. †σήψ snake:

septem 7: SEPTM̥ (-*m* for -*n* from the ordinal SÉPTM̥-MOS, see *decem*) for SEPTM̥ ἑπτά, OIr. *secht n-*, Got. *sibun* E., Arm. *evthn*, Zd. *haptan-* Sk. *saptá*, cf. Lit. *septyni* OSlav. *sedmĭ* (= *sept-mĭ).

septuāgintā 70: formed on anal. of *octuagintā* 80, i.e. **octūāgintā* **octō-āgintā*, see *trīgintā*.

sequor follow (E. *sue*): SEKV- ἕπομαι, MIr. *sechur* I follow, Got. *saihvan* see E. ('follow with the eyes'), Lit. *sĕkti* follow, Zd. *hac-* Sk. *sac-* accompany.

serēnus dry, **serescō** Lucr. 1. 806 get dry:

sēria jar: 'heavy,' sq.

sērius grave: SVER- OHG. *swāri* heavy Got. *svērs* honorable, cf. SVER- Lit. *swerti* weigh.

sermō speech: 'connected' discourse, fr. *serō²*.

serō¹ sow: SES- W. *haidd* barley (= *hei-ja *hes-ja), Zd. *hahya* corn Sk. *sasydm*, cf. Plin. 18. 141 *secale* ('rye') Taurini sub Alpibus *sasiam* (so Stokes conj. for *asiam*: hence Span. *jeja*) vocant.—Perf. *sēvī* from SĒ- *sēmen*, Part. *satus* from SE-.

serō² join (E. *concert seraglio*): SER- εἴρω (= *ἔρ-jω), cf. SER- Lit. *sēris* thread.

serperastra splints (for term. see *mediastīnus*): fr. **serperus* Adj. of sq.

serpō creep: ἕρπω, Sk. *sarp-*.

†**serpyllum serpullum serpillum** thyme: ἕρπυλλος, fr. ἕρπω creep, spelt as though direct fr. praeced. (cf. *salm-acidus* sour from ἅλμη brine, with *s-* from *sāl*).

serra saw:

serum whey: SER-, cf. SOR- ὀρός, Sk. *sárasas* juicy.

sērus late (Fr. *soir* evening): OIr. *sīr* long.

servô keep:

servus slave (E. *serf*): fr. praeced., 'protégé'.

†**sēsamum** sesame: †σήσαμον, for **σάμσαμον*, Arab. *semsem* Zenker 518 b Assyrian *samassammu*.

sēscēnāris of 600 pounds' weight (Graevius) Liv. 41. 15 *bovis*: fr. *sēscēnī* 600 (= *sex-cent-nī, sex + centum).

†**seselis** hartwort: †σέσελις:

sēsqui- 1½: fr. *sēmissi-* (see *sēmīs*) + -*que*.

†**sētanium** medlar: 'fresh,' σητάνιον (Neut.) of this year, fr. **σῆτες* Att. τῆτες this year, = **τϝ-ῆτες* fr. τό this + term. -VO- + ἔτος.

sevērus serious: 'fixt,' Lit. *segù* I fasten.

sex 6 (E. *siesta*): SĒKS Got. *saihs* E., Sk. *shdsh*, cf. (1) SJEKS OSlav. *šestĭ*, (2) SVEKS ἕξ, Lit. *szeszi* (unless these two are from SEKS), OIr. *sē* W. *chwech*, (3) VEKS *Fέξ*, Arm. *veths*, UKS Pruss. *uschts* sixth, (4) KVSVEKS Zd. *khshvash* 6.

sī sei if: proclitic form of *svai* Osc. *svai*, *al*: from svo- Got. *sva* so E.? Hardly add *el* if, which rather = Lit. *jei*.

sībilus sīfīlus whistling:

sīc thus: = *so-i-ce* (see *hīc*), so Enn. *sam* eam, *ó* he, OIr. *sē* this Neut., Got. *sa* he, Zd. *ha*- Sk. *sás*.

sīca dagger: cf. Lit. *sykis* stroke.

siccus dry (E. *sack* sherry): = *sit-cus* fr. *sitis*, cf. MIr. *seisc* (= *sit-kios*).

sī-cubi wherever: from *sī*, see *nĕ-cubi*.

sīdō settle: = *si-sdō-* ZD- Arm. *n-stim* I sit down (Bedrossian), cf. SED- *sedeō*.

sīdus constellation: praeced., 'fixt,' as opposed to the moon.

signum mark: SIG-, cf. *sigilla* images:

sileō am silent (Got. ana-*silan* abate, of wind): 'settle down,' fr. *sedeō*.

siler brookwillow: 'growing by rivers,' cf. *Siler Silarus* river in Lucania:

silex flint:

sili-cernium funeral feast: 'meat at which they sat' (the old Rom. fashion) instead of reclining, fr. *sedeō* + *cĕrsna* dinner, OUmbr. *çersnatur* cenati, see *cĕna*.

silīgō winter-wheat (σιλίγνιον):

siliqua pod: fr. *silex*, 'hard'.

†**silūrus** shad: †σίλουρος: Egyptian, Plin. 9. 44 silurus in Nilo.

sīlus snubnosed: SVĪ-, see *simus*.

silua silva wood (E. *savage*):

simia ape: fr. *sīmus*.

similis alike: from *sŭmŭlus* SOM-ĻŌS ὁμαλός level, SOM- ὁμός in common, Got. *sama* same E., cf. SM̥- ἁ- together ἅ-μα with, Got. *sums* some E. E. game-*some*, Arm. *ham*- together, Zd. *hama* like Sk. *samás*, and SŌM- OSlav. *samŭ* ipse, see *semel simul*.

simītū at once (for term. see *pītuīta*): SM̥-, see *simul*.

simplex simplus simple (for terms. see *duplex*): ·SEM-, see *semel*.

simpulum ladle: fr. sq., cf. OUmbr. *seples* Abl. Plur.

simpuvium bowl:

simul at once (E. *assemble*): = *simulum* SM̥-ĻO- cf. OIr. *samal* likeness, from SM̥- see *similis*.

simultās quarrel: 'match,' fr. *similis*.

sīmus snub-nosed: σῖμός, SVĪ-, see *sīlus*.

sīn but if: = *si-num* 'if now'.

†sināpis mustard (MHG. *senf*): *σίνᾱπυς Dor. for †σίνηπυς, cf. (σ)νᾶπυ: Egyptian (Plin. 19. 171 semen optumum Aegyptium)?

sincērus clean (for term. cf. *sev-ĕrus*): fr. *sin-cus* simple, SEM-, see *simplex*.

sinciput half a head: *sēmi-* + *caput*.

sine without: SN- *ἄνευ*, Zd. *hanare*, cf. *ἄτερ*, Got. *sundrō* privately E. *sunder*, Sk. *sanitár* without.

singulī each: dialectic (?) for *sinculī* Dimin. from *sincus*, see *sincērus*.

singultus sobbing: fr. *singuliō* Vb., SING- cf. SĪG- Ags. *sican* sigh E.?

sinister left (for term. cf. *magister minister*): SEN- *senex*, 'elder' (a euphemism like *εὐώνυμος* 'well-named, left,' and Ags. *vinster* left fr. Sk. *van-* to desire).

sinō leave (E. *site*):

hardly cf. ONor. *svina* subside (of a swelling) SVI- cf. SVĪ- Ags. *svima* dizziness E. *swim*[2] am dizzy.

sīnum bowl:

sinus fold:

sīparium curtain: = *sīlparium* fr. *supparum*.

†sīphō pipe: σίφων:

sirempse (Plaut. Amph. 78) siremps (for loss of -*e* see *instar*): = *sur-em-p-se* Inf. Perf. of *surimō* take up, Fest. *surĕmit* Perf., from *sus* + *emō*; so that *siremps lex esto quasi* = 'let an assumption be law, as though,' &c.

†sirpe (see *caepe*) silphium: for *sirpium*, *σίρφιον* by-form of †σίλφιον: sistō stop: formed from Inf. *sistere* = *si-stă-re* Redupl. of STA- see *stō*, cf. *ἱστάναι* place (= *σι-στά-ναι*).

†sīstrum rattle: σεῖστρον: Egyptian (as used in Egypt), but formed quasi fr. σείω shake.

†sisura coverlet: σισύρα:

†sisymbrium mint: σισύμβριον, Redupl. (with θ softened in Ion. before υ, cf. ἐρυσίβη πίσυνος) fr. θύμβρα savory, see *thymbra*.

sitis thirst:

†sittybus label; *σίττυβος, σίττυβον piece of leather:

situla jar:

†smaragdus emerald (E.): †σμάραγδος (for σ- see *murra*[1]), cf. Sk. *marakatam*.

†smyrna myrrh: †σμύρνα, see *murra*[1].

sobrīnus cousin (E. E. *cozen*): = *svesr-īnus* 'sister's son,' Lit. *seserynai* Plur., svESR- Lit. *sesers* sister's, and (with -*t*- from the words for 'brother') svESTR- OIr. *sethar*, Got. *svistar* sister E., Pruss. *swestro* OSlav. *sestra*, cf. svESŌR- *soror*.

sōbrius sober: 'free from drunkenness,' *sō-* by-form (see *dōdrans*) of *sē-*, + *brius* see *ēbrius*.

†soccus slipper: *σόκχος, Zd. *hakha* sole, cf. Hesych. †σύκχος Phrygian shoe.

socer father-in-law: SVEKŪR- *ἐκυρός*, Lit. *szesziùras*, Zd. *qaçura* Sk. *çvá-çuras*, cf. Arm. *skesur* mother-in-law, see *socrus*.

socius ally: SOKV- *ὁπάων* attendant, cf. SEKV- *sequor*.

sōcors dull: fr. *sō*- see *sōbrius* + *cor* wit.

socrus parent-in-law: SVEKRU- W. *chwegrwn* father-in-law, OSlav. *svekrŭ* (-*k*-, for -*s*-, from Teutonic?), cf. SVÉKRON- Got. *svaihra*, see *socer*.

sodālis fellow: 'going' with one, see *solum*.

sōdēs pray: = *saudēs*, *sī audēs* 'if you are inclined,' cf. Aen. 2. 347 audere in praelia.

sōl sun: SAUL- W. *haul*, Lit. *sáule*, cf. SAUEL- Got. *sauil*, from SĀUEL- *ἥλιος* (= *σἄϜέλιος*).

†soldūrii vassels: Gaulish, †σιλόδουροι (Athenaeus).

solea slipper: 'for going in,' see *solum* (as *ἐμβάς* fr. *βαίνω* go).

soleō am accustomed: 'go my way,' see *solum*.

solidus firm (E. *soda solder soldier*): SĻ-, cf. SĻ- *salvus*.

solium seat: = *sodium*, OIr. *suide*, SOD- cf. SED- *sedeō*.

sollemnis sollennis (quasi fr. *annus*) appointed: 'coming when the round is completed,' fr. sq. + *amnus* round, Osc. *amnod* circuitu.

sollus whole: Osc. *sollo* totum (Fest.): SÓLVOS, *οὖλος*, Zd. *haurva*- all Sk. *sdrvas*.

sōlor comfort: 'make to go,' SŌD- cf. SOD- sq. ?

solum ground: 'for going on,' SOD- *ὁδός* way, OSlav. *hoditi* walk.

sōlus alone (E. *sullen*): 'by oneself,' from *sō*- (see *sōbrius*).

solvō loose (E. *assoil*): 'let go,' fr. *sol-vus* Adj. from SOD- see *solum*.

somnus sleep: SVOP-NOS Lit. *sápnas*, Zd. *hvafna*- Sk. *svdpnas*, cf. SVEP-NOS Ags. *svefn* dream, SUP-NOS *ὕπνος* sleep, OSlav. *sŭnŭ*, Arm. *khun*, SŪP-NOS MIr. *súan*; fr. *sopor*.

sons guilty: SONTI- cf. SŅTI- OHG. *sundea* sin Ags. *syn* E.

sonticus serious (of a reason or disease): SVENT- *αὐθ-έντης* (fr. *αὐτός*) perpetrator (E. *Effendi*) *αὐθεντικῶς* authentically, Got. *svinths* strong, cf. SVŅT'- Ags. *sund* sound (Adj.) E.

sonus sound (E. E. *sonnet*; OIr. *son* word): SVEN- OIr. *senim*, Ags. *svin* song, Zd. *qan*- to sound Sk. *svan*-.

sōpiō lull: fr. *sōpus* Adj. (see *cōmis*) fr. sq.

sopor sleep: SVEP- Ags. *svefan* put to sleep E. *soft*, Zd. *qap*- to sleep Sk. *svap*-, cf. SUP- OSlav. *sŭpati*, see *somnus*.

†sōracum hamper: σώρακος:

sorbeō swallow: SRBH- OSlav. *srŭbanije* swallowing, Arm. *arbi* I drank, cf. SROBH- *ῥοφέω* swallow, SRĒBH- Lit. *sriẽbiu*.

sorbum sorvum (Plin.) service-berry (E.): SŖV-, cf. SROV- *ῥοῦς* sumach *ῥο(Ϝ)ιά* pomegranate, Sk. *sravāt* a plant.

sordēs dirt: SVṚD- ἄρδα, cf. SVORD- Got. *svarts* black E. *swarthy*, see *sudsum.*

sōrex saurex (Plaut. Poen. 1313 Goetz) shrew-mouse: SAUB- cf. SUB-ύραξ (Nicander).

soror sister: SVESŌR OIr. *siur*, Arm. *khoir*, cf. SVESOR- Zd. *qaṅhar-* Sk. *svdsar-*, see *sobrīnus.*

sors lot (E. *sorcery*): SṚTĪ- OIr. *sreith* row, fr. *serō*[2], 'connected'.

sōspes sīspes (i.e. *sūspes*) safe :

†**spādīx** nut-brown : 'palm-coloured,' σπάδιξ palm-branch:

†**spadō** : σπάδων :

spargō scatter :

†**spartum** esparto-grass : σπάρτος : 'used in making ropes,' fr. σπάρτον rope, SPṚT- see *sporta*, cf. SPORT- Lit. *spartas* band.

†**sparus** spear: Gaulish? cf. Ags. *spär* E. *spar* (W. *par*), and SPER- Ags. *sper* E.

†**spatha** broadsword : σπάθη broad blade, Ags. E. *spade.*

†**spatium** space : Etruscan (see *idūs*) for *spadium* from σπάδιον Aeolic for στάδιον race-course.

speciō spiciō see (E. *pillory spice spite*): SPEK- OHG. *spehōn* watch E. †*spy*, Arm. *spasem* I await, Zd. *çpaç-* look Sk. *spaç-* perceive, cf. SPOK- SKOP- σκοπέω.

specus cave: 'refuge,' SPEK- SKEP- (cf. praeced.) σκέπας shelter.

†**spēlaeum** cave : σπήλαιον :

†**spēlunca** cave : σπήλυγγα (see on *pertica*) Acc. of σπῆλυγξ, fr. praeced.

spernō sever, despise : 'kick off,' Ags. *speornan* kick E. *spurn*, from SPER- NHG. *sperren* struggle E. *spar* Vb., cf. SPṚ- σπαίρω, Lit. *spìrti* kick, Sk. *sphur-* jerk.'

spēs hope: SPĒ- 'go on,' Lit. *spēti* have leisure OSlav. *spēti* advance, Sk. *sphā-* grow fat ('advance'), cf. SPŌ- Ags. *spōvan* succeed E. *speed.*

†**sphaera** ball : σφαῖρα :

spīca spēca (rustic, Varr.) point (E. *spigot spike spoke*) :

spīna thorn : SPĪN- cf. SPIN- OHG. *spinulā* pin.

†**spinter** (Neut.) bracelet : 'compressing,' = *spincter* (with term. on anal. of *tūber*), σφιγκτήρ muscle, fr. σφίγγω bind.

†**spinturnix** (with term. from *cōt-urnīx*) avis carbonem ferens ex aris Plin. 10. 36: fr. *spintēr*, σπινθήρ spark.

†**spīra** coil : σπεῖρα : SPER- cf. SPṚ- Lit. *spirà* ball.

spīrō breathe : 'emit' breath, = *spūrō* fr. *spū-rus* Adj. fr. *spuō.*

spissus thick : = *spid-tus* Part., SPID- Hesych. σπιδνός close Hom. σπιδής broad.

†**splēn** milt : σπλήν, see *liēn.*

splendeō shine (Lit. *splendžiu*) : = *splēnideō* fr. *splēnidus* yellow, Adj. fr. praeced. (cf. *ārdeō* fr. *āridus*).

spolium spoil:

†sponda side of a bedstead: 'place of preliminary libation' before getting into bed, σπονδή libation, see *spondeō*.

†spondālium hymn: fr. *spondālis* Adj. of *sponda* libation, σπονδή, see sq.

spondeō promise (E. *spouse*): SPOND- cf. SPEND- σπένδω offer.

†spongia sponge: σπογγιά, fr. †σπόγγος, see *fungus*.

sponte freely:

sporta basket: 'plaited,' SPṚT-, see *spartum*.

spūma foam: fr. sq.

spuō spit (E. *scupper*): SPJU- πτύω, W. *ffwn* a puff, Arm. *thukh* saliva, cf. SPĪV- Got. *speivan* spit E. *spue*, SPJEU- Lit. *spiduti* OSlav. *pljuti*, and STJŪ- STĪV- Sk. *shthīv*-.

spurcus dirty: SPṚK-, cf. SPORK- Sk. *sparç*- touch.

squālor roughness: = *squādor*, cf. sq. :

squāma scale: = *squād-ma* fr. praeced.

squilla prawn: σκίλλα:

st Interj. : cf. E. *hist whist*, and PST ψύττα, French *pst*.

†stadium furlong: στάδιον, Aeol. σπάδιον (see *spatium*) :

stagnum pool (E. *stanch staunch tank*): from *steg-nús* Adj., cf. στεγανός close, fr. στέγω hold water, see *tego*.

stāmen warp (W. *ystaf*): cf. στήμων, Got. *stōma* stuff: 'set up,' fr. *stō*.

†statēra steelyard : στατήρ a weight, from STA- cf. STĀ- *stō*.

†stega deck: στέγη roof, see *tego*.

stella star: *stēla* (French *étoile*), = *ster-la*, STER- ά-στήρ, W. *seren*, Got. *stairnō* Ags. *steorra* E., Arm. a-*stl*, Zd. *çtare* Sk. *stár*- : fr. *sternō*, 'strewn' about the sky ?

stelliō stēliō stilliō newt: praeced., 'marked with stars'.

stercus stircus dung: cf. *sterquilinium* mixen : Metath. (quasi fr. *sternō*) of *squertus* *squortus* SKVṚT-, cf. SKVẸT- W. *ysgarth* offscourings, SKVŌRT- σκώρ dung.

sterilis barren: STER- στεῖρος, Got. *stairō*, Arm. *sterj*, Sk. *staris* barren cow: 'hard,' cf. στερεός solid, Ir. *seirt* strength.

sternō spread (E. *stray street*): STER- OSlav. *strēti*, Zd. *çtar*- Sk. *star*-, cf. STṚ- OIr. *srethi* substernendum, Ags. E. *storm*, STṚ- *strāvī* Perf. *strātus* Part., στρώννῦμι στορέννῦμι στόρνῦμι; also STREV- Ags. *streovian* strew E., STROU- Got. *straujan* Ags. *streā* straw E., STRO- Lit. *strója* stall.

sternuō sneeze: PSTER-N- Arm. *phṙngal*, cf. PSTṚ-N- πτάρνυμαι : fr. sq., 'make a noise with the nose'.

stertō snore: PSTER-, cf. PSTṚ- OIr. *srenim*.

stilla drop (E. *still* Subst.), **stilicidium** (fr. *cadō*) dropping: *stīla*=*stīr-la* fr. *stīria*.

stilus stake : = *studus*, STÜDH- Ags. *studu* pillar E. *stud*[2].

stimulus stake, goad (MIr. *sibal* thorn, pin) : = *stib-lus* STÜB- (or STÜBH-), see *stipula*.

stinguō quench : 'strike asunder,' STINGV- Got. *stiggan* push.

stipendium pay : = *stip-pendium*, fr. *stips* + *pendō*.

stipes log : STŨP- ONor. *stúfr* stump, Sk. *stũpas* tuft, cf. STÜP- στύπος stump, Sk. *stupás* tuft.

stīpō press (E. *costive stevedor*) : STŨP- cf. *stuppa* :

stips gift :

stipula stalk : = *stupula* (whence the forms in the Romance languages, and W. *soft* stubble, OHG. *stupfilā* E.) *stub-la* STÜB- (or STÜBH-) OSlav. *stũblo stĩblo* stalk.

stipulor bargain : 'take earnest-money,' fr. *stips*.

stīria drop :

stirps stock :

stīva plough-handle : 'tail,' STĪV- cf. STIV- OHG. *stiuz* haunch.

stlātārius stlattārius deceitful : fr. *stlāta stlatta* pirate vessel (not 'broad,' as Fest., quasi fr. *lātus* Adj.) :

stloppus scloppus slap : onomatop.

stō stand (E. *stage stanchion stanza*) : STĀ- ἵστημι set, Lit. *stóti* tread OSlav. *stati* stand, Zd. ςtā- Sk. *sthā-*, cf. STĀI- OHG. *stān* E. *stay stow stithy*, and see *dēstinō*.

stolidus dull : STĻO-DO- cf. STĻ-DO- Ags. *stolt* rash E. *stout* : 'set,' see *praestōlor*.

storea mat : 'spread out,' STŖ- cf. STER- *sternō*.

†**strabō** squinting : στράβων, STŖB-, cf. STREB- στρεβλός crooked.

strāgēs overthrow : 'making a strewing,' = *strā-āgēs* from STŖ- see *sternō* + ĀG- amb-āgēs circumlocution, see *agō*, cf. sq.

strāgulum coverlet : 'made for strewing,' = *strā-āgulum* from STŖ- praeced. + ĀG- co-āgulum bond, see *agō*.

strāmen straw : STŖ-MN στρῶμα bed ; 'strewn,' see *sternō*.

†**strangulō** choke : στραγγαλάω, STŖNG- στραγγαλίς knot ('tight') στραγγεύομαι hesitate ('am tied') στράγξ drop ('pressed' out).

†**strēna** strenna omen : Sabine for 'health' (Lydus de Mensibus 4. 4), cf. sq.

strēnuus brisk : STREN- στρῆνος health, cf. STŖN- Ags. *styrn* stern (Adj.) E., Pruss. *sturnawiskan* earnest.

strepō make a noise : onomatop.

striāta scallop : 'fluted,' fr. *stria* furrow :

strīdō creak : onomatop.

†**strigilis** scraper : quasi-Adj., for *strigila *stregida* from Acc. of *στρεγίς* by-form (cf. φάρυγα later φάρυγγα) of †στρεγγίς στλεγγίς.

strigōsus thin : 'drawn together,' STRŨGV- cf. STRŨNGV- sq.

stringō[1] bind, draw tight: STRŪNGV- cf. STREÜGV- στρεύγομαι grow weary ('am tied'), STRÜGV- *striga* row of hay ('raked together'), see *struō*.

stringō[2] strip off, pluck: STRŪNGV- cf. STBŪGV- Lit. *strūgas* shears, STRÜGV- OSlav. *strŭgati* shave.

stringō[3] graze, touch lightly: STRINGV- cf. STRIGV- Got. *striks* tittle ('stroke' of the pen), STRĪGV- OHG. *strihhan* to smooth E. *strike* *stroke*.

strix strix screech-owl: cf. *strīga* witch ('bloodsucker,' as the screech-owl was supposed to be): 'squeaking,' onomatop., cf. στρίζω τρίζω squeak.

struō arrange: 'bind together,' = *struō *strūvō STRŪGV- cf. *stringō*[1].

studeō am eager: PالسTUD- cf. PSTEUD- σπεύδω hasten, PSTOUD- Arm. *phoith* zeal.

stultus foolish: STL̥-TÓS Part., see *stolidus*.

stupeō am amazed: 'am struck,' STUP- ἀπο-στυπάζω beat off, cf. STUMP- OHG. *stumbal* mutilated; also TUP- τύπτω beat, OSlav. *tŭpati* throb.

stuppa stūpa stīpa tow (E. *stuff*): στύπη: ·compressed,' see *stīpŏ*.

stuprum dishonour (E. *strumpet*): 'being beaten,' see *stupeō*.

suādeō recommend: 'cause to please,' SVĀD- Ags. *svēte* sweet E., cf. SVAND- ἀνδάνω please, OIr. *sant* desire, Zd. *qand-* be merry (Spiegel), SVAD- Sk. *svad-* sweeten, SUD- Got. *suts* pleasant, see *suāvis*.

suāsum dark colour: = *suarsum *svard-tum* Part. Neut. from SVE̥D-, cf. SVR̥D- *sordēs*.

suāvis sweet (E. *assuage*): = *suād-vis*, ἡδύς, Sk. *svādŭs*, see *suādeō*.

suāvium (quasi fr. praeced.) **sāvium** kiss: popular perversion of *vāsium*, *bāsium*.

sub under (E. *sudden* *suzerain*): = *sup* (see *ob*) *s-upo* 'there-under,' from so see *sīc* + ὑπο ῦπο, OIr. f-o, Got. *uf* E. *eaves often*, Zd. *upa* to Sk. *úpa*.

sūber cork-tree: 'with wrinkled bark,' σύφαρ old skin:

sub-lestus slight: from LAS- Got. *lasivs* weak E. *less*, OSlav. *loŝĭ* cheap, + Part.-ending.

†sublica stake: Volscian (Fest.): = *sub-liga* (see *pertica*) fr. *ligŏ*.

sub-līmis high: 'obliquely up,' fr. *līmus* Adj.

†subō: *συβάω, fr. Hesych. σύβας lewd:

sub-olēs sob-olēs (dialectic, cf. Cato *jogālis* for *jugālis*) offspring: see *adolescō*[2].

subtēmen subtegmen woof: fr. *tegō*, 'covering' the warp.

subtīlis fine: = *sub-tēlis* fr. *tēla*, 'suited for weaving'.

subūcula shirt: fr. *sub-uō* 'put under' from *avō*, see *exuō*.

subulcus swineherd: from SU- see *sūs*, with term. from *bubulcus*.

sūcus succus juice (E. *sewer*) : SŪKV- OHG. *sūgan* suck, cf. SUNKV- Lit. *sunkti* pour out : see *sūgō*.

sudiculum flagri Plaut. Pers. 419 whipping-post : Dimin. of **sude* Neut., by-form of sq.

sudis stake :

sūdor sweat : SVOID- Ags. *svāt* E., Zd. *qaēdhem* (Fick), cf. SVID- Arm. *khirtn*, Sk. *svid-* to sweat, SVĪD- Ῑδos sweat ἱδρώς, W. *chwys*, Lett. *sviedri*.

sūdus clear : = **sūs-dus* 'dry,' SAUS- αὖos dry Hesych. σαυσαρός (dialectic), Ags. *scārian* dry up E. *sear sere sorrel* Adj., Lit. *saūsas* dry OSlav. *suhŭ*, cf. SUS- ἀ-υσταλέos squalid Odyss. 19. 327, Zd. *hush-* to dry Sk. *çush-*.

suescō am wont : SEVÓ- *suus*, cf. Perf. *suēvī* (disyllable) from SVÓ- ὅs his, OSlav. *svoj* one's own, Zd. *hva-* Sk. *svas-* : 'have my own way,' with meaning extended to all persons.

†sūfēs suffēs consul (at Carthage) : Punic (Fest.), Heb. *shofēt* judge.

suffiō fumigate : = **sub-fuō*, DHU- smell, see *fimus thymum tūs*.

sufflāmen drag : = **sub-flāg-mcn* 'under-beam,' BHḶG- see *phalanx*.

suf-frāgor vote for : from **frāgor* vote :

sūgillō beat black and blue : Dimin. of sq., 'draw blood '.

sūgō suck : SŪGV- MIr. *sūgim*, Ags. *sūcan* E. E. *soak* ; by-form of SŪKV- see *sūcus*.

sulcus furrow : SḶKOS Ags. *sulh* plough, cf. SOLKÓS ὀλκós furrow.

†sulfur sulphur sulpur (Sk. *çulvāris*) brimstone :

sum am : formed from Plur. *sumus*, for **ēm* ES-MI εἰμί, OIr. *am*, Got. *im* E., Lit. *esmi* OSlav. *jesmi*, Arm. *em*, Zd. *ahmi* Sk. *ásmi*, ES- cf. *esse* Inf.

summus highest : = **sup-mus* from *sub* ('upward,' see *super*), cf. Sk. *upamás*.

sūmō take : fr. **sūmus* Adj. 'taking up,' *sus* + Adj.-ending (see *emō demō*).

suō sew : = **sūō* SJŪ- κα-σσύω stitch, Got. *siujan* sew E. E. *seam*, Lit. *siūti* OSlav. *šiti*, Sk. *syū-*.

super over (E. *somersault sovereign*) : SO (see *sub*) + UPER ὑπέρ, OIr. f-*or* (= **f-u-ar*), Got. *ufar* E. E. *orlop*, Zd. *upairi* Sk. *upári* : fr. *sub*, 'more upward, higher,' see *summus*.

super-bus proud : praeced. + term. -BHO-, see *acerbus*.

supercilium eyebrow : 'above the eyelid,' *cilium* eyelid (Fest.), = **cülium*, cf. κύλα Plur.

sup-īnus backward : from **sup* see *sub* 'up,' cf. ὑπ-τιos backward.

†supparum sipparum smock (worn over the *subūcula*, Varr. L. L. 5. 131), topsail : Oscan (Varr.), = **sūparum* 'upper,' see *suppus*.

sup-peditō am at hand : from *sub* + *peditō* go on foot, fr. *pēs*.

sup-plex submissive, **supplicium** offering: fr. **placō = placeō*.

suppus inverted: 'turned up,' = **sŭpus* from **sup sub* (cf. *cŏmis* from *com-*).

sūra soera calf of leg: = **soira*: cf. *sŭrus* stake (cf. ONor. *leggr* leg, trunk of a tree), the calf compared to a shaft:

sūrculus sprout: = **sŭriculus* Dimin. of *sŭrus*, praeced.

surdus deaf:

sus up (in *susque dēque* up and down, *suscipiō suscitō suspendō sustineō sustuli*; also sū-, *surgō* = **sŭ-rigō*, *sŭ-spĭciō*, *sŭ-spĭciō*, *sŭ-spīrō*; and see *sirempse*): cf. NUmbr. *surur* also:

sūs pig (E. *soil* Vb.): sŪ- *ĭs*, W. *hw-ch* sow (not E. *hog*), OHG. *sŭ* E., cf. sᴜ- Zd. *hu* pig.

sū-spĭciō suspicion: fr. *sus* + *spīca*, 'pricking,' cf. sᴘɪᴋ- *sŭ-spicor* suspect, *sŭspectus* suspected.

susurrus hum: = **su-sŭr-us* Redupl. of sᴜʀ-, cf. sᴜʀ- Lit. *surma*, sᴠᴇʀ- Sk. *svar-* to sound, sᴠᴏʀ- OHG. E. *swarm* ('humming').

Not add σῦριγξ pipe, as primarily 'hollow'.

suus (from **suvus*) **sovos** his: sᴇᴠόs, ἑ(F)ός, Lit. *sáwa*, Arm. *iur* (= **sev-r*), cf. sᴠᴏ- see *suescō sē*.

taberna booth (E. *tavern*): 'made of boards,' fr. *tabula*.

tābēs wasting:

tabula board: = **teb-lā*, ᴛᴇʙʜ- cf. sᴛᴇʙʜ- Sk. *stabh-* to prop, sᴛᴇᴍʙʜ- Zd. *çtemb-* Sk. *stambh-*, sᴛᴇ̄ʙʜ- Lit. *stĕbas* post.

taceō am silent: ᴛᴀᴋ- Got. *thahan* Inf.

taeda pitch-pine:

taedet irks:

†taenia fillet: ταινία, fr. **ταινός* Adj., = **ταν-jós* from ᴛɴ̥- see *tendō* (as φοίνιος fr. φοινός, = **φον-jós*).

taeter tēter offensive: *taetro-* = **taed-rŏ-* fr. *taedet*.

tālea staff (E. *tailor* &c. *detail intaglio tally*): OSlav. *talij* young branch.

†talentum talent: τάλαντον: 'weight,' see *tollō*.

tālis such: fr. **tālus* Adj. of **tā* thus, case-form from ᴛᴏ- see *tam*, and see *quālis*.

talpa mole:

tālus ankle (E. *talon*): = **tax-lus*, see *taxillus*.

tam so: = **tām tāme* (Fest.) i.e. **tā-sme* from *tā-* (see *tālis* and *ita*), ᴛᴏ- *τό* this, Got. *thata* that E., Ags. E. *the* Ags. *thes* this E., Lit. *tàs*, Zd. *ta-* Sk. *tá-*; + a case-ending -sᴍᴏ, cf. OUmbr. *pu-sme* to whom, Got. *tha-mma* to him, see *-met*.

tamen yet: 'in spite of all,' Acc. of **tamen* (Neut.) contempt, ᴛᴍ̥-ɴ from ᴛᴍ̥-, cf. ᴛᴍ- *temnō*.

tandem at length: = **tam-dem, tam + -dem*.

tangō touch (E. *taste task tax*; but for *touch* see *dīcō*): TANG- cf. TAG- τεταγών seizing.

tantus so great: formed from *tan-tum* 'only' (taken as Adj. Neut.) i.e. *tam tum* correlative of *quantum*, see *quantus*.

†tapēte carpet (E. *tapestry tape tabard tippet*): *τάπητι by-form of †τάπης δάπις:

tardus slow (E. *tarry*): 'smitten, crippled,' cf. Sk. *taḍ-* beat.

tarmes woodworm:

†tarpessīta banker: *ταρπεζίτης τραπεζίτης, fr. τράπεζα table.

tat tatae Interj.: cf. τοτοῖ, E. *tut*, see *ātāt*.

†taurus bull: ταῦρος (OSlav. *turŭ*), = *τάρϝος, Gaulish *tarvos* OIr. *tarb*.

tax sound of blows: onomatop., cf. E. *thwack*.

taxillus die (E. *tassel*):

†techna techina trick: τέχνη art: TEGH- Ags. *thicgan* touch, cf. TENGH- Ags. E. *thing*.

tegō cover: TEGV- τέγος roof, OIr. *teg* house, Ags. *theccan* to cover E. *thatch* †*deck tight taut*; cf. STEGV- στέγω shelter, Sk. *sthag-* cover.

tēgula tile (E.): TEGV- cf. praeced., and STEGV- Lit. *stėgiu* I cover.

tēla web (E. *toilet toils*): = *tex-la* fr. *texō*.

tellūs earth: = *tĕl-ŏs* (for term. cf. αἰδ-ώς ἠ-ώς) TEL- 'flat,' cf. TEL- Ags. *thelu* board, Sk. *talas* level ground, and TḶ- OSlav. *tĭlo* pavement.

tēlum spear: MIr. *tāl* axe: = *tex-lóm* fr. *texō*, 'shaped'.

temere by chance: Neut. (cf. *facile* Adv.) of *temeris* 'blind,' TEM-ES-, see *tenebrae*.

tēmētum wine:

temnō scorn: 'confuse,' TṂ- see *timeō*?

tēmō pole: = *tex-mō* fr. *texō*, 'shaped,' cf. Ags. *thisle* pole.

temperô qualify (E. *tamper*): 'fix the limits of,' TEMP- Lit. *tempti* stretch, sq.

templum open space: 'expanse,' cf. *ex-templō* 'on the spot,' see praeced.

tempora temples of the head: 'spaces,' see praeced.

tempus time: 'extension,' see *temperô*.

tendō stretch (E. *tent*): fr. *tendus* Adj., TEN- *tenō* whence Part. *tentus* and Fest. *obs-tinet* ostendit, τείνω, Zd. Sk. *tan-*, cf. TON- Got. uf-*thanjan*, TṆ- OIr. *tēt* harpstring (E. *tether*), see *tenuis*.

tenebrae darkness: formed quasi fr. *teneō*, 'detaining,' for *temebrae* *temesrae*, Sk. *tdmisrā*, cf. TEM-ES- OHG. *demerunga* twilight, Zd. *temanh* darkness Sk. *támas*, TM-ES- OSlav. *tĭma*, TEM-S- OIr. *temel*, TOM-S- Lit. *tamsà*; and TEM- Lit. *témti* grow dark, TṂ- Zd. *tam-* perish Sk. *tam-* to faint.

teneō hold (E. *rein tenon*): 'stretch to,' see *tendō*.

tener soft (E. *tender tendril*): TṆ-, see *tenuis*.

tensa car for images of gods:

tentô (quasi fr. *teneō*) **temptô** handle (E. *taunt*) : 'stretch,' see *temperō*.

tenuis thin : TN̄-Ŭ- *τανυ*- long-, Sk. *tanús* thin, cf. TN̥- *ταναός* long, OIr. *tana* thin, Ags. *thyn* E., OSlav. *tĭnĭkŭ*, see *tendō*.

tenus Subst. snare ('stretched out') Prep. as far as ('stretching to') : TEN-, see *tendō*.

tepeō am warm : TEP-, OIr. *tĕ* hot (= *tepent-), OSlav. *teplo* hotly, Zd. *tap*- burn Sk. *tap*- be hot.

ter thrice : = *tri*, *τρί-ς* *τρι*-, Gaul. *tri*-, Zd. *thri*- 3, Sk. *trí*-, cf. TREI- *tres*.

†**terebinthus** turpentine-tree (E. *turpentine*) : †*τερέβινθος*, Syrian (as growing in Syria, Plin. 13. 54).

tergō wipe :
hardly = *trigvō* *τρίβω* rub, or Perf. would be *trixi*.

tergum tergus back : TERGHV- cf. TR̥GHV- *τράχηλος* neck; and STERGHV- *στέρφος* skin.

termes (for term. cf. *līmes* beside *līmen*) bough cut off : 'end,' fr. sq.

terminus termen limit : TER-MN̥ *τέρμα*, Sk. *tarman*† point, from TER- Zd. *tar*- go over Sk. *tar*- pass.

terō rub (E. *try*) : = *triō* (cf. *trīvī* Perf. *tritus* Part.), TRŪ- *τρύω* weary (for the meanings cf. E. *tire* Vb. fr. *tear* Vb.), cf. TROU- Ags. *threāvian* threaten E. *throe*.

terra earth (E. *terrace terrier tureen turmeric*) : = *tĕra* TER- Osc. *teer*[um], OIr. *tir*.

terreō frighten : = *terseō* TERS-, cf. TR̥S- MIr. *tarrach* timid, Zd. *tareç*- be frightened, and TRE-S- *τρέ(σ)ω* flee, Sk. *tras*- be terrified; see *tremō*.

territōrium land round a town : 'land subject to octroi,' formed fr. *terra* on anal. of *portitōrium* 'custom-house' fr. *portus*.

†**tesca tesqua** deserts (an augural term) : Sabine (Schol. Hor. Epp. 1. 14. 19) :

†**tessera** die ('square-sided') : *τέσσαρα* 4, see *quattuor*.

testa brick (E. *test tester*) : = *texta* Part. Fem. from *texō*, 'shaped'.

tēstis witness, **tēsticulus** : = *terstis* *tristis*, Osc. *trĭstaamentud* by will :

texō weave, construct : TEKTH- (see *ursus*) 'shape,' *τέκτων* carpenter, OHG. *dehsen* to shape, OSlav. *tesati* cut, Zd. *takhsh*- hew (Spiegel) Sk. *taksh*- fashion, cf. TOKTH- Lit. *taszýti* hew.

†**thalamus** bower : †*θάλαμος*, Egyptian (Isid. Orig. 15. 3. 6).

†**thēca** case : *θήκη*, cf. *ἔθηκα* I placed, see *faciō*.

†**thēsaurus thēnsaurus** treasure (E.) : †*θησαυρος* *θηνσαυρός* :

†**thēta** TH : †*θῆτα*, Heb. *teth*.

†**thiasus** dance : †*θίασος* :

†**tholus** dome : *θόλος* :

†thōrāx cuirass: θώραξ:

†thunnus tunny: θύννος θῦνος: fr. θύω rush, see *fūmus*.

†thymbra savory: θύμβρα: 'odorous,' DHUMBH- cf. DHŪBH- τύφω smoke.

†thymum thyme: θύμον: DHU- smell, see *suffiō*.

†thyrsus stalk, Bacchic staff (E. *torso*): θύρσος:

†tiāra turban: †τιάρας, Persian (as worn by Persian kings).

tībia shinbone: TOIBH- cf. STOIBH- Lit. *staibiai* shinbones, *staibis* post.

tignum beam: TIG- cf. *tigillum* Dimin.:

†tigris tiger: †τίγρις, oriental (cf. the river-name *Tigris*, Zd. *tighri* arrow).

tilia linden: 'spreading,' = *ptelea*, πτελέη elm (see on *frāxinus*), from PT-, cf. PET- *pateō*?

timeō fear: 'faint,' TEM- see *tenebrae*.

tinea tinia worm: 'tenacious,' fr. *teneō*?

tingō tinguō wet (E. *stain taint Tent*): TŪNGV- MIr. *tummim* I dip (= *tumbim), OHG. *duncōn* dip.

tinniō tīniō jingle: onomatop.

tintinnō tintinō jingle: onomatop. Redupl. of TN-, cf. τιτανισμός singing of pæans Strabo p. 281. 34 Müller and Dübner, Lit. *titinoti* brag.

tīnus laurustinus:

tippūla tīpūla water-spider:

tīrō recruit:

tītillō tickle (for E. *tickle* see *digitus*): Dimin. of *tītō 'inflame,' cf. *titiō* brand (E. *entice*), see Wölfflin's Archiv. 1. 244.

tītivillītium trifle: coined by Plaut., 'nullius significationis' (Fest.).

titubō stagger: Redupl. of TUB-, cf. STŪB- ONor. *stūpa* stoop E.

titulus inscription (E. *tittle*):

†tōfus tufa: foreign, cf. Heraclean τοφιών tufa-quarry:

toga cloak: TOGV- cf. TEGV- *tegō*, and cf. OSlav. o-*stegŭ* garment.

tolerō tulerō bear, tollō raise (= *tol-nō), tolūtim trotting (E. *trot*), tulī have borne: TL̥- τάλαντον weight, MIr. *tlethar* carry off, Got. *thulan* endure Scotch *thole*, Sk. *tul-* lift, cf. TL̥- τόλμα daring.

tōmentum stuffing: TVŌM-N̥- σῶμα body.

tondeō shave:
hardly cf. τένδω gnaw: meaning too different.

tonō thunder: TON-, cf. TN̥- Ags. *thunian*, Sk. *tan-* roar: 'continue,' fr. *tendō*.

tonsa oar: 'bough stript of leaves,' Part. Fem. of *tondeō*, cf. Fest. *tonsilla* stake.

tonsillae (quasi fr. praeced.) tossillae tōsillae tussillae tūsillae toxillae tonsils: TOX-, cf. Fest. *tōlēs* tumor in faucibus:

topiārius ornamental gardener: fr. †*topia* ornamental gardening, landscape-painting, *τόπια fr. τόπος place, 'making the most of a space'.

†tornus lathe (E. *attorney tornado tour turn*): τόρνος: 'boring,' TOR-, cf. TER- τέρετρον gimlet τείρω weary, OSlav. *treti* rub, Sk. *tdrunas* tender, TṜ- OIr. *tarathar* gimlet.

torpeō am stiff (E. *sturdy*): TṚP-, Lit. *tirpti* stiffen.

torqueō turn (E. *tart* Subst. *torch tortoise trousers truss trousseau*): TRKV-ᾰτρακτος spindle, cf. TORKV- OSlav. *traku* bandage, Sk. *tarkus* spindle.

torreō burn (E. *toast*): = *torseō* TṚS- Got. *thaursjan* to thirst E. E. *thrush*[2], Arm. *tharanim* I wither, cf. TṚS- OIr. *tart* thirst, TERS- τέρσομαι dry up, Zd. *taresh-* to thirst Sk. *tarsh-*.

torus knot:

torvus fierce:

tot so many: = *toti*, Sk. *tdti*, cf. *toti-dem*, Loc. of sq. (see *quot*).

tŏtus so great: from TO- see *tam* + a term. *-to-* (see *quotus*).

tōtus tottus whole (E. *teetotum*): fr. *tō* Abl. of TO- see *tam* (and see *cottīdiē*), + a term. *-to-*.

†trabea robe of state: Sabine, as introduced by Numa (Lydus de Mensibus 1. 19).

trabs beam (E. archi*trave travail travel*): TRABH- τράφηξ stake.

trāgula dart attached to a strap: = *trāgla* *trā-veg-la* fr. *trans* + *vehō*, cf. sq.

trahō draw (E. *portray trace* &c. *train tret*): = *trāhō trā-vehō* from *trans* + *vehō*.

trāma woof: 'across' the warp, = *trans-ma* from *trans*.

trāmes crossway: = *trans-m-es* from *trans*.

tranquillus calm:

trans across (E. *trance trespass*): NUmbr. *traf trahaf* (= *trās*), W. *trach* beyond (= *trass* *trans*).

transenna network: praeced., with same term. as *antenna*.

tremō shake (E. *turmoil*): TRE-M- τρέμω, cf. TR-M- Lit. *trimti*, TRE-M-S-OSlav. *tresti*; and TRE- under *terreō* (see *premō*).

trepidus alarmed: TREP- OSlav. *trepetu* tremor, Sk. *trap-* be abashed.

trēs 3: = *trei-es* TREI- τρεῖς, Got. *threis* E., Arm. *e-re-kh*, Sk. *tráyas*, cf. TRĪ- OIr. *tri*, Lit. *trys* OSlav. *tri*, see *ter*.

tribuō assign: 'divide,' cf. sq.:

tribus trebus tribe: OUmbr. *trefi* Abl., MIr. *treb*: 'division,' cf. praeced.

trīcae tricks (E. *intrigue*; but not *trick*):

†trichila bower Caes. B. Ç. 3. 96 (E. *trellis*):

trīgintā 30: formed after *vī-gint-ī* (with *-ā* of old Neut. Plur.) for *triā-conta* τριάκοντα, cf. TRI-KOT- Zd. *thriçata*, TRIN-KÓT Sk. *trinçát*; see *trēs*.

†trigō game at ball: τρίγων: fr. τρί-γωνος triangular, γωνία angle, as being played by three.

†trigonus trūgonus sting-ray: *τρύγονος by-form of τρύγών roach:

tri-pudium a dance: 'striking thrice,' *tri-* see *ter* + (s)POD- see *pudet*.
tri-quetrus triangular: = **tri-qued-rus* 'with 3 points,' see *quadra*.
tristis bitter: Ags. *thrīste* bold:
trīt-avus strīt-avus (Fest.) ancestor in the sixth degree:
hardly cf. STRŎT- OIr. *sruith* ancient, noble.
†**triumphus triumpus** triumphal procession (E. *trump*-card): **τρίομ-φος* by-form (as *πάθνη* of *φάτνη*) of **θρίομβος* †*θρίαμβος* hymn to Dionysos:
†**trochlea troclea** pulley: = **trochilia*, τροχιλία, fr. τρέχω run.
trua ladle (E. *trowel*): TVR̯- cf. TVOR- τορθνη, ONor. *thvara* stirring-stick, TVER- OHG. *dweran* mix up Ags. *thviril* churn-handle E. *twirl*, Sk. *tvar-* hasten.
truc-īdō (for term. cf. *formīdō* fear) kill: 'mangle,' TRUK- W. *trwch* maimed, cf. TRUNK- *truncus*:
trudis pike: TRUD-, cf. sq.
trūdō push: TREUD- Got. us-*thriutan* to trouble E. *thrust threat*, OSlav. *trudŭ* toil.
truncus Adj. maimed, Subst. stem (E. *trounce truncheon trunnion*): TRUNK- cf. TRUK- *trucīdō*.
†**trutina** balance (Scotch *Tron*): τρυτάνη:
trux fierce: TVR̯K-, cf. TVERK- Got. *thvairhs* angry.
†**tryblium** plate: τρύβλιον bowl:
tū thou: TŪ τύ-νη, OIr. *tū*, Got. *thū* E., OSlav. *ty*, Arm. *du*, Zd. *tū tūm*, cf. TU σύ, Lit. *tù*, Sk. *tu-*, TV- Sk. *tvām*.
tū² cry of owl Plaut. Men. 651: onomatop., E. *toowhoo*, cf. Hesych. τυτώ owl.
tuba trumpet (E. E. *trombone trumpery trunk* of elephant): cf. *tubus* pipe:
tūber swelling (E. *trifle truffle*, NHG. kartoffel potato = terrae tuber): TŪM-R̯- from TŪM- W. *twf* growth, Ags. *thūma* thumb E., cf. TUM- *tumeō*.
tuburcinor devour:
†**tuccētum tūcētum** salt beef: Gaulish (Schol. Pers. 2. 42), cf. NUmbr. *toco*.
tueor watch:
tugurium tigurium tegurium (quasi fr. *tegō*) hut: foreign, cf. *attegia*?
tulī have borne: see *tolcrō*.
tum then: = **to-me* (for term. see *tam*), TO- τό-τε, cf. Ags. *th-on* E., see *tam*.
tumeō swell: TUM- Sk. *tumras* strong, cf. TŪM- see *tūber*.
tumultus uproar: cf. Sk. *tumulas* noisy, praeced.
tumulus mound: TUM- τύμβος (= **τύμ-γϝος*: E. *tomb*, whence W. *tom*), fr. *tumeō*.

tundō beat (E. *pierce*): TUND- MIr. *tond* wave, cf. TUD- Sk. *tud*- push; and STOUD- Got. *stautan* strike E. *stoat stutter.*

†tunica shirt: = *ctun-ica* Heb. *k'thôneth,* whence also χιτών.

turba uproar (Fr. *trop* too much; E. *troop trouble*): TVURB- τύρβη disorder συρβηνεύς noisy, cf. STVURB- στυρβάζω stir up.

turbō whirl (E. *turbot*): praeced.

turdus thrush: TURZD- cf. TRUZD- Ags. E. *throstle,* and STROZD- Lit. *strázdas,* cf. Bohemian *drozd* (Miklosich: with *dr-* from OSlav., see note). A different bird (Carmen de Philomela 11 droscam 17 turdus) from Late-Lat. *drosca,* with which cf. Ags. *thryssce* E. *thrush,* OSlav. *drozgŭ.*

turgeō swell: 'am rubbed' (so that a blister is raised), TRG- cf. TERG- *tergō.*

turma torma (late) troop:

turpis ugly: TRP-, cf. TREP- *trepidus,* 'frightful'.

†turris tower (E., Ags. *torr* rock, NHG. *thurm* tower, W. *tŵr*): †τύρρις τύρσις:

turtur turtle-dove (E. *turtle*): quasi-Redupl., for *tetrur* TETR- τέτραξ grouse, ONor. *thidurr* partridge, Sk. *tittirás,* cf. TETR- Late-Lat. *tetrinniō* I quack, MIr. *tethra* scall-crow, and TETER-V- Lit. *teterwa* moor-hen OSlav. *tetrēvĭ* pheasant, Pers. *tczerw* Zenker 273 b.

†tūs incense: = *tuus,* θύος, see *suffiō.*

tussis cough: = *tud-tis* TUD- Got. *thut*-haurn trumpet, cf. TEUD- Ags. *theōtan* howl E. *toot tootle.*

†tūticus public: Campanian (Liv. 23. 35. 13), from TEUTO- Osc. *tovto* people, Got. *thiuda* (and Lat. *Teutones,* E. *Dutch*), OIr. *tūath,* Lett. *tauta.*

tūtus safe: Part. from TŪ- OSlav. *tyti* grow fat, cf. TU- Zd. Sk. *tu*- be strong.

tuxtax sound of blows: Redupl. of *tax,* cf. E. *thwick-thwack.*

†tympanum typanum drum (E. *timbrel*): τύμπανον τύπανον, TUMP- TUP- τύπτω beat, see *stupeō.*

†typus figure: τύπος, see praeced.

†tyrannus despot: †τύραννος:

über Adj. rich, Subst. breast: οὔθαρ udder (for *ὔθαρ, to avoid a double aspiration), Ags. *ūder* E., Sk. *ūdhar-,* cf. Lit. *ūdrŭti* get milk.

ubī where (for term. see *nēcubi*): U- Relative, cf. VO- ὅς who.

ulciscor volciscor take vengeance: 'wound,' fr. sq.

ulcus sore: = *vulcus *velcus,* ἕλκος wound.

ūlīgo moisture: = *ūvili-gō* fr. *ūvilis* moist, see *ūvidus* (cf. *fūligo*).

ulmus elm: ELMOS Ags. E. *elm,* cf. ḶMOS Ir. *lem,* Russian *ilemŭ* (Miklosich).

ūlna elbow : ŌLEN- ὠλένη, cf. ŌLN- Sk. *āṇíṣ* axle-pin ; also OLEN- Got. *aleina* cubit (mis-written for *alina), OLN- OIr. *uille* Acc. Plur. elbow, Ags. *eln* E. *el*-bow *ell.*

†**ulpicum** leek : Punic (Columella 11. 3).

ūltra ūls beyond : ŪD out, cf. UD- *uterus.*

ul-ula screech-owl : UL- ὐλάω bark. Lit. *ulóti* to halloo, cf. *ulūcus* screech-owl (Servius), Sk. *ūlūkas*, and ŪL- ONor. *ȳla* howl.

ululō howl (E. E. *hurly*-burly) : Redupl. of UL- praeced., cf. ὀλολύζω (= *ὐλ-υλ-ύζω), Lit. *ulūlóti* shout.

ūlva sedge : ŪD see *ūltrā*, growing 'out' in the marsh, not in the field.

umbilicus imbilīcus navel : from *ombolos OMBH-Ḷ- ὀμφαλός, cf. MBH-L- MIr. *imbliu*, NOBH-EL- Ags. *nafcla* E., NŌBH-Ḹ- Sk. *nābhīlam*† ; from NOBH- Lett. *naba*, NŌBH- Sk. *nắbhis* : 'centre,' cf. sq.

umbō boss : OMBH-, cf. NOBH- Ags. *nafu* nave (of wheel) E. E. *auger.*

umbra shade (E. *sombre umber umbrage umbrella*) : ONDH-, Sk. *andhás* blind, cf. ṆDH- Zd. *aṅdāo*, see *āter* ; and NODH- Hesych. *νυθός* dark, see *nothus.*

ūmeō hūmeō am moist : fr. *ūvimus Adj., see *ūvidus.*

umerus humerus shoulder : ŎMESOS, cf. ŎMSOS NUmbr. *onse* Abl., Got. *ams*, Arm. *us*, Sk. *dṁsas*, and ŎM- ὦμος.

um-quam ever : *um*- from *u-me (for term. see *tam*), U- see *ubī.*

ūncia one-twelfth (Sicil. οὐγκία, also ὀγκία quasi fr. ὄγκος mass ; E. *inch ounce*) : = *ūnicia fr. *ūnicus* single, see *ūnus.*

uncus hook : = *vuncus VONK- ὄγκος, Lit. *vą̄szas.*

unda water (E. *sound* Vb. *surround*) : = *vunda VOND- Lit. *vandú*, cf. VOD- Got. *watō* Ags. *väter* E., Ags. *vät* wet E., OSlav. *voda* water, VED- Arm. *get* river ; also UND- Lit. *undtl* water, ŪD- OUmbr. *utur*, ὕδωρ (Gen. ὕδατος), UD- MIr. *u-sce* (E. *whisky*), Sk. *údan-*, cf. Zd. *ud-* flow Sk. *ud-* to wet.

un-de whence : from *um Abl. (see *inde*) of U- see *ubī.*

ungō unguō smear : ONGV- OHG. *anco* butter, Sk. *anj-* anoint, cf. ṆGV- OIr. *imb* butter.

unguis nail : ONKHV-, cf. ṆKHV- OIr. *ingne* Acc. Plur., NOKHV- ὄ-νυξ, Lit. *nãgas* OSlav. *nogĭtĭ*, Sk. *nakhás.*

ungula hoof : fr. praeced., cf. NOKHV-EL- Ags. *nägel* nail E. Not add Arm. *mayil* claw.

ūnus oinos one (E. *onion*) : OIN- οἴνη ace, OIr. *ōin* one, Got. *ains* E. E. *any*, Pruss. *ains* Lit. *wiênas* OSlav. *inŭ.*

upupa hoopoe (Fr. *huppe* E.) : OP-OP- ἔποψ (for *ὄποψ ; formed quasi fr. ἐπόπτης on-looker, Aesch. fragm. 291) Hesych. *ἀπαφός*, from its cry *op* or *ap.*

urbs city : = *vurbs VORDH- OPers. *vardana* ; 'concretion,' fr. Zd. *vared*- promote Sk. *vardh*- grow.

urceus pot (Got. *aurkeis*; E. *lurch* Subst.) : = *vurceus* VRKV- OSlav. *vrŭčĭ.*

Hardly add ὄρχα jar.

urgeō urgueō press : = *vurgueō* VRGV- cf. VERGV- *vergō, ἐ-(F)έργω* shut up, VORGV- Lit. *wargas* distress OSlav. *vragŭ* enemy.

ūrīna water: = *vūr-īna* VŌR- Sk. *vār,* cf. ŪR- Lit. *jūrẽs* sea, VOR- *οὖρον* water (= *Fόρ-Fον*), Ags. *vär* sea, Zd. *vairis.*

ūrīnor dive : 'get into the water,' fr. praeced.

urna water-pot :

ūrō burn : EUS- *εὔω* singe, cf. US- Ags. *ysla* ashes, Zd. Sk. *ush-* burn.

ursus bear : ŖKTHOS (see *texō*), *ἄρκτος,* Arm. *arj,* Sk. *ŗkshas,* cf. ŖKTHOS Ir. *art.*

urtīca nettle : = *vurtīca* VRT- see *vertō,* 'altering, poisoning '.

†**tūrus** wild ox : Gaulish (Macrobius), borrowed from Teutonic, OHG. *ūrō.*

usquam anywhere, **usque** continuously : *u-s-* from U-, see *ubī,* + a case-sign, see *abs.*

ūsūrpō use: fr. Adj. *ūsū-ripus* 'getting by prescription,' *ūsū* Abl. + *rapiō,* cf. *ūsū-capiō* acquire.

ut as : = *u-tĭ,* U- see *ubī* + -TI Loc., see *ast.*

ūter skin : *ūtri-* = *ōd-ri-,* ŌD- Lit. *ŭda.*

uterus womb : UD-ŖO- Sk. *udáram,* from UD out (i.e. 'beyond' the stomach, cf. *extrēmus* 'furthest off' from *ex* out) Got. *ut* E., Sk. *ud,* cf. *ὕσ-τερος* behind, *ὑσ-τέρα* womb.

utī utei as : U- see *ubī* + TĪ from TO-, see *tam.*

ūtor oitor use : 'take as my portion,' OIT- cf. *οἶτος* fate ('portion '').

ūva grape : = *ōva* ŌGV-, OSlav. vin-*jaga* Lit. *ūga* berry.

ūvidus hūvidus moist : ŪGV- cf. UGV- *ὑγρός,* MIr. *ūr* fresh, and VOGV- ONor. *vökr* moist E. *wake* of a ship.

uxor (from *vuxor*) **voxor** wife :

vacca cow (E. *bachelor?*) : = *vet-cā̆* (for term. cf. *juven-ca*), VET- Sk. *vat-s-ás* calf, see *vitulus.*

vaccīnium whortleberry : fr. *vaccīnus* Adj. of praeced., 'eaten by cows '.

vacillō stagger : Dim. of *vacō* VAKV- Ags. *vah* crooked E. *woo,* Sk. *vakrás:* also **vaccillō** stagger, from *vaccō *vācō* VĀKV-.

vacō vocō am empty: 'am open to an offer,' VOK- Arm. *vasn* on account of, cf. VEK- *ἑκών* willing, Zd. *vaç-* be willing Sk. *vaç-* be eager.

vādō rush : VĀDH-, cf. sq.

vadum ford : 'passage,' VADH- MIr. *fonnadh* travelling, Ags. *vadan* go E. *wade waddle.*

vae Interj. (*οὐαί*): Got. *vai* Ags. *vā* woe Subst. E. E. *wail wellaway,* Lett. *wai* Interj.

vafer cunning: *vaf-ro-* VAGHV-, Lit. *wagìs* thief.

vāgīna sheath (E. *vanilla*):

vāgĭo cry:

vagus roaming (E. *tcrmagant?*): 'broken,' VAGV- ἄγνῡμι break, MIr. *fann* weak.

vah vaha Interj. : = *vā* (see *aha*).

valeō am strong: GVAL- βάλε oh that ('mayst thou be able'), Lit. *galèti* be able.

valgus awry : = *volgús* VOLGV- Ags. *vealcan* roll E. *walk* †*galop*, Sk. *valg-* to spring, cf. VĻNGV- OIr. *lingid* he leaps.

vallēs valley (E. E. *avalanche*): 'shut in,' cf. sq.

vallum palisade (Ags. *veal* rampart E. *wall*), **vallus** stake for a palisade: = *valno-* : 'enclosing,' cf. MIr. *fál* hedge.

valva door : = *volvâ* fr. *volvō*, 'revolving' on its hinges.

vannus fan (E., OHG. *wanna*):

vānus empty (E. *vaunt*):

vapor steam :

vappa flat wine : = *vāpa*, *vāpus* Adj. fr. praeced. (see *cōmis*), 'that has emitted its bouquet '.

vāpulō am flogged : 'wriggle,' VĀP- *vappō* moth (= *vāpō*), cf. VAP- Ags. *väfer* unsteady E. *wave waver waft*.

varius variegated (E. miniver *vair*): = GVODIÓS (with accent of πολιός), dialectically Varr. *badius* brown (E. *bay* Adj. *baize*), cf. OIr. *buide* yellow.

varix dilated vein : 'blotch,' VŖ- *rarus* pimple, cf. VŖ- Lit. *wìras*.

vārus crooked :

vas surety (E. *engage*) : VEDH-f- cf. ἀ-(ϝ)εθ-λος contest, W. *gwystl* pledge (= *vedh-tlion*), and VODH- Got. *vadi* E. *wed* †*wage*, Lit. *wadùti* redeem.

vās vessel (E. E. *flask*) : OUmbr. *vasus* Abl. Plur :

vāstus waste (E.) : VĀST- OIr. *fás* empty, Ags. *rēste* waste.

†**vātēs vātius** (Caper, Keil 7. 112): VŌTI- Celtic οὐάτεις priests (Strabo 4. 4. 4) OIr. *fáith* prophet, cf. Ags. *Vōden* a god E. *Wednesday*, and Got. *vōds* mad OE. *wood* Adj. ('inspired,' cf. μάντις prophet fr. μαίνομαι am mad), Rhys, Hibbert Lectures, p. 278.

-ve or : -VE ἠ-(ϝ)έ, cf. VĒ Zd. Sk. *vā*.

vē- vae- depreciative particle (*vē-cors vē-grandis vē-pallidus vē-sānus*, see *vēscus vēstibulum*):

vectis lever : 'mover,' fr. *vchō*.

vegeō arouse: = *vogeō* VOG- Got. *vakan* watch E. E. *wake wait* †*bivounc,* cf. VŌG- Zd. *vāza* strength Sk. *vâjas* quickness; also UG- ὑγιής healthy, OIr. di-*uch*-t-rad to wake.

vehemens (-*ehe*- dialectic spelling of -*ē*-, see *aha*; in poetry always a disyllable) **veemens vēmens** violent: 'mad,' *vē-* + *mens*.

vehō carry: VEGH- OIr. *fēn* wagon, Got. ga-*vigan* move E. *wag wagon weigh wall*-eyed *whit wight* ear*wig* †*vogue*, Lit. *wežù* I carry OSlav. *vezą*, Zd. *vaz-* drive Sk. *vah-* carry, cf. VOGH- *ὄχος* chariot.

vel or: 'choose,' Imperat. fr. *volō* (cf. *dīc dūc fac fer* fr. *dīcō* &c.).

vēles skirmisher: fr. **vēlus*, see *vēlōx*.

vellō pluck: = **vel-nō*, VEL-N- W. *gwellaif* shears.

vellus fleece: = **vollus* VOLN-ES-, cf. VOLN- *οὐλος* woolly (= **Fόλνος*), and VḶN- Got. *vulla* wool E., Lit. *wilnos* OSlav. *vlŭna*, Arm. *gaṙn* lamb, see *lāna*.

vēlōx swift: from **vēlus* (see *atrōx*) **veh-ēlus* fr. *vehō*, 'carried away'.

vēlum[1] covering: OIr. *fīal*: = **ves-lum*, see *vestis*.

vēlum[2] sail: = **vex-lum*, see *vexillum*.

vēna vein: = **vex-na* 'conductor,' VEGH- *vehō* + -s- see *vexō*?

venēnum poison (E *venom*): = **venes-num* 'philtre' .(Hor. Epod. 5. 87), fr. *Venus*, sq.

veneror beseech: VEN-ES- cf. *Venus* goddess of love, from VEN- Ags. *vine* lover, Sk. *van-* to love.

venia kindness: = **vonia* VON- *ὀνίνημι* help, cf. VṆ- MHG. *wunnan* be happy.

veniō come (E. *adventure saunter venue*): GVṆ-JŌ *βαίνω* (= **βάν-jω*), for GVM-JŌ, cf. GVEM- OIr. *bēim* step (= **bem-men*, Stokes Remarks), Got. *qiman* come E., Lit. *gemù* am born, Arm. *ekn* he came (= **e-gem-t*), cf. GVOM- Zd. Sk. *gam-* go.

vēnor hunt (E. *venison*): 'gain,' fr. *vēnum*.

venter belly: sq., 'wind-bag'.

ventus wind: VENT- Got. *vinds* E., cf. VENT-JO- W. *gwynt*; from VĒ- (with shortening before -*nt*-) *ἄ-(F)ημι* blow, Got. *vaian*, Lit. *wéjas* wind OSlav. *vějati* blow, Zd. Sk. *vā-*.

vēnūcula vennūcula vēnīcula vēnuncula a grape for preserving: Fem. Dimin. from **vēnūcus* or **vēnūnquus* 'preserved for sale,' fr. sq.

vēnum vaenum sale: VĒN- OSlav. *věniti* sell, Arm. *gin* price, cf. VŌN- *ὦνος*, MIr. *ūain* loan.

Not add Sk. *vasnám* price, for -*sn*- would remain in OSlav.

veprēs briar:

vēr spring: ONor. *vār*.

vērātrum hellebore: 'corrective, purgative,' fr. **vērō* set right, fr. *vērus*.

verbēnae herbage (E. *vervain*): = **verbes-nae* fr. sq., 'shoots'.

verbera whips (Nom. Sing. **verbus*, cf. Plaut. *sub-verbustam* 'slightly beaten'): = **vorbera* VṚB- *ῥάβδος* wand, Lit. *wirbas* rod OSlav. *vrŭba* willow.

verbum word : = *vorbum* VṚDH- Got. *vaurd* E., cf. VORDH- Lit. *wardas* name.

vereor reverence : 'look to,' = *voreor* VOR- ὁράω see, Got. *vars* wary E. E. *ward warrant* &c. *wormwood worthy wraith* †*garnish* &c. †*garret*.

vergō bend (E. *verge* Vb.) : see *urgeō*.

vermina gripes : = *vert-mina* fr. *vertō* (as στρόφος colic fr. στρέφω turn).

vermis worm : = *vormis* VṚM- ῥόμος wood-worm (Lesbian for *ῥάμος), Got. *vaurms* serpent E. *worm*.

verna home-born slave : 'born in a *ver sacrum*' (Nonius). Not = *vesina* from VES- dwell, see *villa*.

verpa πέος, **verpus** circumcised :

verrēs boar : VERS- ἔρραος ram ἔρσαι young lambs, Lit. *werszis* calf, Zd. *varshni* ram, cf. VṚS- Sk. *vṛshṇis*.

verrō vorrō sweep : VṚS- OSlav. *vrūhǫ*, cf. VERS- ἀπό-(F)ερσε it swept away, VORS- ONor. *vörr* pull of the oar.

verrūca wart, steep place (Cato) : 'rising,' = *vorr-ūca* VṚS- Lit. *wirszus* top OSlav. *vrūhū*, cf. VERS- Arm. i-*ver* up, Sk. *várshman*- height.

verruncō turn out : 'rise' (cf. *āverruncō* avert, 'prevent from rising'), = *vorruncō* fr. *vorr-unquus* Adj. from VṚS- praeced. ; whence also *urruncum* (i.e. *vurruncum) top of stalk of corn (Varr.).

vertō vortō turn : VORT- ὄρτυξ quail ('dancing'), Lit. *wartau* I turn over OSlav. *vratiti* turn, Zd. *varet*- turn to Sk. *vartakas* quail *vart*-turn, cf. VERT- W. *gwerthyd* spindle, Got. *vairthan* become E. *worth* (in 'woe worth the day') *weird* Got. and-*vairths* present E. *toward*.

verū spit : GVERV- OUmbr. *berva* Plur., OIr. *beura* stakes : 'of wood,' cf. GVṚ- Hesych. βαρύες trees, Lit. *girè* forest.

vērus true (E. *very*) : VĒR- OIr. *fīr*, Got. tuz-*vērjan* to doubt Ags. *vaer* true E. *warlock*, Lit. *wièra* faith OSlav. *vĕra*.

vervēx berbēx (Petronius 57) wether :

vescor eat : = *voscor*, GVO-SKŌ βόσκω feed.

vēscus small : = *vĕ-squus* from *vĕ-*.

vēs-īca vens-īca bladder : VENS- :

vespa wasp : = *vospa* VOSP- Ags. *väsp* E., cf. VOPS- Ags. *väps*, Pruss. *wobse* OSlav. *vosa*.

vesper evening (OIr. *fescor*) : ἕσπερος.

vester voster your : VOS Sk. *vas* you Enclitic, cf. VŌS *vōs*.

vē-stibulum porch : *vĕ-* + *stabulum* stall, 'inferior building' (cf. *Vĕjovis* 'little Jupiter' Ov. Fast. 3. 447).

vestīgium track :

vestis garment (E. *travestie*) : = *vostis* Got. *vasti* E. †*gaiter*, from VOS- Got. *vasjan* clothe E. *wear*, Zd. *vanh*- Sk. *vas*-, cf. VES- ἕννυμι, Arm. z-*ge*-num I dress.

veterīnus of beasts of draught: 'of yearlings,' VET-ES- see *vetus*, and cf. *vitulus*.

vetô votô forbid: 'speak,' GVOT-, see *arbiter*, cf. GVET- Got. *qithan* speak E. *quoth bequeath*.

vetus old: 'full of years,' VET- *ἔτος* year, Lit. *wétuszas* old OSlav. *vetŭhŭ*, Sk. tri-*vat-s-as* three years old.

vexillum standard: ·carried,' fr. *vexus Part. of *vehō*.

vexô shake: 'move,' from VEGH- *vehō* + -s-.

via vea (Varr.) way (E. *envoy invoice voyage*): OUmbr. *vea*; = *vehā fr. *vehô*, cf. Ags. *veg* E.

vībēx vībīx weal: Lett. *vībele*: 'mark of a whip,' VIB- Lit. *wyburti* wag the tail, cf. VIB- sq.

vibrô shake: VIB- OHG. *wipph* vibration E. *whip wipe wimple quip* †*gimp*, cf. praeced.

vīburnum wayfaring-tree: 'quivering,' VĪB- see *vibēx*.

vicem Acc. change (E. *traffic*): VEK-, cf. VEK-S- OHG. *wehsal* change.

vīcēnī 20: = *vīcent-nī, VĪKNT-, see *viginti*.

vicia vetch (E.; Galen βίκιον bean): 'sown at intervals,' thrice a year Plin. 18. 137, fr. *vicem*.

victima victuma victim: 'return' to the gods, fr. *vectus Part. fr. VEK- *vicem*.

vīcus veicus quarter (E. -*wick* -*wich* in place-names; OIr. *fïch* village): VOIK- οἶκος house, Sk. *vēças* tent, cf. VEIK- Got. *veihs* village, VĪK- Zd. *vīç*, VIK- OSlav. *vĭsĭ* farm.

video see (E. *advise survey view visage vista*): VID- ἰδεῖν to see, W. *gwedd* aspect, Got. *witan* watch E. *wit* &c. *twit* †*guide*, Zd. Sk. *vid*- know, cf. VĪD- OSlav. *vidēti* see.

vidulus wallet (Fr. *valise*?): VĪDH-, cf. VIDH- 'bind,' OIr. co-*beden* connexion, Got. ga-*vidan* bind E. *wallet wattle* &c. *wad weeds wind* Vb. &c.

viduus bereft (E. *void*; OIr. *fedb* widow): = *viduvus *vidovus VIDH-EV- ἠίθεος (= *ἠ-fίθεfος) bachelor, OSlav. *vĭdova* widow, Sk. *vidhávā*, cf. VIDH-U- Got. *vid-u-vō* E.; from VIDH- 'separate,' see *dī-vidō*, ἰσθμός (= *fιθ-θμός) neck of land, cf. VĪDH- Ags. *vid* wide E.

viētus vjētus withered: Part. of *vieō 'overpower,' = *vieō from VĪ- see *vis* Subst.

vigeō thrive: = *vegeō*.

vigil awake (E. *vedette*): see *vegeō*.

viginti 20: dialectic for *vicintī VĪKNTĪ cf. VĪKNTĪ Dor. fίκατι, Zd. *vīçaiti*, VEIKNTI εἴκοσι (with ο, for α, from τριάκοντα), VINKNTI Sk. *viñçati*, VIKNTI OIr. *fichet* Gen., Arm. *khsan*.

vīlis cheap (E. *revile*): 'common, from a farm,' sq.

villa vella (Varr.) farm : = *vīla* *vēla* cf. *vīlicus* bailiff, *ves-la* 'dwelling,' VES- Got. *visan* to stay E. *was wassail west*, Zd. *vañh-* dwell Sk. *vas-*, cf. VOS- MIr. *foss* a staying, Arm. *gom* I am.

villus shaggy hair (E. *velvet*) : = *vellus* from *vollus*, VLNO-, see *vellus*.

vīmen withe : VĪ- *vieō* weave, cf. VI- Sk. *vi-*, and VĪ-T- see *vitis vitta*.

vinciō bind (E. *periwinkle*[1]) :

vincō conquer (E. *vanquish*) : VINKV-, cf. VEIKV- Got. *veihan* fight E. *wight* Adj., OSlav. *věkŭ* strength, and VIKV- MIr. *fichim* I fight, Lit. *wikrus* active.

vindicō vendicō claim (E. *vengeance*) : 'declare the price,' see *vēnum* and *dicō dicō*, with the -*ē*- shortened before -*nd*-.

vinnulus delightful : VEN-, see *veneror*.

vīnum wine (Got. *vein* E. E. *vignette vine vinegar vintage win*-berry) : VOIN- *οἶνος*, Arm. *gini*, Heb. *yāyin* (borrowed from Europe).

viola violet : Dimin. of *via*, cf. *ἴον* (= *Fἴον*).

violō injure : fr. *violus* Adj. from VĪ-, see *vīs* Subst.

vipera adder (E. *wyvern*) : 'wriggling,' VOIP- ONor. *veifa* to wave E. *waive waif*, cf. VIP- W. *gwibio* wander, Ags. *vifel* weevil E., Sk. *vip-* tremble.

vir man : VIRO- OIr. *fer*, Got. *ṛair* E. *werwolf world*, cf. VĪRO- Lit. *wýras*, Zd. *vīra* Sk. *vīrás* hero.

virāgō heroine : 'acting like a man,' fr. praeced. + ĀG-, see *strāgēs*.

vireō am fresh, green (E. *farthingale verjuice*) : fr. Adj. *virus* GVI-RŌS Zd. *jira* eager, cf. GVĪ-RŌS Sk. *jīrás* lively ; from GVI- Zd. *ji-* live Sk. *ji-* quicken.

virga twig (E. *verge* Subst.) : VIDGĀ (see *mergō*), OHG. *wisc* wisp E.

virgō maiden :

vīrus poison : VĪSÓS *ἰός*, cf. VISÓM Zd. *visha* Sk. *vishám* : from VIS- Sk. *vish-* be active ?

vīs Subst. strength : VĪ-s- from VI- *ἴς*, cf. *viētus*.

vīs Vb. thou wilt : VĪ- *ἴεμαι* desire, Sk. *vī-* enjoy.

Vois in the Dvenos inscription (E. Schneider 19) is too obscure to compare.

viscum misletoe : VISK-, cf. VIKS- *ἰξός*.

viscus internal organs : VISK- cf. VIKS- *ἰξύς* waist : 'growth, development,' fr. praeced. (as E. *waist* fr. *wax* Vb.).

vīta life : = *vīvita* GVĪVO-T- Lit. *gywatà*, fr. *vivus*, cf. GVIVO-T- *βιοτή* OIr. *beothu* (E. usque*baugh*).

vitilēna Plaut. Most. 213 (204), corrupt.

vītis vine (E. *vice*[2]) : fr. VĪ-TŌ- Part. from *vieō*, see *vīmen*, cf. *vītex* chaste-tree (Plin.), *ἰτέα* willow, Ags. *vīdie* withe E., Ags. *viḍig* willow E. *withy*, Lit. *wytis* withe OSlav. *vitĭ* twisted, cf. VOI-T- OSlav. *vētvĭ* branch, Zd. *vaēti* willow.

vitium defect (E. *vice*[1]):

vitô avoid: 'feel loth towards, dislike,' fr. **vītus* 'forced' Part. of vī-, *vīs* Subst., see *invītus.*

vit-ri-cus stepfather: 'marrying a widow,' fr. **vid-ra* widow, see *viduus.*

vitrum woad, glass (as of a bluish tint: E. *varnish vitriol*): VIT-, cf. VOIT'- Ags. *wād* woad E.

vitta band: 'woven,' = **vīta* Part. Fem. from vī- see *vieō vitis.*

vitulor keep holiday (E. *fiddle viol*): 'enliven myself,' fr. **vītula* Dimin. of *vīta.*

vitulus calf (ἰταλός; E. *veal vellum*): 'yearling,' see *vetus,* VET- cf. Got. *withrus* lamb E. *wether.*

vīvō live (E. *viands*): GVĪV- Arm. *keam* I live (= **kivam*), Zd. Sk. *jīv-* live, cf. GVEIV- βείομαι shall live, sq.

    Perf. *vīxī* and Supine *vīctum* are fr. *vigeō.*

vīvus alive: GVĪVO- OIr. *bīu,* Lit. *gýwas* OSlav. *živŭ,* Sk. *jīvás,* cf. GVIVO- βίος life, Got. *qius* alive Ags. *cwic cwicu-* (with -c- developed before -*u*) E. *quick whitlow,* cf. praeced.

vix hardly: = **vic-su* (for term. see *mox*), fr. *vicem,* 'at the chance of circumstances'.

vocô call: VOKV- ὄπα Acc. voice, OHG. gi-*wahan* to mention NHG. er-*wähnen,* Pruss. *wackis* war-cry, cf. VEKV- ἔπος word, Zd. Sk. *vac-* speak.

†volaema volēma warden-pears: Gaulish for 'good and large' (Serv.).

volô wish: VOL- cf. VEL- *velle* Inf., Got. *viljan* to will E. E. *well weal wild,* Lit. *wélyti* wish OSlav. *velēti,* Zd. Sk. *var-* choose.

volô fly (E. *volley*): 'drop,' GVL̥-, see *balanus.*

volup agreeably:

    hardly cf. VELP- ἐλπίς hope.

volva vulva integument: VL̥V- Sk. *úlvam* caul, cf. sq.

volvō roll (E. *revolt vault*): VOLV- OIr. *fulumain* rolling W. *olwyn* wheel, Got. af-*valvjan* roll away E. *wallow,* cf. VELU- ἐλυσθείς rolling.

vōmer vōmis ploughshare:

    hardly = **vox-m-is* from VOGHV-S-, cf. VONGHV-S- ONor. *vangs-n̦* (Fritzner), from VOGHV- Hesych. ὄφνίς, OHG. *waganso,* Pruss. *wag-nis* coulter.

vomō: VOM-, cf. VEM- ἐμέω, Lit. *wemiù* vomo, Zd. Sk. *vam-* vomere, and VĒM- ONor. *vāma* qualm.

vorô devour: GVOR- Zd. Sk. *gar-*, cf. GVER- Lit. *gérti* to drink, Arm. *ker* food, GVRO- Ir. *broth,* GVR̥- OSlav. *grŭlo* throat, GVR̥- βιβρώσκω devour βορά food.

vōs ye: VŌ- OSlav. *va* Dual, Zd. *vāo* Acc. Plur., see *vester.*

voveō vow (E.): OUmbr. *vuvçi* a vow:
  not from (1) ɢᴠᴏ- βοή cry or *ἐγ-γύη* pledge, or Umbr. would be *bouçi*;
  (2) ᴠᴏɢʜᴠ- cf. Sk. *vāghát* sacrifice, or Perf. would be *voxī*.

vōx voice (E.): ᴠōᴋᴠ- Sk. *vắk*, cf. ᴠᴏᴋᴠ- *vocŏ*.

vulgus volgus multitude: ᴠᴏʟɢᴠ- Sk. *várgas* class.

vulnus volnus wound: = *volinus* ᴠᴏʟ-ᴇɴ-ᴇs- cf. ᴠᴏʟ-ɴĀ *οὐλή* scar
  ᴠᴇʟ-ɴ- *vellō*.

vulpēs volpēs fox: dialectic for *volquēs*, ᴠᴌᴋᴠ- see *lupus*, beast-names
  being confused.

vultur voltur vulture: ᴠᴏʟ-, ci. ᴠᴇʟ- *vellō*.

vultus voltus face:
  hardly fr. *volŏ*, which gives too weak a meaning.

†**zāmia** loss: ζāμία Dor. = ζημία Ion.:

†**zephyrus** west wind: ζέφυρος, cf. ζόφος west.

†**zōna** girdle: ζώνη, = *ζώσ-νη from ᴊōs- Lit. *jŭsiŭ* I gird OSlav. po-*jasŭ*
  girdle, Zd. *yāh*- gird oneself (Spiegel).

COMPARATIVE ETYMOLOGY

(Letters given in Capitals are those of the Ursprache.)

LATIN.

ɪ remains, see e.g. *is pix vir*; before j it = *ē jējūnus*, see *jentō*; unaccented before r (from s) it = e *anser*. Final it = **e** *ante mare*, which often drops (orig. before an initial vowel), *ad- amb- ast aut et hic ob post quot tot ut, instar siremps*.—Dialectic compression by omission of unaccented i (of whatever origin) between consonants, see *forceps sēsqui- sīnciput, splendeō jūncus ūncia, ōrnō ūsurpō ārdeō, ipse abdōmen, multīcia antestor fastīdium portōrium pōstulō, pōnō sūmō*, and below on v. Contraction : i + hī = ī *bīmus*, **ae** + hi = **ae** *praeda*.

ᴜ *cutis furō lucerna*. After Lingual it = later **v** *calvor mīlvus pēlvis salvus silva, lārva*: Metathesis after ᴅʟ *dulcis*. Final it drops *mox*, see *vix red-*.

ŭ written **u**, later **i**: *clueō culullus domus frutex jungō lacruma lubet lunter luō manubiae numerus pugnus pungō supō surpiculus sus-* opp. *cliens culillus domicilium fritillus igitur lacrima libet linter litō manibiae nimis pignus pingo dissipō sirpus sirempse;* see *fimus ligō miser nimbus redivīvus stipula stringō supercilium tingō* and below on the short sonants. Unaccented before r it = **e** *socer*. Dialectically it = **o** *soboles*.

ᴇ *ego ɟerō sequor*; dialectically it = **i** *cicer cicur filix fistula in milium nisi niteō pinna plicō sileō singulī sinister spiciō tribus via vindicō vitulus*, see *quinque* and below on ᴍ ɴ.—Before nasal + g it = **a** *anguilla frangō*: before l + any consonant but v it = **u** *mulceō ulcus ulmus*, see below on *adulter indulgeō*; before v it = **o** *foveō moveō novem novus ovō sovos* or (see on ᴏ) **u** *juvō pluit viduus*. It = **o** after initial s from ꜱᴠ, *socer sonus sopor soror*, or initial c from ᴋᴠ, *colō coquō corium cortex* (also **u**, *cucumis culina*).—Pretonic ᴇ, unless saved by analogy, = **a**: in Noun-stems in **eá** *palea*, **nó** (**ná**) *alnus catēna magnus stagnum taberna*, **lä** *tabula*, **ró** *aper sacer*, **ká** *vacca*, **í** *ās ratis vas*, **ú** *gradus manus*, **jét** *ariēs*, **íd** *lapis*; Verb-stems in **í** *capiō faciō jaciō sapiō*, **é** *candeō maneō pateō*, **ä** *amō flagrō*, **ísko** *nanciscor paciscor*;

and Prepositions *ad- af.*—Unaccented E (i.e. in any syllable but the first) before two consonants remains *haruspex* or (dialectically, see above) = i see *sēmis*; before a single consonant it = ŭ i.e. u *famulus nŭncupŏ occulŏ* or i *arbiter compitum dīligŏ inquilīnus inquinŏ meminī oppidŏ permitiēs*, unless preserved by 'Recomposition' *ēlegans intellegŏ neglegŏ impetus.*—Final E drops (see on I) in *ceu haud neg-legŏ nŏn vel.*

o *domus ob potis*; dialectically = ŭ, i.e. u or i, *locus-lucŭna-īlicŏ, colober-coluber colpa-culpa dolus-sēdulŏ locusta-lucusta polcer-pulcer, poliŏ-pudet, clupeus-clipeus cunctus-cingŏ recuperŏ-reciperŏ umbilīcus-imbilīcus,* see *cunctor cupiŏ gumia humus luxus murmur umbō umbra ungŏ, cinis imber similis,* and below on ʟ ʀ.—Later = u in atonics *cum* (Prep., cf. *hunc sunt*) and before consonant in final syllable of polysyllables *centum fīlius genus rŏbur* &c. Initial vo remains by analogy in *vocŏ volŏ volvŏ,* else later = ve *vegeŏ vellus venia verbum vertŏ vespa vester* (or, pretonic, va, *varius vacŏ,* see below); so initial vo from GVO = ve *vescor vetŏ.* Initial quo remains by analogy in *quot quotus,* else = que (see on ʀ) or qui (see E above) *quisquiliae* (o *canis* see below).—o before v = a *avis caveŏ cavus fateŏ favilla favus gravis lavŏ paviŏ,* unaccented u (see above on ᴀ) *cxuŏ.*—Pretonic o, unless saved by analogy, = a: in Noun-stems in á *ansa valva ŏ valgus* (or in these two the al may = ʟ̣) iŏ *radius varius* rŏ *amārus atrŏx* (and see *catus*), ĭ *canis*; Verb-stems in é *cracens* (see *gracilis*) *placeŏ,* á *vacŏ.*—o final = e *ille iste tame* (see *tam*).—Contraction : o + o = ŏ *prŏlēs,* and so o + a *cŏgitŏ.*

ᴀ *agŏ caper pater.* Unaccented before two consonants it = e *convexus identidem necesse peregrē sollcmnis sublestus* or i (see above on E) *concinnus,* or, before l + another consonant, u, *adulter,* see *indulgeŏ*; before a single consonant it = o *aboleŏ* (cf. *Hecoba* from Ἑκάβη), later ŭ (see above on O), i.e. u (*contubernium*) or i *adminiculum conquiniscŏ dēstinŏ vēstibulum,* which before r = e *properus reciperŏ sistere.*—Contraction : a + ŏ = ŏ *dŏ, nŏ.*

ī *acclīnis vītex vīvus*; dialectically = ē *avēna, reus* (so *covehriu,* see *cūria* = **co-vēriŏ*), and see *spīca villa.*

ū *cūpa fūmus mūs.*

ŭ spelt ū *fŭcus mŭtulus mŭtus pŭteŏ scrŭta stŭpa,* see *supparum trŭgonus,* or ī *ficus mitulus mitis pituita scrinium stipa, siparium trigonus,* see *flŏ frigŏ gibbus limpidus mīrus spirŏ stipes*: also oe *amoenus* (see below on OI, EU, AU).

Ē *fēmina rēs rēx* (to show the length spelt also ee see *bālŏ penna vehemens* or ehe *ehem mehe vehemens*; later ae *faecundus laevis nae praelum vaenum, †caepe †chaela †naenia †paelex †scaeptrum,* or oe *foecundus foetus moeta*); dialectically it = ī *sinciput subtilis,* see *farīna villa* and perhaps *spīca,* and below on EI, AI.

ō *dōnum nōscō pōtus* (to show the length spelt also **oh** *oh proh*); dialectically it = ū i.e. ū *fŭr hŭc jŭcundus nŭdus nŭtriō praestŭlor ŭlna ŭpĭliō ŭtcr ŭva*, see *septuāgintā*, or ī *renīdeō sīspes* (see *sōspes*).—Pretonic, unless saved by analogy, it = ā *ācer plăcŏ*.

Ī *fāgus māter suādeo* (to show the length spelt also **ah** *ah vah* or **aha** *aha vaha*, see *trans*).

Original vowel-length is often denoted by doubling the consonant following:

Ī *immō, hinniō* (?), *illicō ille millia pilleus villa, cippus lippus quippe, gibbus, littera-littus mittō vitta* (and †*sagitta*?), *crissŏ* (†*sarissa*).

ū *dummētum nummus, cunnus, cucullus culullus culleus, cuppa stuppa* †*supparum suppus, friguttiō futtilis gluttiō gutta muttiō muttō, buccina muccus* †*tuccētum, suggillŏ, fussus russus*.

Ē *penna strenna vennūcula, bellua fellō helluō mustella pelluis sella* (from *sedda*) *stelliō tellūs, susurrus tcrra* (cf. Fest. †*crēterra* from κρητῆρα).

ō *nonne, lollīgō, porricĭŏ*.

Ā *damma flamma lammina, annus pannus,* †*tallĕc allium allūcinor callīgō, narrŏ parricīda sarriō, vappa* (cf. *applŭda sappīnus), attāt battuō quattuor stlattārius, accipiter bacca* †*braccae* †*bracchium flaccus vaccillŏ, nassus*.

Conversely, for a short vowel + two consonants may be written a long vowel + a single consonant, *āmentum cōturnīx stīpendium sūspĭcĭō*.

A long vowel is shortened before

(1) another vowel, or **h** + vowel: ī *dĭēs hĭŏ proprius vĭolŏ nĭhilum*, ū *cruor pruĭna ruŏ*[1] *ruŏ*[4], ē *deinde neŏ rcor* (see *ceu*), ō (from ov) *clŏāca*, ā *trahō*.

(2) **nt** *contĭō fontis ventus* (but *mĕntula nŭntius* probably earlier forms), **nd** *vindicŏ* (but *nŭndinum prĕndō*).

(3) final **m** *clam*, **r** *prŏspcr*, **d** *scd*.

EI remains in Interj. *hei*, else later = ī *dīcō fīdō līveō*, dialectically ē *lēvis* and see *ceu deus*. Before vowel it = e *eŏ qucŏ scrcŏ*, see *trēs*.

OI later = **oe** *foedus* (Subst. and Adj.) *moenia soera*, later still ū i.e. ū *cūnac cūra fūscus lūdus mūnus mūrus mūtō mūtŏ pūmex ūnus ūtor* or ī *clīvus fⁱdus* (Subst.) *tĭbia* or (dialectically, see above on ī) ē *fedus* (Subst. and Adj.): pretonic, unless saved by analogy, it = **ae** *caecus* (later mis-spelt **oe**).

AI later = **ae** *aevum caedō scacva* (later mis-spelt **oe** *coclum coena hoedus mocreō poenitet*), or dialectically ('rustic') ē *cēna glēba hēdus hērēs obscēnus pēne sēculum sēta tēter*. Before vowel, or **h** + vowel, it = **a** *aëneus ahēneus*, in Compounds **e** *prehendō*. Unaccented AI = ī *sī*, and see *olīvum*.

EU remains in Interjs. *ëheu heu heus*, else = $\bar{u}$ i.e. $\bar{u}$ *dūcō gūstó lūbricus lūgeō lūridus lūx nūtó plūma prūna rūctó* or $\bar{\imath}$ *līber*.

OU = later $\bar{u}$ *clūnis cūdō lūcus mūcus pūblicus rūbigō*, dialectically $\bar{o}$ *pŏblicus rŏbīgō*; both with shortening before vowel, *cluâca cloâca*. Pretonic OU, unless saved by analogy, = **au** *auris aurōra fraus*, see *autumô*.

AU *augeō caulis hauriō*; dialectically = $\bar{u}$ (vulgar?) *clūdus cūleus cŭpó frūstrā frŭstum nūgae rūdus sūdus* (also, to show the length, spelt ou *roudus*), $\bar{o}$ ('rustic') *adŏrea clŏdicô clŏdō cŏleus cŏpó cŏrus crŏciō nōgae ŏlla ōmen ōriga ōs ōstium ōtium plŏdo plŏstrum rōdus sŏdēs* and see *fôns*. Unaccented AU = $\bar{u}$ i.e. $\bar{u}$ *adūlor indūtiae obtūrô* or **oe** *oboediō* or $\bar{e}$ *obēdiō*.

ŌU before vowel = ***ōv āv** *octāvus*: *bovis*, like *bŏs*, is un-Roman.
ĀU before vowel = **āv** *nāvis*; before consonant (after loss of i) it = **au** *claudō gaudcō*, dialectically (see above on AU) $\bar{u}$ *clūdō*.

Dialectically **h** is prefixt to an initial vowel, *haud hauriō haveô herus hic hodiĕ hŏrnus humerus* and Interjs. *hau hei hĕja hĕm*. In *hālēc hālūcinor harūndō helluô herciscor hērēs honus* it is doubtful whether it is original or prefixt. It is added between vowels to prevent hiatus in *ahĕneus nihil*.

Sonants.

M = **em** *geminī temnō, decem novcm seplem*, or (see above on E) **im** *simul*; when unaccented in trisyllables it = **üm** i.e. **um** or **im** *aestimô autumô optumus*.

N = **en** *centum dens densus ensis genŭ mens mensus mentum tenuis, ingens juvenis lūmen* (after v with Contraction in *nōnus*; = **e** [or $\bar{e}$?] before **x** *exta*), or (see above on E) **in** *in- infit* (?) *infula inter lingua pinguis, dominus terminus tintinô vīgintī* (= $\bar{\imath}$ before **gn** *ignis*).

L = **ol** *dolô holus polleō stolidus tolerô*, or (see above on O) **ül** i.e. **ul** *culmus fulgeō fulica fulvus gula mulgeō multus pulcer pullus* (Subst. and Adj.) *sculpô stultus tulī, gurguliō prōmulgô, angulus cumulus dīscipulus fīcēdula manipulus saeculum stimulus stipula tabula trāgula*, or **il** *similis concipilô rutilus.*—Initial VL dialectically = **lu** (see below on R) *lupus*, else **vol** *volpēs volva* (and so GVL-, *volô*) or **vul** *vulpēs vulva*.

R = **or** *cor corbis cornŭ dormiō dorsum fornāx forô fors fortis horreum hortor mora mordcō morior orior por- porrum portiō portô portus scortum sorbeō sors sporta storea torpeō extorris* (which before **sc** for ***csc** = $\bar{o}$ *pŏscō*), or (see above on O) **ur** *curculiō curtus furnus spurcus turpis ursus* **er** (for ***ir**, see above on Ü) *iterum uterus auger ūber.*—VR dialectically = **rü** i.e. **ru** *quadru- trua trux* or **ri** *quadri-*; else = **vor** *vorrô* (or, after **t, uor** *quattuor*) or (when initial) ***vur ur** *urgeō urtīca*, later

when initial (see above on O) **ver** *verbera vermis verrō.* So initial
ᴋvʀ = *quor *quur **cur** *currō,* later **quer** *quercus*: initial **ɢvʀ** = *gor
gur *gurges-gurguliō,* dialectically = **vor** *vorō.*

м̤ = **am** *tamen.*—**ṉ** = **an** *anguis manus* or **nā** *gnārus-nāvus nāscor,* which
after **m** = **ā** *germānus hūmānus.*

ḻ = **al** *callum calvus fallō palma*[1] *scalpō* (by Dissimilation **ar** *largus*) or
lā *clādēs clāmō flāvus flō lātus* Part., see *clam flaccus.*—**ʀ̤** = **ar** *ardea*
arduus argentum armus ars carduus carpō farciō haruspex marceō margō
parō quartus varix (which before **st** = **ā** *fāstīgium*) or **rā** *crābrō crāssus-*
crātis frāxinus grānum grātus prātum prāvus rādīx rāmus rārus strāmen.

Consonants.

м remains, see e.g. *medius*: = **n** before **ᴊ** *lanius veniō,* **t** *centum quantus*
d *deinde,* **c** *nunc nuncubī,* **s** *ansa mensa*: before **l** it = **p** †*plumbum,*
before **r** it = **b** *brevis* (see *hibernus*), and so before **ʙ** *tūber.*—Omitted
before **nc** *nūncupō,* **sq** *sēsqui-,* and between **r** and **c** *forceps.*—Final **um**
drops (originally before an initial vowel) in *crās* (?) *dōnec nihil nimis*
procul quīn sed simul sīn.

ɴ *nemus*: = **m** before Labial *semper imbuō*: assimilated before **r** *irrītō.*—
ɴм in Derivatives = **rm** *carmen germen nōrma* (in Compounds = **mm**
immūtō): **ɴᴛ** before **n** drops with compensation[1] *vīcēnī*: **ɴs** dialectically = **s** with compensation *vēsīca,* dropt with compensation before
m *īmus trāma* **v** *trāvehō.*

ʟ *lingō*: by Dissimilation it = **r** *caeruleus largus* or (in a Compound)
drops *multīcia.*—**ʟɴ** from **ʟᴇɴ** remains *ūlna vulnus,* else = **ll** *bulla*
callum collis follis fullō pellis procella pullus vellus, antecellō fallō pellō
percellō polleō recellō tollō vellō: **ʟs** = **ll** *collum.*

ʀ *ruber*: by Dissimilation it = **l** *colurnus* (?) or (before **c**) **n** *cancer*:
before **l** in Compounds it is assimilated *intelligō pollingō,* in Derivatives dropt (with compensation if required) see *stella stilla.* Dialectically omitted after **st** *clandestīnus frūstum mediastīnus praestigiae.*—
Dialectically **ri rī rü** become **er,** *hibernus lucerna noverca ter cervīx,*
acerbus quater terō, see *tēstis.*—**ʀs** = **rr** *cerrītus currō errō farra garriō*
horreō horreum parreō parricīda porrum terreō torreō verrēs verrūca, but
before **t** = **s** with compensation *fāstīgium fāstus tēstis,* before **n** drops
cēna: unoriginal **rs** remains *accērsō dorsum ursus,* but dialectically =
ss *dossum pessum* or after a long vowel **s** *suāsum* and so (with compensation) before **c** *pōscō.*

---

[1] I.e. the vowel is lengthened to make up for the dropping of one or more of the
following consonants: the syllable thus retains its weight though its elements are
reduced in number.

J initial *jecur jocus juvenis*, drops before i *iciŏ igitur*. Between vowels it usually drops, see *plūs*, but remains (lengthening the vowel before it) in Reduplication *jējentŏ jējūnus*, onomatopoeic words *ējulŏ*, and terminations *saturēja*. It = i (in the classical dialect) after Liquid *lanius veniŏ, alius folium liēn ōpiliŏ saliŏ, caesariēs,* v *viētus* (?), d *medius,* c *socius* : drops after h *herī* p *spuŏ* s *suŏ*.

V initial *vehŏ vir vocŏ*: remains before u + l *vulgus vulnus vulpēs vultur vultus vulva* (unless c follow, *ulciscor*), drops before u (or ū) + any cons. but l, *uncus unda urbs urceus urgeŏ urtīca uxor ūrīna*: drops before Lingual *lāna liquŏ rādīx repens.*—Intervocalic v drops (dialectically) before u *reus deus* †*oleum* (*dea olea* are due to analogy), **saluus* (whence *salvus*) from **salūvus*; and after u *duo exuŏ pluit puer suus tuus viduus* (but uv remains after j *juvenis juvŏ* or before i from J *exuviae pluvius*). Unaccented vi or ve later (1) after a short vowel drops the i or e and vocalises the v: thus ov = ou = ū *būbulus cūria nūndinae* or dialectically ō *fŏmes cŏntiŏ fŏns nŏndinae nŏnus,* av = au *audeŏ autumŏ raucus saucius*; (2) after a long vowel or diphthong drops entirely (for *claudŏ gaudeŏ*, in which the i first drops and then āv becomes au, see above on ĀU): *trahŏ, fūlīgŏ vīta fībula nitor ūlīgŏ ūmeŏ, aequus praecŏ praedēs.*—Postconsonantal v remains after Lingual *alvus arvum*, but dialectically = b *gilbus corbus ferbeŏ sorbum*, or (as in Oscan) assimilates after l *mella mollis palleŏ sollus* (cf. *mīlliŏ* beside *mīlvus*); remains (spelt u) after q from K *equus*, and after s *suādeo-suāvis* (but *sē sērius sī sordēs*: drops before ū *sūdor*); is vocalised later after n *tenuis*, t *quattuor*, d *arduus duellum* (but, later still, initial dv = b *bellum bis bonus*, medial dv = v *suīvis*); drops after f (from DH) *fallŏ foris forum*, and in an atonic syllable after d *dē dis-dīrus.*—Final v (after loss of -e) = u *ceu* (cf. *neu seu*).

P *nepŏs pater plēnus*; drops initially before t *tilia* (?) s *sabulum* (?) st *sternuŏ studeŏ*, and between s and t *hostis* (in Compounds the s drops, Fest. *vŏ-pte* = vōs) or l *liēn*. It assimilates before Labials *summus suffiŏ*, = m bef. n *damnum omnis somnus*. Final P remains, *volup*; *ab ob sub* were originally used only before Mediae, and the b drops with compensation before s-p *āsper* or m (from S-M) *ŏmentum*.

B (rare) *labium lambŏ lūbricus*; dialectically = v *sēvum* and perhaps *arvīna ferveŏ* †*vārŏ vatillum vervēx*. Before n it = m *dominus*; before l from D it remains in *pūblicus*, elsewhere = p *amplus duplex cxemplum maniplus* (so before l from D *dīscipulus manipulus*): before original ḷ it = p or dialectically m, *concipilŏ-cumulus stipula-stimulus*.

BH initial before vowel = f *far ferŏ fungor* &c., dialectically h *haba hara* (?) *hariolus herba horctum horreum* and perhaps *harēna hircus* (sometimes omitted, *ariolus, arēna ircus*) or b *barba battuŏ bulla* im-*buŏ*: before Lingual it = f *frangŏ frāter frīgŏ* dē-*frūtum* &c., dialectically b *blaterō*.—Medial it dialectically = f *scrōfa*, else b *glūbo ambi- albus orbus* &c., which before n = m *amnis scamnum*, before ḷ either remains *scabellum* or (dialectically) = p *scapulae*, before pl drops *amplus*.

T *pater tendo trēs*; drops between r and m *vermina*, p and s *ipse*, KV and v *quartus*, later between s and l *līs locus*, and when final after s in Nom. *os*. Before Nasal it = s *resmos pesna*, later drops with compensation *rēmus peena* (so nt, *sescēnt vīcēnī*) or doubled consonant *penna cunnus*: before l it drops if initial *lātus* (Part.), if medial = c *saeclum* (see *līs*) and so before ḷ *saeculum*. Assimilates before c *ecce siccus vacca*, cf. *ecquis*: drops before s *nox*.—TT = ss *fessus passus* or (after consonant) s *densus dorsum hirsūtus mensus*, but before r = st *capistrum lustrum*: tt from ti-t = t after consonant, *antēstor fāstidium portōrium*.

D *dīcō duo rōdō*: dialectically = (1) l (as in some Oscan dialect, see †*famulus*), initial *lacrima largus lautia līmpidus lingua*, between vowels *adūlor aemulus* (?) *ancīle* (?) *aquilus baliolus calamitās consilium-solium-consul-exul* †*famulus mīluus* (?) *mulier oleō poliō reluvium remc-līgō* (?) *scālae sileō squālor stilus* †*strigilis*, before consonant *almus mella* (*sella*) *ūltrā-ūlva*, after consonant *amplus-duplex pūblicus* and *mālus*: (2) r (cf. Varr. L. L. 5. 110 'perna a pede,' quasi *pedre*), *apor ar careō cūr* (cf. *quirquir* = quidquid Varr. L. L. 7. 8) *mereō muria* (?) *varius, accērsō mergō virga*, and (perhaps Dissimilation, for l) *glārea merula plōrō*.—Before m it drops with compensation *āmentum flāmen squāma*: before l it assimilates *allex*: before r it remains dialectically *quadru-* and by analogy *quadra*, else = t *atrōx nūtriō tactrum ūtrem* and so before ṛ *uterus*: before d drops with compensation *crēdō*: before c assimilates *accērsō*. For dv see on V.—DT = ss *assis pessulus cassus gressus lassus spissus* or (after long vowel, diphthong, or consonant) s *suāsum caesius tonsa*, but before r or ḷ = st *frūstrā* (*pestulus*). —D after n dialectically (cf. Campanian *ipsannam* = operandam) assimilates in *grunniō* †*mannus*, cf. Plaut. Mil. Glor. 1407 dispennite . . . et distennite.

DH initial = f *faber faciō fellō fūmus furō, fallō foris, frūstum*. Medial it = b (dialectically f) before r *glabro- lībra rubro- umbra*, after r *arbor barba verbum*, after m or n *lumbus* (*īnfit*), and in the classical dialect after u or ū *jubeō rubeō* (*rūfus*) *ūber*: elsewhere it = d *caedō fidēlia fidēs*[1] *fodiō gradus rudis vadēs vadum vidulus viduus* (which, see above on D, dialectically = l *caelebs melior stilus*, or r *caerimōnia merus ergā firmus*), and so between r and original v *arduus*. (This d before r = t *vitricus*, and so before ṛ or ḷ *iterum rutilus*.) Final it = d *ad-*, dialectically f *af*.—DHT = ss *assula*, after consonant = s *infensus*, but before r or ḷ = st *monstrum* (*astula*).

K = c *acclīnis cis decem*, later dialectically = ch *pulcer*: before v it = q *aquilus equus queror* or (after loss of v) c *canis*: dialectically = g in *singulī vīgintī*. Before Nasal it = g in the accented syllable *dīgnus magmentum*, dropt by analogy *dēnī*: before t dialectically assimilates †*brattea*, or drops with compensation *cōturnīx sētius* (cf. *pōstulō* from **pōscitulō*, and see *percontor*).—KS = x *coxa dexter ex saxum scx* (dialectically ss †*amussim assis nassa pessimus tossillae*), or, before sc, s with compensation *compēscō dīscō pōscō* (see also on *misceō*), and so before c *sēscēnī*: before l this drops with compensation *āla māla talus*, cf. *paullus tōlēs* (see *tonsillae*). So KTH = x *texō*, or s before t *testa* or after r *ursus*: before a Liquid this drops with compensation *tēla tēmō*.

G *ego genus regō*. This in the accented syllable remains before m *agmen sagmen* (?), in the unaccented syllable drops with compensation *subtēmen sufflāmen*: before initial n it (later) drops *narrō nāscor nāvus nictō niteō nōscō*: drops before medial j *mājor*.—GS = x, which before l drops *pālus*.

GH before vowel = h *haedus haruspex hasta helvus hiems holus homo horreō hortor hortus humus* (dialectically omitted *anser* and sometimes *aedus aruspex olus ortus*), *vehō* (dialectically omitted *via*, and with contraction *bīmus*): dialectically f *folus fovea*, g *geminī gilvus gutta* (which before final a = c, *praefica*, see below on GV). Before or after consonant it = g *glārea grāmen grātus* (so before l *trāgula*), *angō fingō lingō mingō pinguis*, which before j drops with compensation *ājō mējō*, and so in the unaccented syllable before n *inānis*, before t = c *nectō vectis*, + s = x *vexillum* (dropt before Liquid *vēlum*, see *vēna*): dialectically f *flāvus, infula*.

KV (1) as a 'fixt' velar, with no sign of labialisation in any language, = c *callum carpō cicer collis cortex coxa culcita dulcis lucerna lūcus mūcus secō vacillō* and before consonant *crāssus crepō* (dialectically assimilated before t *blatta*; before j it = g *pulegium* or drops *bājulus pūlējum*). This c, + s, = x *axis exta lūx*, see *nox*; which drops before Liquid *lūmen lūna*. (2) as a labialisable velar = qu (i.e. qv) *aqua conquinisco coquō frequens inquilīnus liquō loquor quaerō quatiō -que queō quercus quī quinque* (dialectically, as in Oscan, p *crepō palpō prope quippe*), also later written c *arcus ceu colō coquō corpus jecinoris jocus locus quercus*: always written c before u (*oblīquus* late) *cum* (Conjunction) *cūra jecur oculus* or consonant (dropping before d *dōdrans* and later between r and t *fortis*), e.g. before original J *farciō līcium prōvincia socius* (before n this c = g *lignum*), and so when final *ac nec*.

GV (1) as a 'fixt' velar = g *garriō gelus gibbus, augeō ligō*, which before t = c *auctumnus luctor*, dialectically dropt *autumnus*. This g, + s,

= **x** *auxilium*, dropt before **m** *ōmen*.   (2) as a labialisable velar = **gu**
(i.e. **gv**) *inguen stinguō*, also written **g** *fīgō flīgō cingō tingō ungō ergā*
(which before final **a** in trisyllables, on analogy of *fabrica manica
pedica* &c., = **c** *fulica pertica †sublica*, cf. *†amurca †spēlunca*, see on
praefica under GH): always written **g** before **u** *angulus gurges-gurguliō*
or consonant *āgnus gravis-congruō* (before **t** this **g** = **c**, later dropt
after **r** *fertum*).—Dialectically: (1) in the Roman dialect it = **v**,
initial *valeō varius verū vescor vetō vīvō volō vorō*; medial *cōnīveō sevērus ūva ūvidus* (with contraction *fībula nītor nūdus ūmeō*), dropping
after **u** *fluō fruor struō* (before **i** from J the **v** remains, *fluvius*): (2)
in the Oscan dialect it = **b** *badius baculum bardus bitūmen bōs, blandus
brūtus*.

GHV (1) as a 'fixt' velar (see above on GH), before vowel = **h** *habeō
haereō hilum-hīra hordeum hostis prehendō* (dialectically omitted *abdō-
men-abundō īlia-īra ordeum*, and with contraction *praeda prēndō*):
dialectically **f** *famēs fel fīlum fostis fūnis* (?).   Before or after consonant it = **g** *glaber gradus, indulgeō-largus*, which before **t** = **c** *lectus*:
dialectically **f** *fremō friō*.   (2) as a labialisable velar = **gu** (i.e. **gv**)
lingua ninguit, also written **g** *ningit tergum*, which + **s** = **x** *nix*:
dialectically before vowel = **f** *forceps*.   Between vowels **v** *brevis levis
nivem*.

KHV (1) as a 'fixt' velar = **g** *congius*; after **s** = **c** *scindō*.   (2) as a
labialisable velar = **gu** (i.e. **gv**) *unguis*.

s before vowel *saliō sequor solum*: between vowels = **r** *erus furō ūrō
quaerō auris* &c. (*ōrnō* from **ōsinō*; *anser arbor vōmer* with **r** from
oblique cases), omitted after **r** + vowel *cruor prior- proprius pruīna
ruō*[1] and (before **v**) *privus rivus*, but later remaining *prūriō rōrārit*.
Intervocalic **s** remains in Compounds *positus* and Reduplication
susurrus, dialectically in *nāsus*, and (perhaps to denote a soft **s**, Eng.
z) in *caesariēs casa miser pūsus quasillum vāsa*, and in the loan-words
asinus bāsium blaesus cāseus cisium gaesum lāserpīcium: in *causa quaesō
†rosa* the **s** is from **ss**, in *fūsus* from DT.—**s** remains before **v** *suāvis*
(see above on **v**), and before Tenues *spēs stō sciō*, dialectically,
dropping initially in *parcus pendō pīlō poliō, tabula tegō tergum tībia
titubō tundō turba turdus trītavus, cauda caveō cernō cerrītus corūscus*.
It drops before **f** *rēfert*, and, with compensation if required, before **m**
mīca mīluus (?) *minae mordeō* (see *sum*) *dūmus prīmus sūmo tam -met*,
n *neō nix nurus alnus annus avēna cānus* (?) *fānum farīna līnum pānis*
(?) *perna pōne pōnō prūna venēnum verbēnae*, **l** *labō langueō lūbricus pīla
prēlum quālum vēlum*[1] (and so after loss of interconsonantal **p** *līen*,
see *splendeō*, and, later, **t** *lāmina-lātus līs locus*).   Before **r** initial it
= **f** *frāga frīgus*, before **r** medial it dialectically = **f** *infrā*, else = **b**

cerebrum crābrō fibra membrum sōbrīnus tenebrae.—Dialectically it suffers
Metathesis with c *aesculus ascia luxus viscum viscus*, see *assula pessulus.*
z before d drops, with compensation if needed, *audiō crūdus foedus* (Adj.)
hordeum mālus nīdus pēdō prīdem sidō sūdus turdus.   ZDH = st *cūstōs
hasta.*

[Genesis of Latin Letters.

(I give first the Latin letter, then the various letters (or combinations
of letters) of the Ursprache, or of older Latin, which it may represent.)

a = A *agō*, AI before vowel or h *aēnus ahēnus*, O pretonic *canis* or before
v *cavus.*— = āve before h *trahō*: = e pretonic *gradus* or before ng
frangō.—a- may = ha- *abundō anser ariolus*: am an al ar may respectively = Ṃ Ṇ Ḷ Ṛ *tamen anguis calvus arduus.*
ā = Ā *fāgus*: = Ṇ̄ after m *germānus hūmānus*, = Ṝ before s *fāstīgium
fāstus suāsum.*— = ab before s *āsper*, ad before m *āmentum*, ag or
āg unaccented before nasal *sufflāmen inānis*, ans before m *trāma*,
as before l *quālum* and so *mālus*, ax before l *āla pālus*: = ō pretonic
ācer or before v *octāvus.*—nā lā rā may = Ṇ̄ Ḹ Ṝ *gnārus clādēs grāmen.*
ae = AI *aevum.*— = aevi *aequus praedēs* aevo *praecō* aehi *praeda*, aes
before n *caena*: = ē (late) *laevis*: = oe pretonic *caecus.*—ae- may =
hae- *aedus.*
au = AU *augeō*, pretonic OU *auris* or OUZ before d *audiō.*— = avi *raucus
autumō* āvi *gaudeō.*

b = B *baubor*, BH medial *glūbō*, DH medial *lābor ūber barba lībra*, M before
r̥ *hibernus tūber*, S before medial r *cerebrum.*— = v dialectically after
lingual *gilbus sorbum.*—b- may = BH- dialectically *battuō blaterō imbuō*, GV- *baculum brutus*, M- before r *brevis*, dv- *bonus*: -b may = -p
from -PI *ob* or -PO *sub.*

c = K *centum*, KV *arca*, K-V *canis*, KHV after s *scindō.*— = g before t
lectus luctor nectō or final a in trisyllables *fulica praefica*: = t before
guttural *ecce ecquis* or medial l *saeclum* or ul (Ḷ) *saeculum.*—c- may
= SKV- *caveō*: -c may = -ce *sic* or -cum *dōnec.*
ch = c (dialectically) *pulcer*: in loan-words χ *chrȳsos.*

d = D *dō*, medial DH *gradus arduus.*— = t dialectically *edepol.*—d- may
= dv- pretonic *dis-*: -d may = -de *haud*, -DU *red-*, -DHI *ad-*.

. **e** = E *ferō*, EI before vowel *eō*, I before r in the unaccented syllablè
anser or final *ante*, o later after initial **v** *vespa*.— = **a** unaccented
before two consonants *peregrē* or r *properus*: = **en** (N̯) before **x** *exta*,
ēv before u *deus* and by analogy *dea*: = **ē** before final r *prōsper* or d
sed.—**ee** or **ehe** may = **ē** *veemcns vehemens*: **em en** may = M̯ N̯ *temnō
dens*, and -**em** may = -**en** (-N̯) *decem*; **en** before **t** may = **em** (M̯)
centum: **er** may = R̯ unaccented *uterus*, BI *hibernus* BĪ *cervix*, RŬ
acerbus socer.

ē = Ē *rēs*, EZ before d *pēdō*.— = **ed** before **s** *ēsca*, **ec** before s *compēsco* and
dialectically before **t** *sēlius*, **ehe** *mēntula prēndō*, **en** before s *vēsica*,
ent before n *vicēni*, **er** before s *tēstis*,.**es** before l *vēlum*[1], **et** before **m**
rēmus, **ex** or **ēx** before liquid *tēla-tēmō vēlum*[2]-*vēna* (?), **ēm** from
ēmi *sēsqui-*, **ēs** before consonant *rēfert*: (later) = **ae** *sēculum cēna*: =
unaccented **au** *obēdiō*: = **ī** *lēvis*, I before j *jējūnus*.

eu = EU onomatopoeic *heus*.—-**eu** may = -**ēve** *ceu*.

f = BH initial *fāgus frangō* and dialectically medial *scrōfa*, DH initial
faciō and dialectically medial *infit* (?) *rūfus*, DHV initial *fallō foris*, GH
initial *folus flāvus* and dialectically medial *infula*, GHV initial *fremō*,
s before r initial *frīgus* and dialectically medial *infrā* (and so before
f *inferus*).— = **b** before f *suffiō*.—-**f** may = -DHI *af*.

g = G *genū*, GV *garriō fligō āg̩nus gravis*, GH *gilvus glārca grāmen trāgula
fingō*, GHV *glaber largus ningit*, KHV *congius*.— = **c** before **n** *dignus
lignum*.
gu (i.e. **gv**) = GV after **n** *inguen*, GHV *ninguit*, KHV *unguis*.

h initial = BH *herba*, GH *hiems*, GHV *haereō*: intervocalic = GH *veho*.—
prefixt *herus*, inserted *ahēnus*, to show vowel-length *ah vaha* (cf.
NUmbr. *preplohotatu* beside *preplotatu*, see *trans*).

i = I *pix*, J after consonant *veniō*.— = **ī** before vowel or h *diēs nihil* and
so by dissimilation **ir** *prior*: = unaccented **a** *dēstinō* and so *concinnus*:
= **e** *felix dīligō*, **eh** before vowel *via*: = **u** (Ŭ) *cliens* and from o *clipeus
ilicō quisquiliae*.—-**i**- may = ji- *iciō igitur*: **im in** may = M̯ N̯ *simul
inter dominus*, **il** may = unaccented L̯ *similis*.

ī = Ī *vīvus*, IZ or ĪZ before.d *nīdus prīdem*, EI *fīdō*, E before **nq** *quinque*,
ō *stīpa* and so from. EU *liber* OI *tībia* Ō *sīspes*.— = **in** (N̯) before **gn**
ignis, **ins** before m *īmus*: **ihi** *bīmus*, **iji** *bigae*, **ivi** *fibula nitor vita*.—**ī**-
may = **hī**- *ira* or **hīs**- before **l** *īlia*.

j initial = J semivowel *jecur* or 'spirant' *jugum*: medial = J semivowel
ējulō satureja jējūnus, **gj** *mājor ājō* and this from **cj** *pūlējum*.

l = L *lingō*, dialectically D *lacrima solum*: by assimilation N *bulla* R *stella* v (dialectic) *sollus* s *collum*, in compound d *allex.*—l- may = VL- *liquō* TL- *lītus* SL- *langueō* SPL- *liēn* stl- *lis*: -l may = -le *vel*, -lum *nihil*.

m = M *māter*: = b before in (N) *dominus* or ul (L) *cumulus* or n *scamnum*, = n before p *semper*, = p before nasal *summus damnum*: = mbi before p *amplus.*—m- may = SM- *mīca*: -m may = -me *tam*.

n = N *nebula*, M before J *veniō*, by dissimilation R *cancer.*— = m before c *nunc* d *deinde* n (popular etymology) *sollennis* s *ansa*; = t before n *penna*; = d dialectically after n *grunniō* †*manus*; by contraction = men *nūncupō* ni *jūncus* nte *antestor.*—n- may = GVN- *nitcō*, SN- *neō*: -n may = -ne *nōn*.

o = O *ob*, before vowel OU *cloāca*, E after initial c (KV) *colō* or s (SV) *socer* or before v *novus.*— = unaccented a *aboleō.*—o- may = ho- *ortus*: ol or may = L R *tolerō cor*, and or- may = hors- (GHVRZ-) *ordeum*.

ō = Ō *dōnum*, OU *rōbīgō* ŌU †*bōs*, AŪ *dō* ĀŌ *nō.*— = oa *cōgitō* ōo *prōlēs*, ove *nōndinae* ovi *fōmes*, ō-que *dōdrans*: by compensation = oc (dialectically) before t *cōturnīx*, op-s before m *ōmentum*, orc (RK) before s *pōsco*, os (from o-si) before n *pōnō*: = au *cōpō*, aux before m *ōmen*.

oe = OI *foedus* Subst., OIZ before d *foedus* Adj.—(late) = ae *hoedus coena* or ē *foetus*: = unaccented au *oboediō*.

p = P *pix*, PJ before vowel *spuō*, M before l †*plumbum*, dialectically KV *prope.*— = pt from pti before s *ipse*; b before l (D) *duplex* ul (L) *discipulus scapulae stipula.*—p- may = SP- *parcus*.

qu (i.e. qv) = KV *aqua* KVTV *quartus*, K-V *equus*.

r = R *regō*, s after r *errō.*— = rc before t *fertum*, rt before m *vermina*, by contraction ri *ūsūrpō* rmi *forceps* rti *portōrium*: dialectically = d *accērsō mergō ergā*: by dissimilation = l *caeruleus largus*: = n before m in derivatives *carmen* and before r in compounds *irrītō*: later = s between vowels *crus* and so si *ōrnō.*—r- may = VR- *repens*: -r may = -re *instar*.

s = S *sequor*, SJ before vowel *suō*, between vowels z (?) *miser* DT *fūsus suāsum*, after consonant TT *dorsum mensus* DT *tonsa.*— = ss between vowels *causa*, d before tr *frūstrā monstrum*, t before n *pesna* and after r (D) *accĕrsō*, **x** between vowels (dialectic) *pausillus* and before tenuis *sescēnt testa* and after r *ursus.*—**s**- may = sv- *sūdor sē sī*, PST- *sternuō* : **ss** may = TT *fessus* DT *cassus* DHT *gressus* DHS *jussi*, dialectically rs *pessum*, in Greek words ζ *massa* : **sc** may dialectically = **x** *ascia luscus viscus* : **st** may = dt (before ɫ) *ostula*, ZDH *cūstōs* : -s may = -ss (ST) in Nom. *os*, -**se** *siremps*, -**ssum** *crās* (?).

t = T *tam*, D before r *atrōx* or **er** (ʀ) *utcrus* or **il** (ʟ) *rutilus*, DH before r *vitricus* or **er** (ʀ) *iterum.*— = **tr** dialectically after s *mediastinus*, by dissimilation **til** *multicia* ; **c** dialectically before t *blatta.*—t- may = PT-*tilia* (?) ST- *tegō* : -t may = -te (TI) *et post.*

u = U *cutis*, Ŭ *clueō*, dialectically O *clupeus*, E after **c** (ᴋᴠ) *cucumis* or before **lc** *ulcus* **lm** *ulmus*, **v** after d *duellum arduus* **n** tenuis t *quattuor.*— = ū before vowel *ruō*[4] and after r, from ŪS *cruor* or OUS *ruō*[1] ; = **uv** before vowel *fluō*, unaccented **ov** before vowel *exuō viduus* : = unaccented **a** *concutiō adulter indulgeō* **e** †*famulus*, **o** in final syllable before consonant *genus.*—**ul ur** may = ʟ ʀ *tuli discipulus curtus* : **ul** may = **lu** after d *dulcis* : **lu**- may = ᴠʟ *lupus*, **ur**- may = ᴠʀ *urgeō.*— **u**- may = **vu**- *uxor.*

ū = Ū *fūmus*, Ū *stūpa*, EU *dūcō*, OU *clūnis*, dialectically Ō *fūr* OI *cūra* AU *clūdō cūpō* : UZ *sūdus* ŪZ *crūdus.*— = **eu** (ĒJO) *pius* : = unaccented **au** *adūlor* : = **us** before **m** *sūmō*, **ūx** before nasal *lūmen lūna* : = **uvi** *jūmentum* **ūvi** *fūlīgo* **ūmeō** **ovi** *būbulus cūria* **ōvi** *nūdus* **ove** *nūndinae.*— ū- may = **vū**- *ūrīna.*

v = V *vehō*, GV *valeō ūva*, GHV between vowels *brevis.*— = medial **dv** *suāvis* : dialectically = **b** *sēvum.*—Spelt **u** after guttural or **s**, *aqua equus anguis suādeō.*

x = KS *coxa* GHS *vexillum*, KVS *exta* GVS *auxilium* GHVS *nix*, KTH *texō.*— -**x** may = -KSU *mox.*

y = ʋ †*thymum* : wrongly for **u** (from unaccented E) *corylus.*
ȳ = ū̆ †*pȳramis.*

z = ζ †*zephyrus* †*zōna.*

Any doubled consonant may simply denote that the preceding vowel was originally long.]

UMBRIAN.

(O = Old Umbrian, the language of the first 4⅔ of the Eugubine Tables;
N = New, of the remaining 2⅓.)

o in O = u see *adoleō voveō*. So ō = u O *duplex*.—ŭ (from o) = u O *arbiter*.

ī = N ei *quī*.—Ā = a *vās* N *trans*, also written **aha** N *trans*.

EI = e O *clitellae*.—AI = e O *silicernium* N *cēna*.

OU = u O *pūblicus*, o N *rūfus*.—AU = u O *aut*, o N *fons*.

M before s = **n** N *umerus*.—NS final = f N *trans*, remaining when from **nos** N *fons*.

R with Metathesis of **e** *precor* : RS remains O *silicernium* N *pāreō*, before **n** = s in N *cēna*.

J (Lat. i) lost after ç (from K) O *duplex*.—V remains O *voveō*.

BH = f *tribus*.

D medial = O **đ** *adoleō ar duplex famulus pūblicus*, N **rs** *almus ar*.—DH = f N *rūfus*.

K dropt before s *precor* ; = O ç N **š** before e *silicernium cēna* or original J *duplex*.—GH = h *hortor*, dropt between vowels *via*.

KV = p N *quī quis*[2].—GV initial = b O *verū*, medial = p O *arbiter*.

S between vowels remains after long vowel *hōrnus vās*, = r after short vowel N *sus*.

OSCAN.

(Brackets denote that the word is from Roman grammarians, not epigraphic.)

I written í see *tēstis*.—O = u *quī*.

ĭ = i *quī*; in Volscian = ē, written **eh** *cūria*.—ū after dental = iu *lympha*.

Ē written **ee** *terra* or **íí** *fēstus* : Ā written **aa** *famulus*.

OI remains in Paelignian *cūra*.—AI written **aí** *bītō sī*, later **ae** *diaeta* or ē (*haedus*).

EU = **úv** *līber* : OU = **ov** *tūticus* : AU = **av** *aulem*.

R = **or** quattuor : Ā = **ar**, + inserted **a** *argentum*.

V remains after s *sī*, assimilates after l (*sollus*), drops after t *quattuor* **k** *aquila*.

BH = f *anfractus habeō* (and *harēna hircus*?)

T later assimilates before **d** *meddix*; final = **d** *edepol.*—D dialectically = l (*famulus*).

K *aquila* later spelt **c** *carō cedo.*—GH = **f** (*haedus*; and *harēna hircus?*).

KV = **qu** or **c** after **r** (*hircus*) **s** (*tcsqua*), elsewhere = **p** *quattuor quī.*— GV = **b** *bitō cedo.*

S remains between vowels Paelignian *cūra* (*harēna*) and before nasal *fēstus* Paelignian *primus.*

GREEK.

Vowels remain (both ʊ and ʊ̈ written *υ*): *υ* dissimilates to *o* see *cucŭlus ŭlŭlō*; *υ* initial is aspirated *sub super uterus ūvidus*; *o* dialectically = *υ* *calix crāssus folium mola nox post prytanis umbra unguis.*—πρόσθεσις[1] of ε before initial double consonant *satrapa* **r** *ardea rēmus rica ripa* F *urgeō* (lengthened in a polysyllable to *η viduus*); of *o* before **m** *mingō* **n** *unguis* **r** *regō ritus*; of *a* before double consonant *stella* **m** *malus* l *dēlibūtus* F *vas ventus.*—ἀνάπτυξις (insertion of a vowel between two consonants) of ι *largus sināpi tunica*, *υ corymbus*, *o sculpō*, *a palma*[1] *phalanx scrībō.*

Long vowels remain: *ū* initial is aspirated *sūs*, before an aspirate = *ου über*; *ā* in Ionic = *η anser campus stō* &c.; *η* shortens before vowel *neō.*—πρόσθεσις of *ω* before **r** *rūmor.*

Diphthongs remain: ōι = φ *ōvum*, ōυ = .*ου bōs*, Āυ = *αυ nāvis.*

Μ = *αμ* before vowel *humus*, *a* before consonant *metus similis.*

Ν = *αν* before vowel *sine tenuis*, *a* before consonant *centum inguen pinguis* &c. or final *decem novcm septem.*—Ν̄ = *νă* (Ionic *νη*) *anās.*

Ḷ = *αλ calō fullō palma*[1], before consonant also *λα planta*: VḶ = *λυ lupus.*—Ḹ = *λω flāvus* or *ολ largus polleō sulcus tolerō.*

Ṛ = *αρ argentum gravis jecur* &c., before consonant also *ρα cor quartus turtur* &c.—Ṝ = *ρω ardea sternō vorō* or *ορ carduus haruspex parō.*

Liquids remain:

Μ before lingual = β *blitum brevis*; final = *ν centum hiems semel.*— ΜS = *νs* = *νν* = *ν membrum*, see below on ΝS.

Ν before labial = μ *corymbus*, before guttural = γ *ancora longus angō*; assimilates after l *polleō pullus* Adj. and with compensation *vellus.* —ΝS before a vowel = Lesbian *νν μῆννος* Gen. (see *census*) = *ν* Ion. *μηνός χηνός* see *mēnsis anser* (Nom. μήν χήν take their *ν* from the oblique cases): ΝS final after a long vowel shortens the vowel and then becomes s with compensation Dor. μῆς Ion. μεἰς see *mēnsis*: unoriginal *νs* (from *ντ*) = *s viginti*.

ʙ initial suffers *πρόσθεσις*, see above, or (dialectically) aspirates *ardea rāpum*.

ᴊ semivowel when initial = ' *hōra jecur jocus* : elsewhere

(1) with liquid : ᴍᴊ = vj = *ιν cōmis famēs veniō* : ɴᴊ = *ιν tendō* : ρj = *ιρ curtus periculum spīra sterilis hortor* : λj = λλ *alius praestōlor*.

(2) with explosive : ᴘᴊ = ττ *spuō* : ᴛᴊ after consonant = σ *mūcus* : ᴅʜᴊ = σσ *bardus medius* : ᴋᴊ = σσ *conquiniscō dūcō*, and so ᴋᴠᴊ *coquō farciō mūcus oculus pix* : ɢᴊ = ζ *massa mūgiō* : ɢʜᴊ initial = χθ *herī*. So with sibilant, sᴊ = σσ *pinsō suō*.

ᴊ 'spirant' which in all other languages appears as a simple j, in Greek = ζ *jam jugum jungō jūs*[1] *zōna*.

ᴠ = ϝ (dialectically β *saucius*), dialectically omitted, whether initial *vehō vetus vīs* &c. *lacer repens rosa vermis* (the vowel afterwards sometimes aspirated *ulcus vereor vestis*) or between vowels *aevum dīvus ovis* &c. and after ᴅ *bis* ᴅʜ *fallō*; after liquid transposed (as *υ*) *famēs alvus sollus laurus nervus parvus ūrīna*.—τϝ initial = τ *quartus* or dialectically σ *sētanium turba trua*, medial = ττ or dialectically σσ *quattuor*.—σϝ = σ i.e. ' *sē socer suādeō sūdor*, dialectically ' *sordēs sūdor* or σ *sagīna* : medial = σ *blaesus*.

ᴘ and ʙ remain : π initial dialectically = ττ *perna pinsō* ; πσ = ψ, from ττ before *ι dapsilis jocus* or ᴊ *neptis* ; Metathesis of ᴘ (after s) and ᴋ *speciō*.

ʙʜ = φ *ambō* &c. or dialectically θ *flīgo līber* : φ before vowel + aspirate = π *fīdō fundus* (for β see *fodiō*), before τ it = π *cubō scabō* : φσ = ψ *depsō*.

ᴛ and ᴅ remain : τ = σ before *ι potis viginti* (sometimes remains by analogy *mēta*) *υ densus tū* (dialectically remains *tū*), drops before μ *myrīca* and when final *stercus*.—δ before τ = σ *uterus* (δ drops before τρ *findō meditor*), before λ = γ *dulcis*.

ᴅʜ = θ *ūber* &c. ; before vowel + aspirate it = τ *favilla fingō* ; = σ before *ι rōbīgo υ sisymbrium* θ *viduus*.

ᴋ and ɢ remain : ' Affrication ' (i.e. doubling) of κ *cacō lacus* : κ + ϝ = π *procāx*, κ + ᴛʜ = κτ *texō ursus*, κ + σ = ξ *axis dexter ex luxus sex*.

ɢʜ = χ *angō* &c.

ᴋᴠ (1) as a 'fixt' velar = κ *cancer capiō carduus carpō crātēs crūsta cūpa lūx scandō* (by ' Affrication ' κκ *cuculus*), which + σ (from τj or τσ) = ξ *mūcus nox.*—(2) as a labialisable velar = ϝ *oicer linquō sequor* &c. (dialectically ϝϝ *conquinisco*: dropt before ϝρ *quartus*), = ϝ before ε *quattuor -que quinque* or ι *quis*: dialectically κ *arca* (or κϝ *jecur*), and so after υ *lupus.*

GV (1) as a 'fixt' velar = γ *fugiō garriō grūs jungō rūctō tegō.*—(2) as a labialisable velar = β *bōs gravis vorō* &c., = δ before ε *inguen*, = γ after υ see *fluō*: dialectically γ, *grex gurguliō*, which + σ = ξ *ascia.*

GHV (1) as a 'fixt' velar = χ *fremō friō lectus.*—(2) as a labialisable velar = φ *nix*, = θ before ε *forceps*, = χ before υ *levis* (on 'Affrication' see *bracchium*).

KHV whether 'fixt' or labialisable = χ *congius scindō unguis* (by 'Affrication' κχ *soccus*).

S initial before vowel remains only dialectically *sūdus*, else = ' *sal sedeō septem* (whence the dialectic prefix of ', *hama ūrō*, see above on v) or dialectically ' *obsōnō serō*[2] *serum sine socius sōl sollus*; drops before n *nix nō nurus* m (except dialectically) *mūcus mūrēna mūs* l *langueō*, before r = ' *sorbeō sorbum*, remains before tenuis (by-forms without s *pilleus stupeō tegō tergum turba caveō cerritus*) or aspirate *scindō.*--s medial drops between vowels *auris nurus ūrō* &c. (the s preserved between vowels *miser pinsō porrum* was perhaps a soft s); drops, with compensation where required, before m *jūs*[1] *sum* n *līnum zōna* (dialectically without compensation *līnum*, or sn = νν *vestis*): RS remains *torreō verrēs verrō*, later = ρρ *garriō verrēs.*—PST- with Metathesis = *σπ-, whence dialectically either σπ- *studeō* or ππ- *sternuō*: so BZD- = *σβδ- whence βδ- *pēdō.*

IRISH.

I remains; by o- or a- Umlaut[1] it = e *misceō nix vir* &c., by i-Umlaut = ei *siccus*, by u-Umlaut = iu *liquō.*

U remains; by o-Umlaut = o *canis fui inclutus* &c., by i-Umlaut = ui *frigō mulier.*

E accented remains *nemus*; by i-Umlaut = ei *decem genus sterilis*, by u-Umlaut = eu *verū*, by e- o- a- Umlaut = i *fe lō lectus mel ne- nepōs plūs quattuor soror*: unaccented = a *amnis nanciscor sum.* By compensation it = ē *faciō sex tepeō vehō* (by i-Umlaut = ēi *veniō*, by o-Umlaut = ia *vēlum*[1]), or, when pretonic, ā *rēmus tēlum.*

---

[1] The influence of a vowel (or j or v) in the next following syllable; which influence remains even when that vowel (or j or v) has dropt.—' Umlaut' is found also in Teutonic (not in Gothic), Armenian, and Zend.

o accented remains *co*-, by i-Umlaut = ui *dorsum mare margō monile solium ūlna varius* (the **ai** in *laiget saidim*, see *levis sedeō*, is obscure), by u-Umlaut = u *volvō*: unaccented = a *nepōs*.

A remains *cārus caterva taurus*, by i-Umlaut = **ai** *alius alō at* &c., by u-Umlaut later **au** *laurus*; unaccented sometimes = u *arca* e *saliō*. By compensation it = ē and by i-Umlaut ēi *anser*.

Ī by o- or a- Umlaut = **ia** *cribrum piscis*.

Ū by i-Umlaut = ōe *mūtus rūs*, by o-Umlaut = **ūa** *somnus*.

Ē = ī *dē mēnsis sērus* &c. (by a-Umlaut = **ia** *rhētor*), after KV = ō *quinque*; in onomatopoeic words remains *ēn*: unaccented = i *māter pater*.

Ō = ā *dē neō nōscō queror*, by i-Umlaut = **āi** *vātēs*: unaccented = u *soror*.

Ā remains *vallum*, by i-Umlaut = āi *vātēs*.

EI = ē *is*, by i-Umlaut = ēi *linquō*, by o-Umlaut = **ia** *raeda sciō*.

OI = ōi *ūnus*, dialectically **āi** *mūnis* or **ai** *caecus*.

AI = āi *aevum*, also written **ai** *gaesum*, later ē *ai*: unaccented = ī *bitō*.

EU from EV = ū *clueō*, by i-Umlaut = ōi *novem*, by o-Umlaut = ūe *novus* or **ūa** *nō*.

OU = ō *auris lūx*, by o-Umlaut = **ūa** *cuculus rōbur tūticus*. So OU from OV = ō. and by i-Umlaut ōi *ovis.*—ŌU = ō *bōs*.

AU = ō *augeō*. So AU from AV = ō and by i-Umlaut ōi *aveō.*—ĀU = an . nāvis.

M before consonant = **em** and by e- o- a- Umlaut **im** *ambi- umbilicus ungō*; before vowel it = **am** *simul* and by i-Umlaut **aim** *domō*.

N before consonant = **en** *lingua* (which before t or c = ē *ante centum dens tendō necō* or, when atonic, e *inter vīgintī*) and by e- o- a- Umlaut **in** *unguis* and with ἀνάπτυξις **ini** *insula*; before vowel it = **an** *intenuis*, or n attached to the word following *decem novem*.

L̥ = **li** *valgus* and by e- o- a- Umlaut **le** *latus planta tolerō ulmus.*—L̥ = **lā** *palma*[1] *polleō* or **al** *fallō*.

R̥ = **ri** *cor regō* and by e- o- a- Umlaut **re** *sternō stertō* and further i-Umlaut **rei** *sors.*—R̥̄ = **rā** *gurges* or **ar** *arduus mora morbus terreō tornus torreō ursus* (also written **ār** *farciō*) and by i-Umlaut **air** *fertum prōcax*.

M drops with compensation before s *nummus membrum*. So N before t (see above) c *quinque* s *imus mēnsis*. N assimilates after l *ūlna*.

v = f *liquō vir* &c. ; after r spelt b *ferveō taurus*, and so after original n *vidulus* (later assimilated to the n *vadum*): dropt between vowels *aevum divus vīta* &c., before li from ḷ *valgus*, and after t *quattuor* d *arduus dē* s *sex somnus soror suādeō.*—VO = u *vīvus volvō*; VŌ = ūa and by i-Umlaut ūai *vēnum.*—f is in later Irish prefixt to an initial vowel *sub super.*

P before t = ch *neptis septem*, elsewhere drops *pater tepeō somnus planta pro- stertō* &c. (with h later prefixt to the vowel *baxea*).

B final in later Irish = bh *balbus.*—BH = b *ferō orbus* &c., *umbilicus*, later assimilated after m *ambi-*.

T remains; after vowel it = th *at māter vātēs* &c. ; before c it = s *siccus*, before m drops with compensation *dorsum rēmus.*—ST = s *sterilis* &c. *vāstus*, between vowels ss *dēstinō*.

D remains; after vowel it = dh *vadum*, after n it sometimes = t *suādeō*; assimilates before m *mulier* and later after n *menda pondus*, drops before s *edō unda.*—DT = s *cadō*, between original vowels ss *meditor*: D + DH = t *crēdō*.

DH = d *foris rōbur vidulus*, which assimilates before n *gradus*.

K = c, after vowel = ch *decem mox octō* &c. *equus*; drops with compensation before n *faciō.*—KTH = t *ursus*: KS = ss *dexter ex*, which when final drops with compensation *sex*.

G remains *gula nōscō*, after vowel = gh *frīgō*, before t = ch *vegeō*.

GH = g *angō anser lingō* &c., which drops with compensation before n *vehō*.

KV = c *crāssus queror quīnque* &c. (when hard spelt cc *cacō linquō mūcus*), after vowel = ch *liquō nox sequor*.

GV = b *bōs gurges ungō* &c., assimilating before n *vagus* and in later Irish after m (from n) *tinguō*; dialectically = g *lingua margō*, which before t = ch *nūdus*, before r drops *ūvidus*.

GHV = g *fremō lectus levis māchina*, which before t = ch *nix.*—KHV = g *unguis*.

S remains when initial before vowel *simul* or liquid *neō nix nō*; when medial it remains before c *misceō scandō*, assimilates before l *corylus* (or drops with compensation *vēlum*[1]) and after r *terreō*, drops before m *sum* r *membrum* and between vowels *līnum queror soror*; when final it drops *auris bōs cruor gaesum gustō rūs far*, and so after loss of N *canis mēnsis*.

ZD = t *nīdus*.

WELSH.

I remains *flīgō*; by o-Umlaut it = **e** *vidĕō*.

U = **w** *puer socrus spuŏ trucīdŏ.*—ᴜᴠ = **eu** *juvencus.*

E remains *socrus*: by i-Umlaut it = **y** *vas ventus*, by u-Umlaut = **i** *nebula*, by e- or o- Umlaut = **a** *sĕmi- cervus.* By compensation it = **ei** *argentum*, later **ai** *covīnus serŭ*[1].

O after p (from ᴋᴠ) = **w** *quī*; by u-Umlaut it = **au** *seges*, by w-Umlaut = **y** *covīnus.*

A remains *trans*; by i-Umlaut it = **ai** *nānus.* By compensation it = **ae** *ambactus.*

Ī = **y** *crispus quī sūdor.*—ᴜ̄ = **w** *sūs tūber.*

Ē shortened before **nt** *semi- ventus.*—ō̄ = **au** *ŏcior.*—Ā = **aw** *aciēs.*

ᴀɪ = **oe** *saeculum.*—ᴏᴜ = **u** *cluĕō clūnis.*—ā̄ᴜ = **au** *sŏl.*

N = **an** *grūs juvencus.*

L̥ = **lā** *lāna.*—ʀ = **ri** (later **ry** *carduus*), with i-Umlaut = **ei** *rādīx.*—ʀ̥ = **ar** *stercus.*

M before t = **n** *sĕmi-* ; between vowels = **f** *domŏ*, see *tūber.*

N assimilates after l *vellō*: ɴs = **ss** = **ch** *trans.*

J = **i** *juvencus*; between original s and vowel it = **dd** *serŏ*[1]; drops after **ff** (from sᴘ) *spuŏ.*

V = **w** *arvum sex volrŏ* &c. ; initial it = **gw** before e *vas vellō vertō* &c. or lingual *lāna rādīx*, before o drops *volvŏ.*

P between vowels = **b** *vīpera*, elsewhere drops *patĕō puer pūtĕŏ.*—ᴘs = **ss** = **ch** *crispus.*

ʙʜ = **b** *flīgŏ fodiŏ*, after vowel = **f** *nebula*; drops after m *ambactus.*

T remains *trans*; = **th** after vowel *ambactus* or lingual *vertō*; before l it = **d** *saeculum*, but remains between s (from ᴅʜ) and l *vas.*—sᴛ = **s** *stella.*

D assimilates after n *prehendŏ*, drops before s *sūdor*: ᴅᴊ = **dd** *rādīx vidĕō.*

ᴅʜ = **d**, before t = **s** *vas*: ᴅʜᴊ = **dd** *fodiō.*

K = c *cēlō corvus crīspus* &c. *ōcior*, later after vowel = ch *acies trucīdō* or, after o, g *occō*, and so before r *socrus*: KS = ss = ch *sex*.—G drops between vowels *seges* and, with compensation, before t *ambactus* and after r *argentum*.

GH = g, dropt with compensation before n *covīnus*.

KV initial = p *quī*, between vowels b *coquō*; after s it = g *stercus*.

GV = f *flīgō*; as a 'fixt' velar it = g *grūs*.

GHV as a 'fixt' velar = g *prehendō*, as labialisable = b *frīvola*.

S remains; before vowel it = h *saeculum sēmi- sūs* &c., before w (from v) = ch *sex socrus sūdor*; drops with compensation before dd (from J) *aerō*[1].—SP = ff *spuō*.

GOTHIC.

I and U remain, *minor luō* &c.: 'Breaking' of U to au before r *foris*: u inserted between l and k *mulgeō*.

E = i *edō* &c.: 'Breaking' to ai before h *pecū* r *ferō* &c.

O = a *nox* &c.—A remains, *ager* &c.

Ī = ei *linquō* &c.—Ū remains *fruor pūteō*.

Ē remains *vērus* &c.; dialectically = ei *levis rēx*; before i (from J) = a *sēmen ventus*.

Ō remains *flōs pēs praestōlor*.—Ā = ō *frāter stāmen* &c.

EI remains *dīcō* &c.—OI = ai *mūnis* &c.—AI remains *aevum* &c.

EU = iu *dūcō* &c.—OU = au *luō* &c.—AU remains *augeō* &c.—ĀU = au *sōl*.

M = um *homo*.—N = un *dens* &c.

L = ul *tolerō* &c.—B = aur (a 'Breaking,' see above) *grānum gravis mors* &c.

Liquids remain: n before guttural is written g *angō longus stinguō*: n after l is assimilated *collis vellus*.

J remains, whether semivowel *juventa* or 'spirant' *jugum*: drops between vowels *ahēneus*.

V remains *avus duo socrus* &c. (but sv- in enclitics = s *sē*); dropt with contraction between u and u *juvencus*; assimilated after n *genuīnus*; before consonant = u *vīvus*.

P = f *potis* &c., after barytone vowel = b *septem*; dropt before th (from T) *neptis*.—B = p *cubitum lūbricus*.—BH = b *farīna libet* &c.

T = **th** *fräter* &c., after barytone vowel = **d** *ante pater vätēs* &c. ; dropt between **b** (from P) and sonant *septem.*—ST remains *stella stô tundô* &c.—D = **t** *decem* &c.—DH = **d** *gradus* &c.

K = **h** *nox* &c. *equus*, after barytone vowel = **g** *juvencus lacrima paciscor*, and so in proclitic *co-.*—SK remains *cauda piscis.*

G = **k** *frangō* &c.—GH = **g** *haedus* &c.

KV (1) as a 'fixt' velar = **h** *clepō vincō*: SKV = **sk** *caedō caveō scabō*: (2) as labialisable = **hv** *aqua arcus cernuus linquō quī sequor* (when final = **h** -*que*) or (in the neighbourhood of a **v**) **f** *lupus quattuor* (so by assimilation *quinque*).

GV (1) as 'fixt' = **k** *augeō gelū.*—(2) as labialisable = **q** *arbiter ascia nūdus stinguō veniō vīvus*, = **k** before R *gravis* or **j** *fruor.*

GHV (1) as 'fixt' = **g** *hostis.*—(2) as labialisable = **v** *nix*: before **t** = **h** *levis.*

S remains *auris nix locus* &c. ; drops between barytone vowel and **m** *sum*; = **z** after barytone vowel *aes ascia farīna* or barytone vowel + liquid *membrum errô perna.*—ZDH = **zd** *hasta.*

OLD NORSE.

I remains, anciently spelt **y** *bīmus*; later = **e** *līnum.*

U remains; by j-Umlaut it = **y** *grunniō.*

E remains *egeō* &c. ; before **r** it = **ja** *cerebrum*; also spelt **i** *corbis secô turtur*; by **v**-Umlaut = **ö** *inguen.*

O = **a** *trua vômer*; by **u**-Umlaut it = **ö** *ūvidus verrô.*

A remains *agō* &c. ; by i-Umlaut it = **e** *sarciō.*

Ī remains *dīvus rīpa.*—Ū remains *pūteō*; by j-Umlaut it = **ȳ** *confutô ulula.*

Ē = **ā** *vēr vomô*; by j-Umlaut it = **ae** *arbiter.*

OI = **ei** *vīpera.*—AI = **ei** *aestus blaesus scaeva.*—ĒI = **ei** *plūs.*

OU = **au** *clūnis.*—AU remains *hauriô.*—ĀU = **ō** *nāvis.*

R = **ur** *turtur.*—R̄ = **ar** *ardea.*

Liquids remain.—J and V remain, *jaciō vomō.*

P = **f** *damnum plūs pūteō* &c.—B = **p** *corbis titubô.*—BH = **b** *blaterô feriô.*

T = **th** *turtur*, medially written **đ** *arbiter* &c.—D = **t** *damnum* &c.—DH = **d** *confutô.*

κ = h *clūnis* &c., after barytone syllable g *alcēs jaciŏ secŏ.*—G = k *agō* &c.—GH = g *angō* &c.

KV = hv *cernuus queror.*—GV = kv *arbiter inguen,* before lingual k *blaesus ūvidus.*

s remains *hauriō* &c.

ANGLOSAXON.

I remains *acclīnis* &c.; by a-Umlaut it = e *crīspus nīdus.*

U remains *rōbīgō*; by a-Umlaut it = o *dēfrūtum fundus hydrus turdus,* by i-Umlaut = y *cūpa furō gustŏ ūrō.*

E remains *tegō* &c. (inserted between g and l *ungula*); 'Breaking' to eo before h *equus populus* l *alcēs gilvus* r *frāxinus spernō*; = i by i-Umlaut *corpus fremŏ sonus techna tēmō trua veneror* (this i, + uv, = eōv *novus*) or before nasal + another consonant *crepŏ frendō.*

o = a *odium* &c.; =

(α) ä before consonant (1) + another consonant *carpō oppidō vespa,* (2) + e *corylus unda ungula,* (3) final when not nasal *unda ūrīna*:

(β) ea by 'Breaking' before h (in x from hs) *pectō* l *collum culmus fel* (and by i-Umlaut = y *collis*) r *morior pariō porcus*:

(γ) e by i-Umlaut *anās fallō monīle ūlna.*

a remains *agō* &c.; =

(α) ä before consonant (1) + another consonant *apiscor mālus pateō,* (2) + e *anās caper vāpulŏ,* (3) final when not nasal *langueō pāgus parcus quadra sparus*:

(β) ea by 'Breaking' before h (in x from hs) *ascia* l *palleō salix valgus* r *barba*; or by u-Umlaut *battuŏ*:

(γ) e by i-Umlaut *aciēs pāgus salum sapiŏ.*

ī remains *dīvus* &c.—ū remains *mūs* &c.; by a-Umlaut it = ō *mūscus,* by i-Umlaut = ȳ *cutis.*

Ē = ā *sēmi-*; before n it = ō *mēnsis*; by i-Umlaut it = ae *vērus.*

ō remains *flōs.*

Ī = ō *māter* &c.; by i-Umlaut it = ē *fāgus grāmen vāstus.*

EI = ī *līmus raeda.*

OI = ā *hiŏ līmus*; by i-Umlaut it = ae *glūten.*

AI = ā *aes* &c.

EU = eō *fraus* &c.

OU = eā *dēfrūtum* &c.; by i-Umlaut it = ȳ *clueŏ.* So OV before consonant = eā *caveō lavō.*

AU = eā *aurōra.* So AV before consonant = eā *avunculus*; au by j-Umlaut = ī *aqua*

M = um, by i-Umlaut ym *ambi-*.—N̤ = un *manus* &c., by i-Umlaut yn *sons tenuis*.

L = ul, by a-Umlaut ol *palma*[1] *stolidus* or, after palatal, eol *gula.*—R̤ = ur *quercus*; by a-Umlaut or *aper forō portus* or, after palatal, eor *scrūpus*; by i-Umlaut yr *fāstigium fors*.

Liquids remain: n assimilates after l *fel*, drops with compensation before s *anser*.

J assimilates after p *labium*; GJ = cg *aciēs mējō techna*; j drops between a and i *ahēneus*.

v remains, before J written vv, uv *novus*; va (from vo) after l = o *gilvus palleō*; v drops before un *sonticus*, and after final h *equus*.

P = f *pateō* &c.; after barytone vowel = b, between vowels f *aper.*—SP remains *parcus sparus vespa* &c.

B = p *cannabis labium*.

BH = b when initial *fuī* &c. or after m *ambi-*, between vowels f *umbō*.

T = th *tegō* &c.; after barytone vowel = d *anās battuō fors* &c. (see on *māter*).—ST remains *stilus stolidus vāstus*.

D = t *odium* &c.; before t it = s *rōbīgō*; dropt between n and original J *sons.*—DH = d *barba* &c.

K = h *cutis* &c.; after barytone vowel g *cacula circus secō.*—SK remains as sc *caveō cernō scrūpus scrūta*; KS = hs = x *pectō*.

G = c *fāgus* &c.—GH = g *anser via*.

KV (1) as a 'fixt' velar = h, after a barytone vowel g *secō*: (2) as labial-isable = hv *quadra* (which between vowels = v see *aqua*, final = h *quercus*) or, before u, f *quercus*; after a barytone vowel gv, which after n = g *crepō*.

GV = cv *vīvus*, when final c *langueō*.

GHV as a 'fixt' velar = g *famēs fel fremō.*—KHV = g *ungula*.

s remains *nāris līmus collum* &c.; after barytone vowel it = r *ahēneus gaesum glaesum*.

OLD HIGH GERMAN.

(Middle High German marked M.)

I and U remain: I by a-Umlaut = e *pinsō*, and so in original monosyllable *is*: i dropt between consonants M *fulica*, inserted (and by e-Umlaut = e) between r and ch *gurguliō*.

E remains *arvum* &c.; = i by i-Umlaut *depsō echīnus errō fēlīx neptis* or before nasal + another consonant *lentus meminī.*

O = a *rota* &c.; by i-Umlaut it = e *nōdus* M *occō.*

A remains *plāga* &c.; by i-Umlaut it = e *albus.*—a inserted between l and c *alcēdō.*

ī and ū remain.

Ē = ā *neō sēmen sērius.*—Ō = uo *opus plōxenum.*—Ā = uo *rāpum sānus*; in onomatopoeic words remains M *ah.*

OI = ei M *mūtō.*—AI = ei M *ai.*—ĀI = ā *stō.*

N = un *anguis sons* M *venia.*—L = ul and by a-Umlaut ol M *dolō*, by i-Umlaut el *gurguliō* M *fulica.*

R = ur and by ē- or ō- Umlaut or *consternō pōscō*, by i-Umlaut er *gurges.*

Liquids remain: N after c assimilates *mūgiō.*

J remains *jaciō.*

V = w *vocō sērius* &c.: va final after r = o *arvum.*

P = f *neptis* &c., in loanwords written pf *stipula* or ph *plōxenum*; after barytone vowel b *opus rāpum scīpiō stupeō.*

B = pf *būcina*, earlier written pph *vibrō.*

BH = b *flagrō*, in Oberdeutsch (Alsatian and Alemannic) p *fāstus.*

T = d *centō* &c., after barytone vowel t *anās.*—ST remains *stō stupeō.*

D = z *depsō* &c., in MHG. between vowels tz *mundus.*

DH = t *fēlīx.*

K = h *speciō* &c., after barytone vowel g *jaciō.*—SK remains as sc *misceō pōscō screō*: KTH = hs *texō*, and so KS *axis saxum* M *coxa.*

G = h *plāga*, later medially written ch *flagrō* M *fulica gurguliō*; after barytone vowel c *gurges mūgiō.*

GH = g *echīnus hasta.*

KV as a 'fixt' velar = h *secō* &c., also written ch *būcina*; after barytone vowel g *sūgō* M *occō.*—SKV = sc *scīpiō.*

GV as a 'fixt' velar = k or (medially) ch M *fulica* M *ganniō*: as a labialisable velar = gu *balanus gurges gurguliō.*

GHV between vowels = g *vōmer.*

S remains *mordeō* &c.; assimilated after r *errō fāstus*: Metathesis *depsō.*

ZD = st *hordeum* M *pēdō*: ZDH = rt *hasta.*

LITHUANIAN.

I remains: it is inserted between consonant and vowel to denote that the consonant is pronounced soft (as Germ. *k-* in *kind* opp. *kahn*), *vērus mēta luō congruō paviō dīvus caurus hiems caedō* &c.

U remains: lengthened by accent to *ú lynx.*

E remains: lengthened by accent to *é ariēs celsus tencbrac* &c., *ê decem penus volō* &c.: in monosyllables it = i *ex in*: initially it sometimes = a *ego*, and so before w *novus suus.* Inserted between b and z *pᶻdō.*

O = a: lengthened by accent to *á cervus collis fullō* &c., *à chorus mare rota* &c.

A remains: lengthened by accent to *á arō haruspex*, *à blatta quasillum.*

Ī = y *sīca* ỹ *vir* ỹ *linquō* &c.

Ū remains *über ú fūmus û mūscus* &c.

Ē = é *rēpō rēte ě mēnsis.*

Ō = ů *dōnum* &c.; final = ủ *ambō.*

Ā = o *frāter* &c.; onomatopoeic remains as *á āh à mamma.*

EI = eí *cervīx eō*, or *ê acclīnis dīvus.*—OI = ai *nix tībia aí mūnus*, or *ė ūnus.*—AI remains *caesius* aí *haereō*, or = *ė caedō.*—Why these diphthongs sometimes = *è* is unknown.

EU = aů *luō pulmō* áu *spuō.*—OU = au *clūnis* áu *paviē* aů *lūcus* &c.

AU remains *crōciō*, = áu *augeō* aů *sūdus.*—ĀU = áu *sōl.*

M = im *centum emō tremō.*—Ṇ = in *exta ingens mens tintinō*, before gn = u *ignis*: Ṇ̃ = án *anās.*

L = il *balanus polleō vellus* &c.—R = ir *cor grānum quartus* &c.

M drops before s, dialectically without nasalising the preceding vowel *membrum.*—N drops, nasalising and lengthening the preceding vowel, before s *ansa anser* sz (from K) *uncus* ź (from GH) *mingō.*

L and R remain.

J remains, whether as semivowel *jecur* or as 'spirant' *jūs*[1] *zōna*: it is dialectically prefixt to initial i *is* ú *ūrīna* ů *āter.*—TJ before i = cž *pulmō.*

V = w: it is dialectically prefixt to an initial vowel *ūnus.*

P remains.—B onomatopoeic *babae barbarus baubor.*—BH = b *fodiō* &c.

T remains : inserted between **sz** (from K) and r *acerbus*.

D remains : before final iu it = **dž** *caedō odor splendeō*, before **g** it = **z** *mergŏ*, before il (from Ḷ) it drops *largus*.

DH = **d** *arbor* &c.; before d it = **z** *barba*.

K = **sz** *caleō* &c. ; dialectically before **w** it = **sž** *equus*.—KTH = **sz** *texŏ*, and so KS *axis dexter ex lynx sex*.

G = **ž** *lūgeō* &c.; final it = **sz** *ego*.

GH = **ž** *anser* &c.; before t it = **ksz** *angō*.

KV = **k** *caulis* &c., and so before **s** *exta*.

GV = **g** *augeō* &c.; before **sz** (from s) it = **k** *auxilium*.

GHV = **g** *nix* &c., and so before terminational **w** *levis*.—KHV = **g** *un-guis*.

s remains, dialectically with **k** prefixt *alnus aurum* ; but = **sz** after r *crābrō verrēs verrūca* and dialectically when initial before vowel *sarciō* (and *sex*?), medial between vowels *crūsta jūs*[1] *quasillum* or before r *aurōra* or t *auxilium haereō*.—SJ initial = **si** *suō*, between vowels = **ž** *avēna*.—SV = **sw** *sērius*; dialectically it = **s** *sobrīnus somnus*, or, before vowel + **sz** (from KS or K), **sz** *sex* (?) *socer*.

ZD remains *pēdō turdus*.

LETTISH.

Short vowels the same as in Lithuanian.

Ĭ remains *pĭlŏ sūdor vĭbĕx*.—ū *brūtus*.—Ē *lēnis*.

OI = **ee** *mūtŏ*.—AI remains *bĭtŏ vae*. —EU = **au** *tŭticus*.—ŌU = ōw *bōs*.

Ḷ = **il** see *pulvīnus*.

BH = **b** *blatta scrobis umbilicus*.

K = **s** *congius*.

KV = **k** *blatta capiō*.—GV = **g** *bĭtŏ bōs brūtus*.—KHV = **c** *congius*.

s before consonant = **š** *pĭlŏ scrobis*.

PRUSSIAN.

Short vowels as in Lithuanian : e before **sd** = **ei** *pĕdŏ*, e unaccented = **i** *clepŏ*.

OI = **ai** *ūnus*.—OU = **au** *lŭna*.—AU remains *auferō aurum*.

Ṛ = **ir** *armus*, after velar = **or** *crātis forceps*.

M before **s** = **n** *membrum*.

V = **w** *novem* &c. *sūdor*.

P before **s** = **b** *vespa*.—BH = **b** *faba*.

KS = **sch** *sex.*
KV = **k** *clepō,* after a short accented vowel **ck** *cicer vocō* : KVS = **x** *lūna.*
GV = **g** *blandus.*—GHV = **g** *forceps vŏmer.*
s after a short vowel = **ss** *annus.*

OLD SLAVONIC.

I = I.—U = **ŭ**, spelt **ŭ** *nurus* &c. or sometimes I *stipula* ; so initial
JU = *ji, i *jugum.*

E remains ; in monosyllables it = i *ex* ; initially sometimes **a** *ego* and
with j prefixt *ariĕs.*—EV before vowel = **ov** *novus* : EM EN before consonant (except j) = **ę** *membrum quinque* &c. : ER, to avoid a close
syllable, = **rē** *dormiō* &c.

o remains.—ON before consonant (except j) = **ą** *pons* &c. : OL OR = **la ra**
culmus porcus &c.

A = **o** *acerbus* &c. ; initially sometimes with j prefixt, when it = **e** *annus.*
—AN before consonant (except j) = **ą** *angō angulus anser* : AL AR = **la**
ra *palleō barba* &c.

Ĭ = i *trĕs* &c.—Ū = **y** *fūmus* &c.—Ŏ is dialectically spelt i *suŏ.*
Ē remains *vēnum* &c. ; initially with j prefixt, when it = **a** *edō.*—ĒN
before s = **ē** *mēnsis.*
Ō = **a** *nōmen* &c.
Ā = **a** *frāter* &c.

EI = i *mìgrō* &c.—OI = **ē** *poena* &c., initially = i *ūnus.*—AI = **ē** *saepĕs*
&c.—ŌI before vowel = **aj** *ōvum.*
EU OU AU all = **u** *lūx cluĕō auris* &c.—ŌU before vowel = **ov** *bŏs.*

M = **ĭm** *gemō* &c.—N = **ĭn** *tenuis* &c., or, before consonant, when initial
o *ignis,* when oxytone **ę** *meminī,* when barytone **ŭ** *centum.*—Ṇ before
consonant = **ą** *anās.*
L = **ŭl**, written ĭl (as in Russian, *ulmus*), before vowel *tellŭs* ; before
consonant it = **lŭ**, written **lŭ** *mulgeō* &c. Ĭl *levis.*—Ļ = **la** *palpō.*
R = **ŭr**, written ĭr, before vowel *foris* ; before consonant rŭ, written rŭ
mors &c. rĭ *cor.*—Ṛ = **ra** *armus.*

For Nasals before any consonant but j, see above on E O A Ē Ā N.
l is inserted between m and j *humus,* p (from SP) and j *spuō.*
j often prefixt to initial vowel *annus aries echìnus edō emō sum ūva* : so
dialectically **v** *anima hydrus.*

P remains: PT before m = d *septem.*—BH = b *barba.*

T remains; inserted between s (from K) and r *acerbus*; dropt between s (from K) and m *octō.*—TJ = št *pulmō.*

DH = d *barba* &c.; before t it = s *arbor.*—DHJ = žd *medius rōbigō.*

K = s *centum* &c., through foreign influence k *socrus.*—KTH = s *texō*: so KS *axis dexter sex.*

G = z *mulgeō* &c.

GH = z *angō* &c., through foreign influence g *anser grandō.*—GHJ = ž *echīnus.*

KV = k *cervus* &c.; = c before ı *quis urceus* ē *poena,* = č before e *quattuor* or original E *cerrītus*; before t it = š *nox* or, after original N, is dropt *quinque.*—KVJ = č *būcina.*

GV = g *āgnus* &c.; = ž before ı *gemō* ı *vīvus* e *balanus chelys grūs.*

GHV = g *forceps* &c.—KHV = g *unguis.*

S remains *sarciō nix anser* &c.; = h after ı *alnus pinsō* (unless before ŭ *avēna*) ŭ *mūscus nurus verrūca* u *auris clueō jūs*[1] *sūdus* ē *līra,* and dialectically init. before vowel *solum*; = š before ı *crābrō far mūs sublestus* i *musca*; omitted between long vowel and tr *aurōra,* and before plj (from PJ) *spuō.*—SJ = š *quasillum sex suō*: SV remains *socrus suescō,* but = s in enclitics *sē* and dialectically *sobrīnus.*

ARMENIAN.

The vowel of the original last syllable drops, E see *novem,* Ē *frāter māter pater stella,* Ō *soror*: monosyllables excepted, *canis.* Further, in the word in its Armenian form i and u drop except in the last syllable, i *linquō vīgintī* (and so when from E before liquid, *gena gula sternuō*), u *rūctō*; in the last syllable they remain, i *nīdus sūdor,* u *būbō canis foris socer somnus spuō.*

E remains *ego ferō sex*; dialectically (from Arian influence) it = a *argentum decem levis* or (with h prefixt after loss of s) ha- *semper*; = i before n *quinque* (hi- *senex*) r *cor* ž (from GH) see *echīnus*; = o before ı (from s before R) *soror*; by j-Umlaut it = ē *medius*; drops before o (from VO) *novus.*—πρόσθεσις before λ *frāter* r *trēs,* and (as i) before n *novem.*

O remains *lavō orbus* &c., dialectically with h- prefixt *odor*; dialectically (from Arian influence) it = a *molō odium planta vacō.*—πρόσθεσις before r *rūctō.*

A remains *agō arō pater* &c., dialectically with h- prefixt *avus*; by j-Umlaut it = ai *alius.*—πρόσθεσις before m *mēnsis* r *levis* s *stella.*

ī + a = ea *vīvō.*—ū = u *crūs grūs mūs tū.*

ē = i *fellō mēnsis plēnus rēnum.*

ŏ = u *canis dōnum genū*, and so when from compensation *octō umerus*; dialectically with h̄- prefixt *amārus*.

Ā = a *frāter māter*.

EI in last syllable (of the Armenian word) = e *trēs*, elsewhere = i *hiems lingō*.

OI in last syllable (of the Armenian word) = ē *mējō*, elsewhere = *vīnum*.

EU (from EV) = iu *suus*.

OU = oi *fungor studeō*.

ŌU = ov *bōs*.—ĀU = av *nāvis*.

M̥ = am, dialectically with h- prefixt (after loss of s-) *similis*.

N̥ in the originally last syllable = n *decem novem*, elsewhere = an *ingens vīgintī*.

L̥ = al and with g-Umlaut ail *lupus*; dialectically it = aλ *balanus*; before n it = aṛ *vellus*.

R̥ = ar *argentum armus cerebrum* (in these three it might be from R̥̄), *hordeum pōscō ursus*; dialectically it = aṙ *torreō*.

M remains *armus mēnsis*; before original T it = n *veniō*, before n it = u *domus hiems*; drops (with compensation if needed) before s *membrum umerus*.

N remains *nīdus nurus somnus*; drops before s *mēnsis*.

L remains *alius lingō*, after vowel dialectically = λ *mel sal*; dialectically (from Arian influence) = r *levis*.

R remains *orbus socer trēs*; = ṙ before n *foris sternuō* or vowel + n *grūs morior*; dialectically = λ *frāter stella*.

J after r = J̌ *sterilis*, after l gives Umlaut *alius*, and so after J̌ (from DH) *medius*: PJ = ph *lambō*.

V initial remains *sex vacō verrūca*, dialectically = g *lupus unda vellūs vēnum vestis villa vīnum* or (before s) kh *vīgintī*: medial before r it = u *suus*, between (originally) vowels drops *novem novus vīvō* or dialectically = g *lavō*: final (after loss of the final vowel) remains *avus*.

P initial before vowel = h *pater pēs quinque*, dialectically drops *pēs*; after vowel = v *septem*; drops everywhere before liquid *planta plēnus somnus*.

B onomatopoeic *būbō*.—BH = b *ferō fungor orbus*: BHR = λb *frāter*.

T remains after s *stella,* elsewhere = th *octō septem torreō* or (before u) d *tū*; drops before original R *trēs,* = i before (in the Armenian form of the word) r *frāter māter pater* or n *planta*; when final it drops after n (from M) *veniō.*

D = t *decem odium sīdō* &c. or when final th *studeō*: DB = rt *sūdor.*

DH = d -*dō fellō foris*; before original J it = J *medius.*

K = s *acus decem socer* &c.; before t it drops with compensation *octō.*— KTH = j *ursus*: K-V = ś *canis*: KS = ths *sex,* and so KSK *pōscō.*

G = c *agō gena rūctō* &c.; why it sometimes = s *ego* is obscure.

GH = j *angō hiems,* after vowel z *echīnus lingō mējō* or dialectically ź see *echīnus.*

KV = k before consonant *oculus,* kh before vowel *linquō* (= č in *pix,* foreign), g after liquid *quinque arca* (and so *lupus*).—kvtv = thś *quattuor.*

GV = k *balanus bōs veniō* &c.—GHV = g *hordeum levis,* before e = j *forceps.*

S remains before t *sīdō stella sterilis* and after original nasal *umerus mēnsis*; before r it = i *soror*; drops before vowel *sal septem suus* (and see above on prefixt h-) or nasal *sum nurus vestis* or kh *mūs,* after r *verrūca cerebrum hordeum torreō,* and when final after an original vowel *nurus.*—PST = ph *sternuō studeō*: SPJ = th *spuō*: SV = kh *somnus soror sūdor,* or, before vowel + s (from K), sk *socer.*

ZD = st *nīdus.*

ZEND.

I, U, Ī, Ū remain.

E remains before a nasal, see *tabula tenebrae levis*; elsewhere it = a, which by i-Umlaut = ai *holus medius per- super.* It is inserted after r *arbor cortex curculiō delphīnus forceps torreō vertō* (even when final, *inter*), see below on the sonant linguals.

O before m = e *centum domus ego humus*; elsewhere it = a, which by i-Umlaut = ai *ob potis ūrina,* by v-Umlaut = au *sollus.*

A before m = e *scamnum*; elsewhere it remains (in *pater* interchanging as in Sk. with i), and by i- Umlaut = ai *ambi- anima.* It is inserted after r *cor.*

Ē = ā, by i-Umlaut āi *et*: before ṅh it = āo *mēnsis.*

Ō = ā, by u-Umlaut āu *laurus*: at the end of a word it = āo *nōs plūs vōs.*

Ā remains: before ṅh it = āo *nāris.*

OI = aē *poena sūdor vitis*; so AI bītō *saeta.*

OU = ao *clūnis jūs*[2] *lūna*; so AU *augeō.*—ŌU = āu *bōs.*

M = **am** *similis tenebrae.*—Ṇ = **an** *decem in- juvenis novem*, before a Dental aṅ *dens inter umbra*; barytone before consonant a *centum in-*, which by i-Umlaut = **ai** *vīgintī.*

Ḷ = **er** (+ **e**, see E above) *liēn planta.*—Ṛ = **er** (+ **e**) *argentum portus regō*, before **k** or **p** = **ehr** *lupus corpus*, before **u** = **our** *gravis* : VṚ final = **ru** *quater.*—Ḹ = **ar** (+ **e**) *largus*, and so Ḇ *armus regō terreō.*

N before **z** (from GH) disappears, the preceding vowel becoming ā *angō.*
L = **r.**—R remains; it drops before **sh** (from S) *perna.*

J = **y.**

V remains, but after ç (from K) it = **p** *canis equus*, after **th** (from T) it = a 'spirant' **w** *quattuor.* On SV see below.

P remains before vowel or **t** *septem*; before any other consonant it = **f** *somnus planta plūs pōscō prō.*
BH = **b**; later between vowels it = **w** *delphīnus.*

T remains before vowel (yet sometimes as in Sk. becomes **th**, *passus pateō planta rota bītō*); before consonant it = **th** *putus quattuor trēs*; it = **ṭ** at the end of a stem *nepōs* or root *cortex petō planta vertō.*
D remains; between vowels it = **dh** *sūdor*, before **d** (from DH) it = **z** *cor.*—Pretonic DV = **b** *bis.*
DH = **d**, omitted before **n** *fundus.*

K = ç; dialectically **z** *cor*; before **t** it = **s** *octō.*—KTH = **khsh** *texō* : KS = **sh** *coxa dexter ex mox sex*, KSK = **s** *pōscō.*—G = **z**; before **n** it = **zh** *genū nōscō.*—GH = **z.**
KV before original **e** = **c** *celer quattuor -que quinque* (and so at end of root, *coquō lacer sequor* &c.); before any other vowel it = **k** *corpus oculus quī* &c.; before consonant it = **kh** *lūna nox sex.*
GV = **j** before **i** *vīvus* or original **e** *augeō* (and so at end of root, *instigō jungō sagīna*); before any other vowel it = **g**; before consonant it = **gh** *nūdus.*
GHV before orignal **e** = **j** (and so at end of root, *levis*; later **zh**, *nix*); elsewhere it = **gh** *largus.*—KHV before **i** = **c** *scindō*; elsewhere it = **kh** *cymba soccus.*

S =

(1) **h** before **a** *saeta saltus sedeō* &c. (and so at end of root, *zōna*), or between **a** and another vowel *erus*, or between **a** and **m** *sum.*
(2) ṅh between **a** and **a** *soror*, or when final after āo *mēnsis nāris angō villa.*

(3) sh after i *pinsō* u *crūsta gustō ūrō*, r *verrēs* and so orig. *perna*, kh (from KV) *lūstrō sex.*

(4) ç before p t k c n *liēn stella tabula obscūrus scindō neō nix nō.*

SV = q *sagīna socer somnus sonus soror suāvis sūdor.*

SANSKRIT.

I, U, Ī, Ū remain.

E and O alike = a: A remains. But occasionally E and A = i, *menda turtur pater.*

Ē and Ō alike = ā: Ā remains.

EI and AI alike = ē: OU and AU alike = ō.—ŌU = āu see *bōs*; ĀU remains *nāvis.*

M = am *similis tenebrae.*—N = an *ante dens in- inter juvenis*; barytone before consonant it = a *centum ignis in- mens vigintī.*—Ñ = ā *anās.*

L̥ = ūl i.e. ul *calvus tolerō* or il, which + n = in (see below) *callum*; before consonant it = r̥ *planta.*—R̥ = ūr i.e. ur *gravis* or ir *cerebrum haruspex*; before consonant or final it = r̥ *alcēs ars corpus* &c.—L̥ = ūr i.e. ūr *lāna polleō* or īr *largus*, later īl *umbilīcus.*

M assimilated to a following consonant is written ṁ *umerus membrum.* So N is written ṅ *vigintī anser angō.*—N after r = ṇ *lāna polleō*, and later the R (or L) itself disappears *callum palma*[1] *pila ūlna.*

L = r *celer levis volō*, later l *balanus libet lingō* &c.—R remains, later = l *prūna*: after it a dental becomes cerebral and the r itself disappears *crāssus tardus bardus.*

J = y.—V remains, but drops initially before u *volva* or ū *lāna.*

P remains; dialectically = pp *piper pīpilō*, ph *spēs.*

B rare, *gubernō*, onomatopoeic *babae būcina.*

BH remains; before vowel + aspirate it = b *fundus.*

T remains; dialectically = tt *turtur*, th *centō crāssus passus planta rota stō tegō*; after sh it = ṭ *octō*, dialectically ṭh *costus ōstium.*

D remains, even before dh *crēdō*; it is assimilated before t *oppidum* or j *mergō.*

DH remains; before vowel + aspirate it = d *favilla fingō.* After original R it becomes ḍh and dialectically ḷh *bardus.*

K = ç; dialectically h *cor*; before ṭ it = sh *octō*, before ch (from SK) is lost *pōscō.*—KTH = ksh *texō ursus*: KS = ksh *axis coxa dexter misceō mox*, final sh *sex.*

G = j; dialectically h *ājŏ ego magnus.*—GH = h.

KV = k; but = c before i *poena* (see on *quis*[1]) or original E *celer corium quattuor* (and so at end of root, *coquŏ sequor vocŏ* &c.).—KVS (like KS) = ksh *scĭpiŏ*.

GV = g; but = j before ī *vīvŏ* or original E *augeŏ bardus bitŭmen* (and so at end of root, *jungŏ sagĭna unguŏ*).

GHV = gh.—KHV = kh *congius unguis*, before vowel + aspirate = k *cymba*: SKHV before i = ch *scindŏ*.

S remains; but (1) = sh after i *pinsŏ vīrus* (and so órig. *gaesum*), u *clueŏ costum nurus prūna ūrŏ* (and so orig. *ŏstium*) ū *mūs* (and dialectically after a *lascīvus*), r *horreŏ perna verrūca* ṛ *fāstīgium verrēs*, and before vowel + sh *sex* ; (2) = ç before vowel + ç *socer*; (3) dialectically drops before p *liēn* t *instīgŏ*.—SK before original E = ch *pōscō.*

Z before D makes the d cerebral and itself drops with compensation *nīdus.*